Praise for *Wishcraft*

"One of the saddest lines in the world is, 'Oh, come now—be realistic.' The best parts of this world were not fashioned by those who were realistic. They were fashioned by those who dared to look hard at their wishes and gave them horses to ride. . . . I've got about four copies of *Wishcraft*. It has been very popular. . . . I have now included it in *Parachute!*"

—RICHARD NELSON BOLLES, author of
What Color Is Your Parachute?

"Splendid! A companion, a guide, a visionary work!"

—JUDY COLLINS

"The most irreverent and refreshing self-help manual now on the market . . . Feisty, funny, and down-to-earth, this book is bound to benefit all those who sense they may have temporarily lost track of their true goals."

—*New Age* magazine

"Wise, compassionate, and pragmatic. Written by an expert for people of all ages who seriously want that *something* in life."

—THEODORE ISAAC RUBIN, M.D.

"Thanks for *Wishcraft*. I read it through in a weekend and have gone back now to do the excellent exercises. . . . I always hoped someone would step up to the plate and put into words what I was looking for, what I really want. Step-by-step you moved me right into clear sight of it, and the fog has lifted."

—PRESTON S., Des Moines, Iowa

"My family kept pushing self-help books at me, and I have to tell you that *Wishcraft* is the first self-help book that ever spoke to me. I love your down-to-earth approach, your way of planning as a way of creating a 'passionate' path, but most of all your belief that positive thinking isn't enough. What a relief! Okay, finally I'm ready to listen. Thanks."

—JAMES M., Dallas, Texas

"I'm not very good with words, but I do want to say thank you and let you know how much your words have helped me. Your book, by far, is the only one that has helped me out of feeling hopeless and overwhelmed. I've had dreams, but they seemed so impossible that I kept going around in circles, never really getting anywhere. For the first time I'm taking one step after another and each day getting more of the life I want. How did you know how to do that?"

—WALLACE S., Fresno, California

"*Wishcraft* saved me. I know that sounds dramatic, but I love this book, every phrase, every sentence, every exclamation point! I can't thank you enough for writing it. It's amazing what a change happens inside you when you see how sensible it is to only go after what you really want, no matter how unrealistic it seems, and then work toward it with your funny 'backwards planning' flowchart and hand-drawn production schedule! Yes, factories build ships and airplanes this way, and when I thought about it, you were right. I could build my ideal life the same way. And that's what I have done."

—H.K., Michigan

"Thanks for showing me 'how,' Barbara. Six years ago, after eighteen years as a secretary, I read your book and decided I was going to be a teacher. It had always been my dream, but I never finished college and thought I could never do it. I've always been unsure of myself, but I listened to your words and started teaching before I signed up for school! I volunteered as an assistant to someone teaching foreign people how to speak English and I loved it. I returned to college, at the age of forty-six, got my bachelor's degree, and two years ago I walked into a part-time job in a 'real' classroom, and I felt that I had come home. . . . Every time I become unsure of myself, I go back to *Wishcraft,* and the clarity returns. It's easy to talk about a dream, but it's hard to really step forward and do it. Your words are like having a guide in the wilderness."

—BONNIE J., California

"I'm a forty-seven-year-old never-married woman who, up until the age of forty, was living for others. . . . I had a high-powered, megabucks corporate career that always felt wrong. I even hated the showplace home I owned (but seldom enjoyed). After I was laid off at forty, my life finally became my own. With the help of *Wishcraft*, frequent flyer miles, and profit from selling my house, I did everything from trek in Nepal, coach running in Hawaii, get a master's degree, scuba dive in Fiji, and have a baby of my own at age forty-three! Now I teach college part-time and spend the rest of my time doing what I love more than anything—being with my daughter."

—S.M., North Carolina

"After three plus years of consulting your books, I have reached my goal of becoming a tour guide leading tours in Europe. What helped me the most was to keep going and to connect as much as possible with people who could help me. Thank you for writing such helpful books that got me to develop an achievable action plan, which brought me to this point, and for uncovering things that put barriers in our way to accomplishing our life goals."

—T.B., California

"If it wasn't for *Wishcraft,* I very possibly would still be working till midnight for low pay and all the wrong reasons. Now I walk to work, leave at five P.M., and learn. I feel extremely happy and very content. Thank you so much, Ms. Sher."

—V.C., New York

"I hope you won't mind me being so familiar, but to me you are like an old and cherished friend. When I was thirtysomething and newly divorced, I read *Wishcraft,* and it changed my life. Instead of looking for a role model, I decided to be one. I recommended the book to many people, bought copies for people, and loaned my own to many others. I know it helped some of them. Others I don't know about, but you have such a sane and sensible and refreshing message that I always felt like it was one of the best things I could do for them. I just wanted to say thank you and to let you know what a positive influence you have had on my life over the years."

—ANITA L., Colorado

Wishcraft

ALSO BY BARBARA SHER

I Could Do Anything If I Only Knew What It Was

It's Only Too Late If You Don't Start Now

Live the Life You Love

Refuse to Choose

Wishcraft

How to Get What You Really Want

BARBARA SHER

with Annie Gottlieb

BALLANTINE BOOKS · NEW YORK

To my mother,
who has always believed in me.

Acknowledgments

Because I tried to be a good person, fate dropped into my life just the people I needed to get my notions into a book: Rhoda Weyr, my agent; Annie Gottlieb, my collaborator; Amanda Vaill, my editor; and Paulette Lundquist, who did both her job and mine at the office. They are the best team anyone could ever wish for. Without them there would have been no book.

Five men belong here as well: John, who kept me going when the going got rough; Danny, Matthew, Freddy, who were always proud of me (and kept house—such as it was—for ten years); and my Dad, who showed me how to be a person who trusted herself and didn't quit. Without them, there would have been no Barbara.

—BARBARA SHER

Special thanks to my grandmothers, for the gift of words: Anne Preaskil Stern, who taught me the alphabet; the late Dorothy Kuh Gottlieb, who shared with me her passion for books.

And to Jacques Sandulescu, Margaret Webb, Gita, Harry and Jean Gottlieb, and J. Barnes and Mina Creech.

—ANNIE GOTTLIEB

Contents

——————————————— *Four* ———————————————

CRAFTING II: MOVING AND SHAKING

Foreword to the Thirtieth Anniversary Edition

It's hard to believe that thirty years have passed since I held a copy of my first book in my hands, staring at the word *Wishcraft* on the cover and, right under it, my name. My life didn't change, not at first. I was still a hardworking single parent of two boys, as I had been for over ten years, and I was still scraping by financially, to say nothing of the fact that I was almost forty-five years old at the time, which in 1979 was considered a bit old for anyone, especially a woman, to be starting anything.

But that day, as far as I was concerned, I was Cinderella at the ball because I had become a published writer. It was like a dream. I'd always had a secret fear that I would just pass through this life and no one would ever know I'd been here. Now everything was okay. It was on the record. I wrote a book, and I knew it was a good one because it was based on a painstakingly designed, two-day workshop I'd been running for almost three years. I knew how much my workshop helped people. I watched them use my techniques to help one another turn impossible dreams into realities right in front of my eyes—setting up small businesses, finding ways to perform their own plays in New York theaters, getting grants to travel to the Appalachians to take photos of children, getting into (and through) good law schools, finding reliable help for adopting children—dreams as unique as the people who dreamed them.

I hoped *Wishcraft* would help people just as much as my workshops helped them, but I wasn't sure if that was possible. I had recorded every one of the workshops (and at twelve hours each, that was a lot of audiocassettes) because I knew they were well worth saving, and I used those same words in the book. But people worked face-to-face in the workshops, and I was worried that a book wouldn't have the same impact.

I didn't have to worry for long.

A few weeks after *Wishcraft* was published, letters started coming into my mailbox, handwritten letters in hand-addressed and stamped envelopes. A few every week at first, and then more and more until, after six months, I had cardboard boxes filled with letters piled high in my closet. Readers wrote to thank me for being so practical and down-to-earth, for understanding the reality of their lives, and for helping them pinpoint their dreams. They appreciated the fact that I told them to expect fear and negativity, and they loved the complaining sessions I advised.

Some people sensed the workshop origins of *Wishcraft* and turned it into a reading group selection, spending up to a year going through the pages together and achieving all their dreams. Others told me *Wishcraft* was the text in one of their college courses, and others asked for training to lead special Success Teams, using *Wishcraft* as the guide. Most people read the book on their own but wrote that they no longer felt alone. Their letters invited me into their lives, and they wanted me to know that they finally felt seen and understood and helped by *Wishcraft*. It was like nothing I'd ever experienced before.

Thirty years have now passed and I'm still getting thank-you letters, some of them from people who reread *Wishcraft* after many years and want me to know that it has helped them again and again. I'm even hearing from their grown children.

I've been able to keep only a handful of the letters the post office brought me in the first years. I've saved a few more of the emails that continue to arrive almost every day. But no matter how many I receive, I'm still thrilled and honored to read them, and I personally answer as many as I can.

In publishing terms, *Wishcraft* is a success. It has never been out of print since that first hardcover copy I held in my hands in 1979. Publishers were happy to look at my later manuscripts and published more of my books, which have also done well.

Because of *Wishcraft* I became a "somebody." Freelance writers called to quote me in their magazine articles. I've been invited to speak in front of hundreds of audiences, from Fortune 100 companies and international outplacement firms to parents at "unschooling" conferences and gifted children in rural schools. I've spoken in the United States, Canada, Australia, and Western Europe, and even in countries that had just stepped out from behind the Iron Curtain and wanted to learn how to dream again.

At this writing I've done five public television pledge specials and plans are in the works for more. Occasionally, people even recognize me in airports, which surprises me because I'm usually flying in from overseas, tired, tousled, and carrying a dog. I don't look like a celebrity, and they never treat me like one. They talk to me like we've known each other a long time, and that's what I love most of all.

Because in personal terms, *Wishcraft* is a success greater than any I could ever have imagined. I've actually been given the rare and astonishing opportunity to help people go after their dreams by offering them a nonmysterious, nuts-and-bolts way of reaching their goals—even if they think they don't know what their goals are, can't figure out how to believe in themselves, or can't sustain a permanent positive attitude. I make them laugh at their own negativity and show them that they have everything they need inside them to create the life they want, but that isolation is the dream killer and support is more powerful than attitude.

By now that message, first stated in *Wishcraft*, has rung a bell with millions of people. Because of their responses I've been able to earn my living for decades doing the work I love best. Like everyone else, I've been high and I've been low, but I've never been bored. Not for a moment. That has made the last thirty years fly by.

And it all started with the book you are holding now. With all my heart I hope *Wishcraft* will give you the same engaging, meaningful life it has given me. Even more, I hope it will inspire you to help others go after their dreams, too. That would make me happiest of all.

Introduction

This book is designed to make you a winner.

Not the Vince Lombardi, get-out-there-and-stomp-'em kind—unless that's really your heart's desire. But I don't believe it. I don't think most of us get real pleasure out of stomping the competition and ending up all alone on top of some mythical heap. That's just a booby prize we go after because nobody ever told us what winning *is*. I have my own definition, and it's a very simple, very radical one.

Winning to me means getting what you want. Not what your father and mother wanted for you, not what you think you can realistically get in this world, but what *you want*—your wish, your fantasy, your dream. You're a winner when you have a life you love, so that you wake up every morning excited about the day ahead and delighted to be doing what you're doing, even if you're sometimes a little nervous and scared.

Is that you? If it isn't, what would make it that way for you? What's your fondest dream? It might be to live in peace on your own five-acre farm, or to step out of a huge Rolls-Royce with flashbulbs popping; to take pictures of rhinoceroses in Africa, or become a vice president of the company where you now type and file; to adopt a child or make a movie . . . start your own accounting business or learn to play the piano . . . open a dinner theater or get your pilot's license. Your dream will be as individual as you are. But whatever it is—and whether it's grand or modest, fantastic or practical, far away as the moon or just around the corner—as of right now I want you to start taking it very, very seriously.

Contrary to what you may have been taught, there is nothing frivolous or superficial about what you want. It isn't a luxury that can wait until you've taken care of all the "serious" business of life. It's a necessity. *What you want is what you need.* Your dearest wish comes straight from your core, loaded with vital information about who you are and who you can become. You've got to cherish it. You've got to respect it. Above all, you've got to *have* it.

And you can.

Wait a minute. You've heard that before. If you're at all like me, the very words "You can do it!" are enough to set off a little alarm bell in your head. "The last time I fell for *that,* I broke every bone in my body. It's a tough world out there, and I'm not in such great shape in here. I don't think I'm up for any more of that positive-thinking stuff. Maybe *you* can do it. I happen to know from hard personal experience that I can't."

As the bruised veteran of every success book and program that ever promised me ten easy steps to self-esteem, self-discipline, will power, or a positive attitude, I know what I'm talking about when I say this book is different. I wrote it for people like me—people who were born without any of the virtues that made Horatio Alger great and who have given up all hope of ever developing them. Can you persevere? I can't. There is no diet of any kind, physical, emotional, or financial, that I haven't fallen off by Wednesday if I started it on Monday. Self-discipline? I jogged once—I think it was about four years ago. Self-confidence? I've walked out of success seminars bursting with it. It lasted three days. I'm an ace procrastinator; I love nothing better than to watch old movies on the Late Show when I'm supposed to be doing something important. My positive attitudes are invariably followed by gloomy slumps. As a well-meaning but tactless friend once said to me, "Barbara, if you can make it, anyone can."

And I did.

I landed in New York City eleven years ago, divorced and penniless, with two small children to support and a B.A. in anthropology. (I hope you're chuckling, because it means you know exactly what that's worth.) We had to go on welfare until I found a job. But luckily, I found one I loved, working with people, not with paper. Over the next ten years I started and ran two very successful businesses of my own, wrote two books and the training manual for my seminars, and raised those two boys up healthy and sweet. (I lost twenty pounds, too. And I even quit smoking. Twice.) And all this without the slightest noticeable self-improvement. I still can't stick to things. I still have a rotten attitude a lot of the time. But I made it—on my own terms—and I love my life even on the days when I hate myself. By my own definition, I am a winner. And that means you can be, too.

How?

I have the kind of unholy respect for that little three-letter word that someone who's been starving has for bread. If, ten years ago, some kind soul had given me hard information on how to turn my dreams into realities, instead of just assuring me blandly that it could be done, it would have saved me an incredible amount of time and anguish. As long as I kept trying to believe in myself and reform all my bad habits, I kept crashing—and blaming myself. It wasn't until I gave up on ever fixing *me* and tried to improvise a set of aids that would work for me anyway (because I wasn't going to go to my grave without getting what I wanted, whether I deserved it or not) that I stumbled on the real secret behind the scenes of all successful people's lives. It's not superhero genes and a jaw of steel, like the myths say. It's something much simpler. It's know-how and support.

To start creating the life you want, you don't need mantras, self-hypnosis, a character-building program, or a new toothpaste. You do need practical techniques for problem-solving, planning, and getting your hands on materials, skills, information, and contacts. (See Chapters 6, 7, and 8 on "Plotting the Path to Your Goal.") You need commonsense strategies for coping with human feelings and foibles that aren't going to go away, like fear, depression, and laziness. (See Chapter 5, "Hard Times, or The Power of Negative Thinking," and Chapter 9, "Winning Through Timidation.") And you need ways of riding out the temporary emotional storms your life changes can cause in your closest relationships—while still getting the extra emotional support you need for risk-taking. (See Chapter 10, "Don't-Do-It-Yourself.")

That's the "craft" part of *Wishcraft.* It is based on the needs and potentialities of human beings as we are, not as we ought to be. I had to figure it all out for myself, by trial and error. I don't think you should have to do it the hard way. So I'm giving you the results of my experiment: techniques already tested by thousands of women and men who have used them in Success Teams to bring their dreams to life—from horse ranches to hand bookbinding, from choral singing to city planning, from writing children's books to selling blue-chip stocks. The whole second half of this book is a detailed answer to the question, "How?" All I'm going to tell you right now is that you won't have to change yourself because, one, it can't be done, and two, you're fine the way you are. With nothing more than pencil and paper, your imagination, your family and your friends, you're going to create a life-support system that will do much of the hard work for you and free you to function at your best.

But first, of course, you have to know what you want.

The first half of this book is all about wishing. Unlike the skills for bringing dreams into actuality, which are nuts-and-bolts skills like engineering or carpentry, wishing doesn't have to be learned. It's inborn in human beings the way flying is in birds. For your desirous imagination to take wing, nothing—no knowledge—has to be added to you. But it's very likely that something *does* have to be taken away: the spellbinding cultural curse that says, "It can't be done," and the heavy weight of discouragement you may be carrying if you've tried for your dreams before and failed. Because so many of us never were told how to make our dreams happen, after a few tries we assumed it was impossible or horribly difficult. So we adjusted our sights downward and settled for what we thought we could get. But it's a funny thing: the craft of WISHCRAFT won't really work for you unless you bring your highest hopes and deepest dreams to it. Because while technique and strategy are the "how" of winning, wishing is the all-important "why"—the power source that makes all that machinery run.

Our language is full of phrases that tell us wishing is unrealistic and impotent: "Wishing won't make it so." "She wants the moon." "Idle fantasy." "He's an incurable dreamer." That's nonsense. Wishing and dreaming are the beginning of all human endeavor. Look—mankind wanted the moon for thousands of years, and in the twentieth century we got there. That's what *wishing plus technique* can do: it can change reality. It's true that wishing *alone* won't make it so. Like steam without an engine, it just dissipates. But technique without desire is like a cold and empty engine: it won't go. If you've ever found it difficult to do things, stop and consider what you've been finding it difficult to do: typing? digging ditches? mopping floors? You can do them if you have to, but it's awfully hard to get your heart into any of them as a lifetime goal.

There are plenty of hard-working, responsible men and women in our society who do know *how* to get things done but have never felt free to explore themselves and find out *what* they want to do. If you are one of them, the first half of this book will be a revelation. It will show you how and why you may have lost touch with your dreams, and it will give you simple, enjoyable exercises for rediscovering them. And then it will help you shape a real-world goal out of what you love. So far from being "impractical" or "irresponsible," doing what's closest to your heart is like striking oil: you tap into a surge of energy that will propel you to the heights of success.

If, on the other hand, you've picked up this book already knowing what you want and just looking for clear instructions on how to get it, you may be tempted to skip to the "craft" part. Take the time to read "wish" anyway. It will help you define your goals more clearly than you ever have before—which is half the battle toward getting them—and I promise that it will greatly enrich your sense of what's possible in one human lifetime.

The well-known psychotherapist Rollo May once wrote a book called *Love and Will.* This book is about *love and skill*—the two vital ingredients of real success. Here's to yours.

One

The Care and Feeding of Human Genius

–1–
Who Do You Think You Are?

Who do you think you are?

That's a very interesting question. Or it would be, if the people who asked it when we were young had really wanted a thoughtful answer. Unfortunately, they weren't looking for an answer at all. They already had the answers. This is what they were saying:

"Who do you think you are, Sarah Bernhardt? Take that shawl off this minute and finish the dishes." *Or:*

"Who do you think you are, Charles Darwin? Get that disgusting turtle off my dining room table and do your arithmetic." *Or:*

"You—an astronaut? A scientist like Madame Curie? A movie star? Who do you think you are?"

Does that sound familiar? Most of us heard that question at some time during our growing up—usually at the vulnerable moment when we ventured some dream, ambition, or opinion close to our hearts. But imagine those words being spoken in a curious, open, wondering tone of voice, for once—not in that scalding tone of scorn we've all had burned into our brains.

I'd like to invite you to try a simple experiment. I'm going to ask you that question again, only this time *try hearing it as a real question.* Who do you think you are?

EXERCISE 1: Who Do You Think You Are?

Take a blank sheet of paper (we're going to be using a lot of blank paper in this book—it's the staff of life) and, in a few sentences to half a page, answer the question: "Who do you think you are?" I am genuinely interested in the answer. What do you consider the four or five most important characteristics that define your identity? There are no right or wrong answers, and there's only one rule: don't think too long or hard. Put down the first and surest things that come to mind: "This is me."

Now take a look at your answer. There's a better than 50 percent chance that you said something like this:

"I'm 28, Catholic, single, a secretary in an electronics firm, live in Buffalo." *Or:*

"I'm 5'10", 175 pounds, black hair, brown eyes, Italian, former running back, vote Democratic, Vietnam veteran, appliance salesman." *Or:*

"I'm a former teacher, married to a man I love, an M.D. in internal medicine, and I'm the mother of three terrific kids: Marty, 13, Jimmy, 8, and Elise, 5 1/2." *Or:*

"I'm black, born in Detroit, oldest of five kids. My father worked for GM. B.A. from Wayne State. Computer programmer. Marrying my high school sweetheart next summer."

All variants of "This is what I do for a living, here's where I live, I'm married, not married, I make money, I don't, I'm so-and-so's mother, I'm Episcopalian, I'm in school"—the kinds of things we usually tell each other when we meet. When we've exchanged these vital statistics, geographical and occupational details, we feel we've declared our identities and begun to get to know each other.

Well, we're wrong.

There's no question that these things have been important in our lives. In fact, they have usually shaped our lives. They are experience, history, role, relationship, livelihood, skill, survival. Some of them are choices. Some, including many we'd call choices, are compromises. Some are accidents.

None of them is your identity.

This may surprise you, but if I were sitting down with you to help you choose a goal and design a life individually tailored for you, I would not ask you for any of this information. I would not want to know what you do for a living, unless you were really excited by your job. I would not want to know any of the things you put in a resume—your background, your experience, your skills. All too often we are skilled in things we never really chose, things we have had to do—like typing or scrubbing floors (those were my skills)—not things we love.

When it comes to picking out what you'll do with energy and joy, what you can be a smashing success at, your skills are not only unimportant—they can get in the way, unless you assign them to a strictly secondary role. For the moment, I'd like you just to forget about them.

What?

That's right. And just for now, I'd like you to forget your job (unless you love it), your family (even though you love them), your responsibilities, your education, all the things that make up your "reality" and your "identity." Don't worry. They won't go away. I know they are important to you. Some of them are necessary and dear to you. But they are not you. And right now the focus is on *you*.

What I'm interested in is *what you love*.

You may or may not be able to say what that is. If you can, it may be your work, or a hobby, or a sport, or a pastime like going to the movies, or something you've always loved reading about, or a subject you wish you had studied in school, or just something that gives off a special whiff of fascination for you whenever it goes by, even though you know very little about it.

There may very well be several things you feel that way about. Whatever they are—guitar music, bridges, bird-watching, sewing, the stock market, the history of India—there is a very, very good reason why you love them. Each one is a clue to something inside you: *a talent, an ability, a way of seeing the world that is uniquely yours.* You may not know you have it. You may have a case of amnesia about it. That amnesia can be so total that you're not even sure any more what you love. And yet, *that is you!*

That is your identity, your core.

It is something more. Because "who you are" isn't passive or static or unchanging. It is a vital design, as one philosopher put it, that needs to unfold and express itself through the medium of your whole life. And so that unique pattern of talents and gifts that lies hidden in the things you love is also the map to your own life path.

Did you ever go on a treasure hunt when you were a child, or read Poe's "The Gold Bug"? Then you know that the first thing you have to do before you can find the treasure is find the map. It may be hidden, it may be torn in half, or in a million pieces, but your first job is to find it and put the fragments back together, like a jigsaw puzzle. That's what we're going to be doing for you in the first section of this book.

The clues to your life path are not lost. They are just scattered and hidden—some of them right under your nose, in plain sight. They need to be gathered together and carefully examined before you can begin to know how to design a life that truly fits *you,* a life that will make you feel like jumping out of bed in the morning to meet the world, a little scared at times, maybe, but fully alive.

If you are low on energy, if you need a lot of sleep and feel like you're always dragging yourself around at half throttle, it may not be because you need vitamins or have low blood sugar. It may be because you have not found your purpose in life. You will recognize your own path when you come upon it, because you will suddenly have all the energy and imagination you will ever need.

This is part of the secret of all genuinely successful people: they have found their paths. They also happen to have some very special skills for making their visions come true in reality. That is very important, and it's the purpose of the second part of this book to teach you those skills. But first you must liberate your own ingenuity and drive, and the only way to do that is to discover your own path. It is the only path that will ever truly absorb you. And the treasure at the end is success.

Right now I'd like you to do something symbolic. Take that piece of paper on which you answered the question, "Who do you think you are?" Glance through it one more time. Now *crumple it up and throw it in the wastebasket.*

This is the only piece of paper I'm going to ask you to do that with, and as I said, you'll have occasion to write on quite a few sheets of paper as we go along. Alternatively, you might want to save this one as a souvenir. It will serve nicely as the first in a pair of "Before and After" pictures. Call it the souvenir of a misconception. Because if you're like most of us, you are not who you think you are.

Who are you really?

You've forgotten—but you knew once—when you were a very small child. So that's the place to start our search for the lost treasure map of your talents: in the first five precious and mysterious years of your life—the greatest learning period you ever had.

I'll tell you one thing about who you were then.

You were a genius.

YOUR ORIGINAL GENIUS

Now you're probably laughing, but I'm serious. I don't care what you've accomplished in your life or what your I.Q. is—you were born with your own unique kind of genius. And I mean that in the fullest sense of the word. Not genius with a small 'g' as opposed to Albert Einstein. Big "G" genius, *like* Albert Einstein.

We confer the honorific title "genius" only on those very rare people who we believe were born with a mysterious something extra: great brilliance, original vision, incredible determination. And we believe that "something extra" cannot help but express itself with such force that it overpowers the most difficult circumstances. Look at Mozart. Born overflowing with music. Look at Picasso—another genius, the sculptor Louise Nevelson, says Picasso was "drawing like an angel in the crib." Those are geniuses, not you and I. Or so the standard reasoning goes.

OK, let's take the three characteristics I named as defining genius— great brilliance, original vision, incredible determination—and see whether you had them when you were 2 years old.

"Great brilliance" is a little hard to define. We've found out now that we can't test I.Q. very reliably after all. But even if we could, it only measures one very narrow range of knowing and doing. So we'd better call "great brilliance" a special case of "original vision": intellectual vision, as opposed to the artistic or musical kind, or a dozen other kinds of vision we have or haven't discovered yet: political, emotional, athletic, humanitarian . . . you name it.

You had original vision when you were 2 years old. You may not remember, but that's because it's always difficult to remember things we don't have words for. The fact is, in those early years you were seeing the world in such an original way that no one around you could give you the words for it. And if you found the words for it, usually no one could understand them!

If you've ever listened to a very small child—if you're a mother, for instance—you know that they say some pretty strange and amazing things. That is because they are trying to tell us what the world looks like, seen for the first time, from a point of view that has never existed before! Great poets are people who have held on to that ability to see things new and say what they see, but we all had it once. You had it, when you were 2. You were very busy when you were 2. You were not only reinventing the English language for your own purposes, you were, as a physicist friend of mine told me, doing original research into the nature of the universe.

So you had that: original vision. A new way of seeing the world that was all your own.

You also had "incredible determination."

You knew perfectly well what you loved and what you wanted. And you went after it without the slightest hesitation or self-doubt. If you saw a cookie on the table, you didn't think "Can I get it? Do I deserve it? Will I make a fool of myself? Am I procrastinating again?" You thought, *Cookie*. And you cried, you wheedled, you crawled, you climbed, you piled boxes up on the floor, you did everything you could think of to get that cookie. If you didn't get it, you made a fuss, took a nap, and changed the subject. And it didn't stop you in the least from going right for the next wonderful thing you saw.

Notice that you don't need "self-confidence" when you're like that. The word has no meaning. You're not even aware of yourself. You're completely focused on the thing you're after.

Those "rare" and "special" qualities we think distinguish geniuses from all the rest of us? You had them. I had them.

Where did they go?

As long as you were too young to listen to reason or to be trained to do anything "useful," you had a marvelous freedom to be who you were. By the time you were 5 or 6, if not even sooner, the precious right to make choices based on your own wishes began to be taken away. As soon as you were old enough to control yourself and sit still in school, the honeymoon was over.

You have probably forgotten what it was like to walk into the first grade. You'd just had five years of solid experiences—seeing things; knowing things; feeling, hating, and loving things. But schools are not designed to learn from you; they are designed to teach you. Inadvertently, they probably gave the impression that your knowledge, tastes, opinions were of zero value.

Just by ignoring who you were, they cancelled the whole rich inner world you had brought in with you. All they saw was a blank board that they were going to fill up with everything worth knowing. If it was important to you to talk to your best friend, or daydream, or draw, and they were doing multiplication tables, you got punished. If you happened to know how to talk to plants and plants talked back to you, they didn't ask you, "Do you want to learn how to spell, or did you have something else in mind?" They said, "Get away from the plants and let's see how fast you can learn the alphabet."

If you talked to plants, or if you talked to dogs, or if you made sculptures out of mud, or if you were going to be a movie star or ice skate to Eskimo land, you understood very quickly that that didn't count for much. And so, little by little, you forgot it. You developed amnesia about it. *Now* if you walked out into the world and somebody asked, "What are you good at?" you could easily say, "Nothing," meaning "Nothing that anyone would consider important." Or you might say, "Well, I'm good at math," or "I can type." It would never occur to you to say, "I love plants. I can remember all their names, and I think I understand what makes them happy."

All the people we call "geniuses" are men and women who somehow escaped having to put that curious, wondering child in themselves to sleep. Instead, they devoted their lives to equipping that child with the tools and skills it needed to do its playing on an adult level. Albert Einstein was playing, you know. He was able to make great discoveries precisely because he kept alive the originality and delight of a small child exploring its universe for the first time.

The first thing you will need to do is reawaken those child qualities in yourself. So let's go back and try to get a look at the genius you were. That is the first important clue to your life design—to the discovery of what you'll be happiest doing and what you'll be best at.

It's true that original achievements, great works of art, and the kinds of lives that are works of art almost always have their roots in childhood. Ask any famous woman or man, and you will probably find that they remember having a very clear sense of what they were meant to do at a very early age. A *Redbook* magazine article about singer Linda

Ronstadt says that "Her first memory is of saying to her parents, 'Play me some music.' . . . She was four years old and singing with them one evening when she began to harmonize. Her father said, 'You aren't singing the melody.' She said, 'I know.' "* And the sculptor Louise Nevelson, in her memoir *Dawns & Dusks,* remembers, "From earliest, earliest childhood I knew I was going to be an artist. I *felt* like an artist. . . . I drew in childhood, and went on painting daily. . . . As a young child I could go into a room and remember everything I saw. I'd take one glance and know everything I saw. That's a visual mind."†

The only real difference between these people and you is that there is an unbroken continuity between the children they were and the adults they have become. We're going to go to work to reestablish that continuity for you. But first we need to know: who was that child? What did she or he love? The design of your life path is right there in miniature, like the genes in a seed that say it's going to become a tomato plant, a palm tree, or a rose. So I'd like you to think back to your childhood, and see how much you can remember that might point to your own special kind of genius.

Or, since that word still sounds presumptuous to our ears, I've got an even better name for it. Let's call it your *original self.* And I mean that in both senses of the word "original": "there from the beginning" and "unique, new, never seen in the world before."

EXERCISE 2: Your Original Self

Let your mind wander back through your childhood memories— especially the private, special times when you were allowed to play or daydream or do whatever you wanted to do. Now, on a fresh sheet of paper, try to answer these questions:

What especially attracted and fascinated you when you were a child?

What sense—sight, hearing, touch—did you live most through, or did you enjoy them all equally?

What did you love to do, or to daydream about, no matter how "silly" or unimportant it may seem to you now? What were the secret

---

*Elizabeth Kaye, "Linda Ronstadt: Why Is She the Queen of Lonely?" *Redbook* 152 (February 1979): 130.

†Louise Nevelson, *Dawns & Dusks.* Taped conversations with Diana MacKown. (New York: Charles Scribner's Sons, 1976), pp. 1, 13, 14.

fantasies and games that you never told anybody about?

Does it feel like there's still a part of you that loves those things?

What talents or abilities might those early interests and dreams point to?

Marcia, 32, answered this question very poignantly:

"I actually went back to what I'd experienced in the first five years of my life. Since then it's been downhill. This exercise was very emotional for me. I've had a lot of therapy, but I never realized my first five years were so good."

Here are some other answers:

Ellen, 54: "I remember I had this thing about trees. I used to stand and stare up at them and put my arms around their trunks. I think I knew what it felt like to be one."

John, 35: "I was nutty about rhythm. I was always patting out private little riffs on the dinner table. Nobody could eat their dinner."

Bill, 44: "I loved color. I know I was drawing from the time I was old enough to clutch a crayon. I covered sheets of paper, the pages of books, and the wall next to my bed with brightly-colored scribbles."

Anna, 29: "This will sound ridiculous, but there was a commercial on TV in the Midwest for a beer called Hamms that was made in Minnesota. They had this little song—I can still remember the words and the tune: 'From the land of sky-blue waters / From the land of pines, lofty balsams / Comes the beer refreshing / Hamms, the beer refreshing.' It had a haunting sound and Indian tomtoms and they showed a lake sparkling in the moonlight. Well . . . at night in bed I used to put my head under the covers and pretend I was an Indian princess in the Land of Sky-Blue Waters."

If you didn't have a goal when you started this book, congratulations. You may not believe it, but you have just taken your first step toward choosing one.

Ellen's youngest daughter just left for college, and Ellen is looking for a career. She could have been—and still could be—a botanist, a forester, a gardener, a poet or a painter, or even a psychotherapist.

John is a skilled machinist. He doesn't know much about music, but he could have been—and still could be—a fine jazz drummer or dancer.

Bill is a lawyer, like his father. He makes a good living and he likes his work OK—but he has a gifted artist or interior decorator hiding inside just waiting to be discovered.

Anna is an editorial secretary in a publishing house. She had, and still has, the kind of imagination it takes to be a writer or film director or an editor-in-chief.

What was your answer? What does it tell you about what you want and what you could be good at?

Now comes the real question.

How was Albert Einstein able to become Albert Einstein, while Marcia, Ellen, John, Bill, and Anna—and maybe you—have not made the fullest use of your talents?

If we really did all come into the world with full-sized helpings of originality and drive, how do you explain Albert Einstein? Mary Cassatt? Luther Burbank? Margaret Mead? They had to make it through the first grade. They had to grow up and pay the rent. How did they manage to keep their treasure maps intact? They must have had some mysterious quality—strength of character, perseverance, self-confidence, self-discipline, belief in themselves, even an instability verging on madness—something that puts those "special" people in a separate category from you and me.

It's true. The "geniuses," the truly successful, the self-fulfilled, did have something we did not. But there is nothing the least bit mysterious about it. It's not something you have to be born with, nor is it a character virtue you must develop over years of lonely struggle. I'll tell you exactly what Albert Einstein got.

Soil and air and water and sun.

ENVIRONMENT

If a seed is given good soil and plenty of water and sun, it doesn't have to try to unfold. It doesn't need self-confidence or self-discipline or perseverance. It just unfolds. As a matter of fact, it can't help unfolding.

If a seed has to grow with a rock on top of it, or in deep shade, or without enough water, it won't unfold into a healthy full-sized plant. It will try—hard—because the drive to become what you are meant to be is incredibly powerful. But at best it will become a sort of ghost of what it could be: pale, undersized, drooping.

In a way, that's what most of us are.

I am talking about nurture, nourishment, care. I am saying that the difference between a genius and you and me is in our environment—and that means our first environment, our childhood family.

In essence, what Albert Einstein got was this:

Somebody—I don't know who, his mother, his father, his grandfather, his uncle—somebody told him it was fine for him to do whatever he wanted to do. They saw something in him, something stubborn, shy, special, and they respected and cherished it. And I wouldn't be at all surprised to learn that somebody gave him a compass, a gyroscope, some books, and a conspiratorial grin, and then let him alone.

It's that simple. And that rare.

It's hard for us to believe in ourselves if no one has ever believed in us, and it is almost impossible for us to stick to our own vision in the face of overwhelming discouragement. And we cannot so much as build a bookshelf if no one ever told us we could do it, gave us the materials, and showed us how. That's our nature. That's how we are.

In the age of ecology, we ourselves are the only creatures we would ever expect to flourish in an environment that does not give us what we need! We wouldn't order a spider to spin an exquisite web in empty space, or a seed to sprout on a bare desk top. And yet that is exactly what we have been demanding of ourselves.

As a result, most of us are not aware that we didn't grow up in an environment that nurtured genius. We just think *we* aren't geniuses, and blame heredity or our own lack of character for the spot we're in. Whatever was amiss with the environment we grew up in, we figure "geniuses" had it just as bad or worse. *They* just had the mysterious fortitude to overcome it. We don't see that grandmother or special teacher who was there with the right kind of love and help at the right moment. We wouldn't recognize the key features of a nurturing environment if we fell over them.

In the next chapter, I'm going to show you what that environment really is, and just how it differs from the one most of us grew up in. And then I am going to demonstrate to you that all genuinely successful people—the ones who love their lives—have had that environment . . . or some parts of it . . . or they've figured out how to create it for themselves.

And then we are going to start creating it for you.

–2–
The Environment That Creates Winners

I am going to ask you some questions now about the family you grew up in.

If your answer to all or most of these questions is "Yes," congratulations. I'm jealous. You are one of the rare and lucky ones. You had the great good fortune to be raised in *the environment that creates winners* —the optimum environment for the growth and flourishing of human beings.

The fact is that very few of us were lucky enough to grow up in such an environment. I certainly wasn't. It wasn't our parents' fault. They weren't raised in that kind of environment either, and they couldn't have had any idea how to create one. Given their own upbringing, it's moving that most of them still managed to provide us with at least one or two features of that environment—because they loved us.

Every "Yes" you can answer to one of these questions is something inside you that you can build on—the beginning of a bridge between your child genius and its full adult expression. For every "No," I'll invite you to give a little thought to how your life could have been different if you'd been able to answer "Yes." Even if you answer every one of these questions "No," don't despair. With the help of this book, you will be able to build that bridge now.

Here goes.

In your family, when you were growing up:

1. Were you treated as though you had a unique kind of genius that was loved and respected?

I hope you are lucky enough to be able to answer "Yes" to this one. Unfortunately, if you are like many of us, you not only weren't treated as if you were precious and special, but if you let it slip that *you* thought you were pretty hot stuff, you probably got cooled down fast.

The sad thing is, our parents sometimes did this because they loved us, and they wanted to protect us from the kinds of disappointment and humiliation they had suffered. A lot of them went out there with nothing on their side but their own frail, brave conviction of specialness, and they got clobbered. And they figured maybe if they cut our expectations down to size for us—nipped them in the bud, so to speak—we could avoid that pain. Sort of a bitter way of saying, "Don't try that, honey, you'll only get hurt. Believe me. I've been out there. I've tried."

Of course, sometimes there was a darker motive. Jealousy. Your parents may never have felt that they had the right, much less the opportunity, to get what they wanted out of life. Let's face it. How many of our mothers really had a chance to do anything but keep house, raise babies, and maybe work to supplement the family income? How many of our fathers really got the chance to explore their own talents and interests? Most of them had to start earning a living and supporting a family when their own lives had hardly begun. My parents were like that. If yours were, how do you imagine they felt when you came along? Proud. Delighted. Hopeful. But then you began to grow . . . and demand . . . and suddenly they saw blooming in you all the qualities they'd had to squelch in themselves: open, shameless wanting; free fantasy; originality; ambition; pride. They saw you grabbing the limelight when they had never gotten enough of it. They had learned at great inner cost to be modest and self-sacrificing and resigned—often for your sake—and they said, *"I* learned that lesson. You'll learn it too."

As very small children, we sense that message. We'd rather forget our destiny than risk hurting or angering the person whose love is life itself to us.

So perhaps, whenever that stubborn "special" feeling does raise its head, it may be immediately followed by a wave of shame and an automatic little tape recording that says "Who do I think I am?" If that happens to you, it's a sure sign that your answer to Question Number 1 was "No."

Think about it: how might you and your life have been different if you had been treated differently? Where might you be today?

2. *Were you told that you could do and be anything you wanted—and that you'd be loved and admired no matter what it was?*

This is nothing more than love and respect in action. To truly cherish someone's genius is to give it complete freedom to choose its own mode of expression—and then to support and honor that choice.

This means that when you came home from school and said, "I've decided I'm going to be a doctor when I grow up," or "I'd sure like to be a movie star," or "I want to be a clown in the circus," your parents said with real enthusiasm, "That sounds great! I think you'd be really good at it."

Instead, what most of us heard was something like this:

"A doctor? Well, dear, you could become a nurse." Or:

"If it was so easy to be a movie star, everybody would be doing it. Stop daydreaming and start thinking about the kind of grades you'll need to get into college." Or:

"Ugh, what a disgusting idea. The circus is so dirty."

And so on.

This is where both our present behavior and our future ambitions began to be shaped to fit our parents' ideas about what it was possible and proper for us to be, even if that was very different from what we really were and yearned to become. A steelworker's son born to be a brilliant scholar may be in trouble. So may a lawyer's daughter who dreams of being a jockey. Many families believe that certain occupations are either "beyond us" or "beneath us," and they pass these preconceptions on to the child, so that the range of available possibilities is restricted from the start.

Of course, one of the most powerful sets of shaping preconceptions is, "What is a boy?" and "What is a girl?"

If you're a man, when you were growing up I'll bet there was one pair of words you never heard set up against each other with regard to you and your life, and that is *selfless* and *selfish*. These words are for women. Oh, from time to time your mother may have told you you were selfish, but she didn't really mean it. After all, you were different from her. You were supposed to be so absorbed in your own activities that you were more or less oblivious to the state of order or disorder in your room and the subtle mood changes of the people around you. You got love for being precisely that way—active and self-absorbed and good at things. (Good at *what* things is the rub, but I'll get back to that in a moment.)

If you were a little girl, you probably weren't told you were selfish unless you tried to do something you wanted to do that wasn't for anybody but you. And then—especially if you got so wrapped up in it that you forgot to be nice to your baby brother or to set the table—it was made swiftly clear to you that you lacked the quality that makes for lovable people and you'd better shape up.

Women are raised for love. That is, we have been raised to give it in order to get it. Our upbringing trained us to nurture other people. We're supposed to be good to our children so that they can grow up and realize themselves. We're supposed to back up our husbands so that they feel free to go out and realize themselves. In other words, the flowers are to grow, and guess what that makes us? Fertilizer—to put it politely. That's how most of us were taught we would get love—not by being flowers ourselves. If we dared to flower—to be active and self-absorbed and good at things—nobody would feed our roots, and we would die. At least, that's how it felt.

The psychologist Abraham Maslow has written that all human beings have a *hierarchy of needs.* Our more basic needs have to be fulfilled before we can even start thinking about the higher ones. First come food and shelter—the physical, survival needs. Then come the emotional needs—love for ourselves as we really are and a sense of belonging. Only when all those needs are fulfilled do we really feel secure enough to seek self-realization. Love is such a fundamental need that people go where the love goes just the way the roots of a plant turn toward water and the leaves turn toward light. Our culture trains us to take certain roles by putting the love in that direction—and we just grow that way! And the fact is that in our culture, until very recently, most men have gotten love for realizing themselves; most women have gotten it for helping other people realize themselves.

That means a man can—if he's lucky—fulfill his whole hierarchy of needs with the same actions. Did you ever hear of a little boy who thought he was going to have to make a choice between a career and a wife?! On the contrary, the better he is in his career, the better the wife he's able to get! If you were a little girl, however, somewhere in the back of your mind you probably knew that that was one of the choices you were going to have to make. You could go ahead and be a success, sure, but you'd be loved just about as much as Joan Crawford was in all those movies, which is not at all. No wonder so many women feel divided about success if not downright terrified of it! We're being forced to choose between two of our own human needs—a higher one, self-realization, and a more basic one, love. And that's an impossible choice.

Little girls are being brought up differently these days. But if you were born before, say, 1968—and it's safe to say that covers almost every reader of this book—chances are you bear at least some of these marks of a nice old-fashioned girlhood:

1. You find it difficult to think in terms of what *you* want—to be, to do, to have, to see—because you've never been encouraged to think that way.

2. Even if you've managed to keep your dreams alive, you may have trouble taking them seriously, because you've never been taken seriously. Your talents and interests were considered, at best, qualities that would make you more attractive to a man, provided you didn't develop them seriously enough to threaten him!

3. You don't know how to ask for help in getting what you want, because you feel you're supposed to give help, not get it.

4. Even if you can ask for help, you don't know how to put human resources to work for you in an effective, task-oriented way. Most women are personality-oriented. We are hypersensitive to personalities and feelings, and we tend to get bogged down in them.

5. By far the most devastating: you are afraid that if you dare to go after what you want, you'll be all alone, because that's selfish—and selfish means alone.

Take heart. We'll be talking about all these problems—and finding real solutions for them—as this book goes along.

Men have other problems.

If you are a man, the odds are that you were taken seriously—maybe too seriously. You knew very early that you were going to be expected to earn your living when you grew up . . . but your parents may have had some very definite ideas about just how you should earn that living.

They wanted you to be a success, all right—their kind of success. You had to get into a good college or make the Law Review, or take over the family business. You certainly had to do something "masculine." Whether your family's idea of a man was a professor, a company president, or a longshoreman, it's likely to have been rather clearly defined, if not rigid. And your childhood play and daydreams were expected to conform to that idea. If you were a boy who happened to like to read a lot, or play the piano, or play with dolls (dolls are toy humans and little boys, being human, are often interested in them), what did you do if your dad got a sick look in his eyes? You put down your book or doll and picked up your baseball glove and went out and threw a few with him. As a result, as early as the age of five you may already have had a full-blown case of amnesia about what *your* unique talents and interests were. I suspect that there are a lot of poets and chefs and dancers walking around out there disguised as lawyers, even from themselves.

Whether you're a man or a woman, if your answer to question No. 2 was "No," think about it: how might you and your life have been different if you had been lovingly told that the whole world of human possibilities was open to you to take your pick? Where might you be today?

3. *Were you given real help and encouragement in finding out* what *you wanted to do—and* how *to do it?*

This one is terribly important. Because without it, even if you *did* get No. 1 and No. 2, they may not have been much use to you. In fact, they may have done you more harm than good. Ask those of us who were told we could be whatever we wanted—and then weren't told how.

What this means is that if you said, "You know, I'd really love to be a scientist," or if you spent your free time drawing or taking things apart to see how they worked, your parents noticed your interest, gently encouraged it, and helped you feed it by putting all kinds of resources at your disposal: books, materials, people. They helped you get a library card and showed you where the science shelf was. They helped you set up a terrarium, or they gave you a microscope or a good set of pastels for your birthday. They introduced you to a scientist or an art teacher or an inventor or a mechanic who was actually doing something that clicked with your interests and was happy to let you watch—and teach you how.

In other words, they used their adult knowledge of the world to show you some of the wonderful things that could be done—and were being done—by people like you.

Many parents, with the best will in the world, didn't do this because they thought it would be "pushing" you. Or it may have been a sneaky Puritan test of your motivation: if you really cared, you'd have the ingenuity and the guts to go find out for yourself. But when you're 5 years old, or 8 years old, how are you going to know that there are pastel chalks in all the colors of the earth and sky unless somebody shows them to you? When you're 10, or 12, you take a look at the awesome competence of a grown-up dancer or doctor or carpenter, and you're just not going to see how you'll ever make it—unless someone takes the trouble to tell you that she or he started at the beginning, like you, with nothing but curiosity and love. Talent is inborn. Know-how is acquired. And you don't acquire it out of the air; you acquire it from the people who've got it. If your family was confident and aware enough to help you get in touch with even a small part of the big and thrilling world of grown-up play—the world of skills and activities and ideas—you're in luck.

Relatively few women have gotten this kind of help, and most of them come from wealthy or accomplished families, like Marya Mannes and Margaret Mead. More men got it because it's considered important for a boy to develop skills and interests. But on the other hand, he may also be expected to do it all by himself. Now here's a very interesting question:

If you did get No. 1 and No. 2, but not No. 3, did you blame yourself for not becoming all they said you could become?

I'll bet at least once, and probably eleven times, you've pulled yourself together, decided you could really make it, walked out the front door, and then not had the slightest idea where to go next. Of course not! *Nobody ever told you.* But instead of walking up to somebody and saying, "Excuse me, but where do I go next?" you said to yourself, "Here I've been secretly thinking I was something special. It's not true. I'd better be content with just typing 80 words per minute and being a good person." And you went back in the house and sat down, glad that nobody had seen you. That lasted maybe a year or two, until the dream-hunger rose up again and you tried again and wound up standing on that same sidewalk, thinking, "That's twice. That proves I'm a dummy." And all because nobody ever told you that you're supposed to walk out that door ignorant, and that you are then entitled to get all the information, instruction, help, and advice you need!

If your answer to No. 3 was "No," think about it: how might you and your life be different if you had been helped to decide *what* you wanted to do—and then helped to learn *how* to do it? Where might you be today?

4. Were you encouraged to explore all your own talents and interests, even if they changed from day to day?

That means when you came in at the age of 7 and said, "Mama, I am going to be a movie star," she said, "You know, you might be good at that." Then she got out the Super-8, let you put on her makeup, took a movie of you, let you see it, and showed you and your best friend how to use the camera. And two days or two months later, when you announced, "I've given up my career as an actress. I've decided to be a fireman and rescue people," she said, "Sounds good to me. Want to go over to the firehouse and look at the engines?"

The key word is *explore.* Childhood is a great time for trying out all the myriad possibilities of your being. (Adulthood isn't a bad time for doing that, either, as you'll find out as we go along.) And taking a child's talents and interests "seriously" does not mean expecting a 7-year-old to choose her lifetime career.

If your answer to No. 4 is "No," how do you think your life might be different today if you'd been encouraged to explore *all* your talents and interests? Because most of us do have more than one, you know.

5. Were you allowed to complain when the going got rough, and given sympathy instead of being told to quit?

This one breaks down into two parts:

5a. Were you allowed to complain when the going got rough?

That means it was OK to come in and say, "It's too hard. I can't. I won't. I'm going to flunk. I don't know how. They yelled at me. I hate it. I've changed my mind. I'm never going to do anything again." And . . . they listened. They didn't get hysterical and say, "I knew it—she can't make it. I was afraid of this." And they didn't get furious and say, "Stop that! Pull yourself together!" They really listened, so that you felt that they cared about you, and that doubt, fear and discouragement were normal, acceptable feelings—not shameful or frightening ones.

5b. Were you given sympathy instead of being told to quit?

A lot of us—especially women—were given sympathy as a *part* of being told to quit. "Welcome home, poor darling. You're right, it is too hard. Of course you should give up. Go to bed and relax. It doesn't matter. We still love you. We'll take care of you."

I know a woman, very unsure of her capacities as a student, who started medical school at 27. She was overwhelmed by the masses of material she had to learn, but she was struggling bravely through it all when her father called her up one night and said, "You know, we'll still love you if you fail." Of course he was trying to be kind, to take the pressure off. She could have killed him.

What we really needed, and what practically none of us got, was to be told, "Yeah, it sounds awful. Really rough. I remember when I was in school—it's murder." And then, when you'd griped and moaned your heart out for fifteen minutes and were feeling lighter: "Finished? All right, come on. Time to get out there and try again. Yes, it *is* hard. And you can do it." And maybe even: "I'll help."

If your answer to one or both parts of No. 5 was "No," how do you think your life might have been different if you had been given that kind of tender toughness?

6. Were you bailed out when you got in over your head—without reproach?

This one really breaks down into two parts, too.

6a. Were you bailed out? If you got into trouble and called Mama and Daddy, did you get help? A lot of us did.

6b. But without reproach? Not likely. Most of us vividly remember the scoldings on the way home in the car when we'd done something a little too adventurous or impulsive and had to be hauled out of the drink by the scruff of the neck. A lot of that anger was just the anxiety and pain of parents who would have liked to spare us the uncomfortable but priceless experience of making mistakes. Some of it may have been embarrassment at the way our conduct reflected on them. But trying something and messing it up is a complete and self-contained learning experience. Just about all a parent or teacher can do is point that out. Throwing anger or blame at somebody who's already smarting from a mistake only damages the learner's feeling of self-worth and his or her eagerness to try things again. Yet how rare it was to be told, "Mistakes don't mean you're bad. They're how you learn."

If your answer to No. 6 was "No," how might your life be different if you had been told just that?

Now comes the toughest and most important one of all:

7. Were you surrounded by winners who were pleased when you won?

That is: were the people in your family people who had really gotten what they wanted out of life—who had gotten their chance, and taken it—so that when *you* won, they felt great about it?

They didn't have mixed emotions. They cheered: "Terrific! Another one on board! We are some bunch of talented people."

That sounds like Heaven to almost all of us. We live in a society that has made it heartbreakingly, unnecessarily difficult for people to get what they want, or even to believe that they should or can get it. So most of us grew up surrounded by people who'd either never had a chance, or who'd had a chance but no support or encouragement. They had *not* gotten what they wanted—and they either blamed circumstances ("hard reality"), or they blamed themselves. Either way, they could not be anything but ambivalent about the prospect of our success . . . afraid for us if we tried, helpless to help us, jealous and lonely if we made it across the line into the winners' world.

Have you caught on to the secret? This one single quality of the ideal family is the key to them all. *The environment that creates winners is almost always made up of winners.* That doesn't necessarily mean famous people, hot shots, or superachievers. It does mean people who are contented and curious, open and vital, who trust life and respect themselves—so that they can allow and encourage you to make your own unique experiment.

People who are happily absorbed in what they are doing are real, reachable "role models" for their children. Their kids can observe, close up, *how things really get done*—not by magic, but step by possible step—whether it's practicing the piano or building a bookshelf. What's more, parents who are "winners," so far from "not having time" for their children's interests, are the most likely to encourage them, too, to experience the satisfaction of doing things they love. And they will know, because they've done it themselves, how to help their children get in touch with the skills, information, and resources they need. People who have tried, failed without blame, tried again in a different way, and succeeded—and all winners, without exception, have done this countless times—will be able to help their children overcome discouragement and learn from their mistakes.

Because information about what it really takes to win has not been made freely available in our society, there has been almost no way to learn it except by being lucky enough to get close to people who are doing it. If you didn't grow up in a family of winners, there was really only one other way to learn the secrets of winning. And that's the long, hard way I did it—by trial and error, against tough inner and outer odds: fear, loneliness, and ignorance.

I want to change all that. I don't think anybody should have to do it the long, hard way. Life is too short, and the unique human potential of each one of us is too precious to waste. The purpose of this book is to give you the inside dope on what it really takes to win. But first, I'd like you to ask yourself a question that may be a little painful. Daring to answer it, in spite of that pain, is an important first step on the road to success.

Suppose you had grown up in a family of winners—people who had gotten what they wanted out of life, who knew how to help you get what *you* wanted, and who were nothing but delighted when you got it.

How do you think you and your life might have been different? Where might you be today?

I'm going to run through the list of qualities of that ideal family once more, and as I do, you'll have an opportunity to pull together all the thoughts you've had in the course of this chapter.

EXERCISE 3: What You Might Have Been

Remember what you learned in the last chapter about "your original self"? Now imagine that that gifted child—you—had grown up in a family in which you were:

- treated as though you had a unique kind of genius that was loved and respected . . .
- told that you could do and be anything you wanted—and that you'd be loved and admired no matter what it was . . .
- given real help and encouragement in finding out *what* you wanted to do and *how* to do it . . .
- encouraged to explore *all* your own talents and interests, even if they changed from day to day . . .
- allowed to complain when the going got rough, and given sympathy instead of being told to quit . . .

- bailed out when you got in over your head—without reproach . . .
- surrounded by winners who were pleased when you won.

What do you think you would be doing now? What would you already have done? What kind of person would you be?

Think BIG. Be as extravagant and far-fetched as you like. What I want to hear is the big one, the dream you think you would have gone for if everything had been on your side. If you really think you might have been President of the United States, say the President of the United States. After all, we're only talking "what if." All the rules of "reality" and "possibility" and "modesty"—even the law of gravity, if it cramps your style—are hereby suspended for the duration of this exercise. We'll deal with them later. Right now, I want your imagination free to fly just as far as it can in whatever direction it chooses.

The pain can come in as it dawns on you how much you might really have done if your circumstances had been different. But uncomfortable as it is, that is a *good sign.* It means you are beginning to cherish and respect yourself—and without that, you'll never know how much you still can do. So just let any anger or pain lend your imagination defiant wings. Your capacity to do will depend on your capacity to dream, so prove that *that* capacity, at least, has survived intact.

What might you have been?
I'd have been a famous movie star and gotten bored with it and given it up already!
Here are some answers given by a roomful of perfectly "ordinary" people:
"I'd either be Judy Collins or the president of a corporation."
"I'd be a whole lot richer."
"A great surgeon."
"The Sarah Bernhardt of the 1970s."
"I'd have my own company."
"A traveling news correspondent."
"A top administrator in the school district."
"I'd be an architect."
"A world-famous organist."
"An anchorwoman."
"This is very immodest, but I'd be the president of General Mills."

Stop right there! I asked you to throw out modesty, but this woman —it *was* a woman—said, "very immodest." That's an important thing to notice about women: whenever we confess to having big dreams or ambitions, we get embarrassed and apologetic. Show me a man who feels that it's "immodest" to head for the top of any business or profession! You don't have to dream of being Barbara Walters or the president of a corporation—to open a plant store or learn to play the guitar is every bit as fine an ambition—but if that *is* the kind of thing you yearn for, don't apologize!

"I'd have made a movie, traveled all over the world, and had several hit records."

"I would have given Mme. Curie a run for her money."

"I'd have three Olympic gold medals."

"I'd be the female counterpart of Johnny Carson."

"I'd have published a novel, and I'd play folk guitar, and I'd be studying mime, sign language, drums, Spanish, and Japanese!!"

"I'd be a multilingual interpreter at the UN."

"I'd be the originator and head of a very unusual kind of textile center—a design and manufacturing center for fabrics and a learning institution. Or I'd be a painter. Or an anthropologist. And a folksinger in twenty languages on the side."

Yes. There's evidence that we are all, at least potentially, "Renaissance people"—that a single human brain contains many more capacities than we realize.

Now look at your answer. Were you as daring as the people quoted above?

Examine your answer carefully. Make sure you're not pulling your punches, settling for the "possible" or the "realistic." If you are, stop and readjust your sights upward. Remember, this is fantasy. We're talking about you as you would have responded to a loving, encouraging, instructive environment expressly designed to cultivate your genius.

I'll bet you would have done some pretty fantastic things.

Would you still like to do them? Or a lot of other things that are just as fun and grand?

You still can.

I don't care how old you are, or what your past history has been, or what your present circumstances are: you can still do and have and be anything in the world you really want. And the way you do it is by creating the environment that creates winners around you *now*.

BEYOND "FREUDIAN FATALISM"

"But isn't it too late?" you may be asking. "The damage is done. OK, I can see how growing up in that kind of family would have made me creative and strong and unafraid. But I didn't. So I've already lost my best years for learning skills, and I don't have any of those fabulous inner strengths that are built by good early nutrition—self-confidence and self-esteem and the courage to take risks. I'm going to have to limp along through life without them—unless I can undo some of the damage in therapy, and that's a long, slow process."

I believe in therapy. But if I'd waited for it to fix me up, I'd have been 90 before I walked out the door. It's not only that untying all those emotional knots takes time. (After all, it took years to tie them, and deeply impressionable years at that.) It's that *understanding is one thing and action is another.* You can spend years understanding your fear of water and still never walk to the edge of the pool and jump in.

But you don't have to be doomed to a half-life by the environment you grew up in. Put us in a nourishing environment, even late in a hard life, and we burst into bloom. The misconception I call "Freudian fatalism" has had its day. Now many therapists themselves are rejecting the idea that character is almost irreversibly stamped by the early years of life. They have discovered that we never lose the capacity for growth —or for new learning.

But we never lose our basic needs, either—for food and shelter, acceptance and love. And if you know somebody who's winning and *loving* it (and that's the only definition of winning I'll accept), you can bet that there's a source of support and nourishment in that person's life. And I don't mean only in the past. I mean right now.

You know that "self-reliant" entrepreneur who made it to the top by lonely struggle? He's got . . . a wife. A woman who cheered him up when he was low, listened to his gripes, told him he could do it, typed his proposals, and fed him his dinner. In Chapters 5 and 10, you'll learn to create that kind of support for yourself without taking over anyone else's life—whether you're a man or a woman.

He has something else, too. A little black book full of phone numbers he knows he can call—classmates, cronies, colleagues, friends—whenever he needs information, advice, an introduction, a loan, or an expert's services. That's called *the old-boy network,* and you will learn to create one for yourself in Chapter 7, even if you're not old-boy yourself, or if you're a girl.

And how about that ever so "self-disciplined" novelist who turns out a complete first draft in nine months, when you can't get past page one? She has a structure. A deadline. An expectant editor waiting for her work. A place to sit down undisturbed. A certain number of hours a day. A regular daily output of words or pages. Someone to give her a cup of coffee and a sendoff like Odysseus in the morning, and then meet her at three and say, "How'd it go?" and maybe even read what she's written. Virginia Woolf had Leonard. George Eliot had George Henry Lewes. Gertrude Stein had Alice B. Toklas. Soil and air and water and sun.

You know how hard it is to get anything done entirely on your own. You look for any reason to stop, or you forget, or your pencil breaks, or your finger gets stuck in the typewriter. You don't do it. *And nobody notices.* The times in your life when you have gotten things done, it was probably in a situation where somebody set tasks for you and would have noticed and minded if you didn't do them—like when you worked in an office, or when you got assignments and papers in school. That isn't a terrible weakness. It's human nature. A structure is to us what a loom is to a weaver, or a doorframe to a spider. That's why the first thing all "self-motivated" people do is to set up a structure that will not only help them but *make* them do what they want to do! You will learn to create that kind of structure for yourself in Chapters 6 through 11: a plan that breaks down your goal into manageable tasks and assigns them to you one by one, and a *report-in system* that puts your boss and conscience outside yourself.

To succeed in our thin and chilly atmosphere, you need a Portable Life Support System, like the backpacks the astronauts wore on the moon to give them oxygen, comfortable pressure, and communication. The rest of this book is going to be your Portable Success Support System. It will provide all the features of the environment that create winners. Since you are a unique individual, you will adapt this support system to your own needs. Which parts of it you find most useful will depend on which features were missing in your past:

- *If you were never treated as if you had a special kind of genius that was worthy of love and respect,* you will find that genius alive and well in Chapter 3, "Stylesearch."
- *If you weren't told that it was fine to do and be anything you wanted,* Chapter 4, "Goalsearch," will help you find what's exactly right for you out of all the possibilities in the world.
- *If you weren't helped to figure out what you wanted to do—and HOW to do it,* Chapter 4 will take care of the "what"; the whole "craft" section of the book will show you HOW.
- *If you weren't encouraged to explore ALL your own talents and interests,* Chapters 3 and 4 (and especially "Five Lives," p. 83) will introduce you to some you didn't even remember you had—and show you how they can all be active in your life.
- *If you weren't allowed to complain and given sympathy instead of being told to quit,* you'll have a ball in Chapter 5, "Hard Times, or The Power of Negative Thinking."
- *If you weren't bailed out of trouble without reproach,* you'll find ample permission to goof up in Chapter 9, "First Aid for Fear."
- *If you weren't surrounded by winners who were delighted when you won,* Chapter 7 ("Barn-Raising"), Chapter 10 ("Don't-Do-It-Yourself"), and the Epilogue ("Learning to Live With Success") will show you how you can encourage your friends and family to win with you. But this whole book was written in the hope that we can gradually change the desert around us—with its rare, lush oases of celebrity—into a worldwide garden of winners who are delighted with and for each other.

Two

Wishing

– 3 –
Stylesearch

I'd like you to begin making your life come true by taking a loving look at your own style: how you dress, how you decorate your apartment or house, what colors and foods and movies and music and books you like, all the thousand little details of choice and preference by which you please yourself.

We ordinarily think of personal style as something that "doesn't matter"—fun, but rather trivial and optional; a private game we play in our leisure time after we've dealt with the serious business of life. Style seems like the last place you'd be likely to find the key to success. And yet, after your memories of what you loved best as a child and your fantasies about what you'd have loved to be, your style is your most precious clue to your genius.

Just because it isn't considered "important," style is the biggest field of free play and free choice left to you. Your deepest resources—your talent, your imagination, your identity—cannot be completely suppressed. They *must* declare themselves. And they do—in the one "safe" area society has left free from expectations or consequences. Your style only needs to be noticed and taken seriously to start furnishing rich clues for the direction and design of your life.

If this sounds a little exaggerated, you can demonstrate its truth for yourself. Here's a simple exercise that will reveal the unsuspected importance of your style. It was originated by Jack Canfield, Director of the Institute for Wholistic Studies in Amherst, Massachusetts, and it's one of my favorites.

EXERCISE 4: Pick a Color ("I am blue")

Choose a color that appeals to you. It doesn't have to be your all-time favorite, or a color you especially like to wear—though it may be. The best way to pick one is to look at a selection of colors, and I'd also like you to have your color in front of you while you do this exercise. So you might glance through a brightly colored magazine . . . or look around for a color that catches your eye in a painting or print, a chair or a rug, in the room where you're sitting right now . . . or if you have a child's box of crayons, or a set of chalks or paints, that will give you an excellent range to choose from. (Remember the delicious feeling of choice you got when you opened a brand-new box of forty-eight sharp-pointed crayons and decided which one to draw with first: silver? flesh? forest green?)

Now I would like you to role-play that color. That means you are going to pretend you *are* that color and speak for it, since it cannot speak for itself. It can't tell us what it's like to be royal purple, or buttercup, or black. You will have to tell what it's like to be your color.

Take a sheet of paper, and start by writing, "I am red" . . . or "I am yellow" . . . or "I am cerulean blue"—whatever color you've chosen. Do *not* say "I like blue because . . ." or "I think blue is . . ." From this moment on you *are* that color.

Now, in a few words to a few sentences, tell what qualities you have *as that color*—not as yourself. For instance, "I am dark blue. I'm quiet and deep like the ocean." Or, "I am yellow. I'm cheerful, intelligent, efficient but warm." (Don't let these responses influence *your* response. There are no right answers to this exercise. If you happen to find black a cozy color, or you think white is depressing and blue is cheerful, great!)

This is a deceptively simple little exercise, and it has so much to tell that I'm going to break its revelations down into three parts, each of which will lead to questions and exercises of its own—choice and identity, uniqueness *vs.* competition, and assets and "objectivity."

I. CHOICE AND IDENTITY

The first thing you may have noticed is that it took you a while to pick your favorite color. You found yourself being very particular and choosy, and it was hard to make up your mind. That happens to a lot of people, and there's a very good reason for it: you didn't want to pick a color that wasn't right.

Somewhere down deep, not much is left to you on which to take a stand—so you'll take it on preferences. You'll fight for your tastes. When it comes to color, or whether you want to eat Chinese or fried chicken, or how you want your house to look, or how you wear your hair, or whether you prefer Elvis Presley or opera, you will take a life and death stand—because that's where your integrity is.

You choose your color so carefully because subconsciously, half-consciously, you know that style is anything but trivial. When you pick your color, or your records, or your necktie, or the print for your curtains, you are doing far more than just pleasing or indulging yourself. You are declaring yourself. You are saying, "This is who I am." That's why those "little" choices are so important to you.

With this in mind, let's take a closer look at your style.

EXERCISE 5: The Private-Eye Game

Play detective. Snoop around your own house or room as if you were a private-eye trying to find out who lived here just from the style revealed in the house. After all, in a way you *are* learning about a stranger. You are following the tracks and examining the fingerprints of a unique individual you do not know who happens to be you.

Look in the clothes closets, the kitchen cabinets, the book and record shelves. Look at the furniture, the rugs, the curtains, the pictures on the walls, the food in the refrigerator, the colors, the state of clutter or order, the arrangement of space. Make an inventory of as many characteristics and interests as you can find.

For instance, would you say that the person who lives here is organized or scatterbrained? Sociable or solitary? Sensual or intellectual? Or some of both? Would she rather read fiction or history? Does he prefer Bach or Eric Clapton? Or both? Do the furnishings this person chose show a preference for rough, natural materials or for finished, classy ones? Does the house or apartment have a striking central feature, or a favorite lived-in place: the kitchen, a writing desk, a fireplace, the stereo? What are the clothes in the closet saying about the person who chose them? (I have never met a person who wasn't carefully costumed!) And so on.

When you've gathered all the clues you can, sit down and read through the detective's profile you've compiled. It is a portrait of yourself.

Are you surprised?

Ruth, a 38-year-old English teacher, was. She had never thought of herself as a visual person. If you'd asked her, she would have said she was primarily interested in literature and music, and didn't know anything about painting. And yet she had covered one whole wall of her apartment with cork board, and pinned up an arrangement of postcards that revealed an instinctive sense of color and design. She'd done it simply because she liked them—because they looked pretty and made her feel good! She'd never given it a second thought. Only when she played the Private-Eye Game did it dawn on her that she was, in fact, a highly visual person who needed to—and knew how to—please her own eye.

Margaret, 26, works as a computer programmer in an office that requires her to dress neatly and conservatively. She thinks of herself as efficient and tidy. When she goes out on weekends, she likes to wear splashy, glamorous clothes—big hats, plunging necklines, capes, and spangles. When she looked at all her evening dresses hanging together in her closet, she felt like Clark Kent looking at Superman's cape. Those clothes added up to a second secret identity: an actress or adventuress, reckless and dramatic, with a love of costume and gesture.

Bill, an accountant who does a lot of his work at home, had devised his own color-coded, fast-access filing system, which he thought of as nothing more than a convenience. When he looked at it with the eye of a detective, he realized that it showed real logic and ingenuity—a talent for organization and design.

Jacob, a 45-year-old bachelor poet-in-residence at a small New England college, recorded the fact that his house had not one center, but two: the library and the kitchen! His spice racks were as carefully stocked as his bookshelves, his copper pots were as lovingly polished as his sonnets, and he had to admit that the man who lived here was considerably more sociable and sensual than the melancholy recluse he'd thought he was.

The Private-Eye Game may give that kind of pleasant shock to *your* self-image. In any case, it is bound to enrich it. Your tastes and choices often reveal aspects of you that you aren't very conscious of, or have never taken seriously. If you've been thinking of yourself as an indistinct person with no special talents or interests, this exercise will lay that idea to rest! You may be puzzled at how you can parlay the discoveries you've made into a goal, activity, or profession, but don't worry about that now. In the next chapter I'll be showing you how to shape a goal—one that is possible in the real world—out of all these characteristics of yourself. Right now, your job is just to have fun discovering them. You're getting to know your multitalented self.

The same goes for you if—at the other extreme—you are already a very goal-directed, even single-minded person. Your style may serve as a safety-deposit box for all the other talents you're not using right now —like Ruth's visual ability. You need to be aware that those talents are there. You don't have to become a dilettante or "spread yourself thin," but you should know that your life will be richer, your energy more abundant, the more of your inborn gifts you can bring into play. In the pages ahead you'll find out how to make room in your life for all of them.

Your style is the place where you still exercise the creative power to shape your world and design yourself. *It is proof that you haven't lost that power at all.* All you need is permission, encouragement, and guidance to expand it into a wider domain: your whole life.

II. UNIQUENESS VS. COMPETITION

Now I'm going to go back to the color exercise and show you another very interesting facet of it. Just take a look at some of the responses other people gave.

"I am red. I am intense, hungry, and angry, like fire."

"I am red. I'm lively and giving."

"I am red. I am a firelit living room with a red velvet couch—I am fiery and passionate, but also cozy and warm."

"I am red like blood—very deep and very vital."

"I am blue. I'm cold, distant, but intelligent."

"I am blue. I'm soothing and serene."

"I am blue—electric blue—crackling with energy."

"I am yellow. I am a new kitchen with lots of sun and flower pots. I am cheerful and like company, order, and comfort."

"I am yellow. I'm quiet, simple, straightforward, sincere."

"I am yellow. I'm heavy, rich and valuable, like gold, like cream."

One thing you can't help noticing right away is the striking variety of answers. But even more important, look how completely different the same color appears through different people's eyes! This can be true right down to the physical level. I have seen two people look at the same color and heard one say "I am rust" and the other say "I am rose."

Do you remember when we were talking about early childhood, and I said that each one of us sees a different world? There it is—in this simple-minded little exercise on color. Your style is a style of perception, a way of seeing and feeling the world, that is unique—as unique as your fingerprints. You are born with it, and it develops as you grow, and it is not like anyone else's in the world. It is literally incomparable.

There is only one way you can compare people with each other, and that is to select one single feature that can be measured quantitatively. Take height. Obviously, some people are taller and some shorter. That doesn't tell you much about them as individuals, but as far as it goes, it is a valid basis for comparison. Unfortunately, in our society comparison, in turn, often becomes the basis for *ranking*. We have an obsessive need to know who is "better," so we take a single quantitative yardstick —like grades in school, or income—and we evaluate a whole individual by his or her performance on that one scale. When you really think about it, this is as absurd as declaring that tall people are superior to short people, or that an orange is better than a rose because it weighs more! And yet we've all been trained to think this way, to compare ourselves to others and worry about whether we "measure up."

Think about it. When you walk into a room full of strangers, don't you immediately, half-consciously "case" it according to your own favorite standard—smart/dumb, rich/poor, pretty/ugly, accomplished/not accomplished, or whatever—and then rank yourself? For instance, if pretty/ugly is your private yardstick, you may think, "Let's see . . . I've got more taste than she does, but that one over there has prettier eyes than I do, and . . ." It's embarrassing to admit, but very few of us are completely immune to this game.

But what would happen to this ranking system if you met people—

and they met you—in terms of individual style? Suppose, for instance, you were going to meet the people who "spoke for their color" in the examples above. How would you rank their answers? Where would you rank your own? Which one do you think is "best"?

Of course. You couldn't even compare them, much less rank them. Because the truth is that human beings are not comparable. You can't compare us any more than you can compare roses and oranges, or mountains and the sea, or France and England. You might prefer living by the sea to living in the mountains. You might rather take your vacation in England than in France. And you certainly like some people better than you like others. Preferences are perfectly valid . . . they're just your style asserting itself again. But you'd feel pretty silly saying, "England is a better country than France," or "The sea is better than the mountains." And it's every bit as silly to go around saying, "I'm better than Mary, but Joe is better than me."

The notion of competition—the idea that there is someone out there just like you, only better—is untrue. What's more, it keeps your attention focused away from yourself, on the struggle to meet the ill-fitting standards of other people, instead of looking inside and discovering your own. The things that are unique and incomparable about you are the only basis on which you can design a life that will truly satisfy *you.* And it is you who must be satisfied. There is no authority outside you who can tell you what's right for you.

When you become aware of your own uniqueness, that's when you really begin to cherish and respect yourself—and to respect others! If you met people on the basis of their style, you would respect each one instinctively, and they would respect you. And there would be genuine mutual interest and curiosity. If we're not in competition with each other—if we're not threatened by our differences or busy trying to rank them—then our differences become resources. I'm not like you, and I don't want to be like you, because then I wouldn't have anyone around me who could tell me anything I didn't know, show me anything I couldn't see. I'd only have me. I want you, too, because you're different.

III. ASSETS AND "OBJECTIVITY"
When you were speaking for your color, did it strike you that you felt free to say *anything?* "I am red; I'm intense and angry. Well, of course it's OK to say I'm angry! I'm red, aren't I?"

Or did you find that you had some difficulty saying things like "I am intelligent, I am passionate, I am sad, I am giving"? Did you feel at all shy about it?

That was a pretty thinly veiled exercise, wasn't it? I'm sure you realized rather quickly that you were talking about yourself—or at least a facet of yourself. If you had been asked to pick your favorite color on a different day, it might have been a different color. But certainly this color represented a part of you . . . and it revealed some pretty intimate things about you, too. That's why it may have been hard for you to talk about it. You were breaking a rule of our culture, the rule against saying, "I am the kind of person who . . ."

How many of us walk through life saying to ourselves and everyone else within earshot, "I'm a passionate person! I may not be organized, but I've got fire and drive"? No, we say, "Lord, I'm fat." That's because we learned very early that to speak honestly about ourselves—and especially to say anything good about ourselves—was taboo. If you're like me, more than once in your life you've walked up to a prospective lover or employer and, convinced that you were being honest and "objective," said, "I want to know everything that's wrong with me in advance!"

Luckily, there are a few loopholes in the taboo—a few places where you *are* allowed, just as a game, to say "I am the kind of person who." Magazine quizzes are one such place. Astrology is another. That's why magazine quizzes and astrology are so popular! Notice that your sign of the zodiac doesn't say you're perfect. It says you're good at this, you're bad at that, these are your wonderful qualities, these are your awful qualities. And you love them all. I'm a Leo. That gives me an excuse to say, "I'm a showoff, I'm a ham, I'm an amateur at everything, I need a lot of affection"—and all without the slightest bit of embarrassment.

That's real objectivity—the kind of loving objectivity that says you're fine and fascinating just the way you are. But take off the mask of your astrological sign, and all of a sudden you're not allowed to say those things any more. *A direct statement about yourself is considered objective only if it is negative.* If it's positive, it is considered *subjective.* And "objective" means it is accurate, and "subjective" means it is conceited self-delusion.

We all have negative tapes running constantly in our heads, reciting our shortcomings, until we know what's wrong with us backwards, forwards, and upside down. Very few of us have positive tapes to tell us all the things that are right with us! And yet, *only when you have a clear, unembarrassed view of your own assets do you have a truly objective picture of yourself*—one you can draw on to design a creative and satisfying life. And so you sorely need some positive tapes that you can play whenever the negative ones get too insistent.

Positive information about yourself isn't as hard to come by as you may think. If you were asked to sit down and give a thoughtful, accurate inventory of your best friend's good qualities, could you do it? Sure—in about two minutes. Well, your best friend can do the same for you. The truth is, you're not hiding your good qualities from anybody except yourself. They're as plain as the nose on your face to anybody who knows you—or even just meets you. You would be surprised and delighted if you could really see yourself through other people's eyes. And so that's exactly what I'm going to invite you to do in this exercise.

EXERCISE 6: Seeing Yourself as Others See You

This exercise comes in two versions—one for extroverts and one for introverts (there's another fun classification for you). If you've got even a little nerve, try Version No. 1. If you're shy but imaginative, you may feel more comfortable with Version No. 2.

VERSION NO. 1: PRAISE BE!

Pick somebody you love and trust—a good friend, or your mate, lover, or child. Sit down with a pen and a piece of paper (no erasing!) and ask him or her to spend about three minutes telling you precisely what's good about you. And you write it down, word for word. This is going to be your positive tape, so get it right.

Don't let your partner get away with saying something vague, like "You're nice," or even "You're wonderful." That's the only kind of praise most of us have ever gotten, and it doesn't help. You need to hear things like: "You have a delightful imagination, you're articulate, your energy is contagious, and you help everyone around you to see the world in fresh, new ways." Or: "Do you know that you move beautifully? You're really graceful—and really giving and kind. You touch people a lot, and you mean it. Anybody in trouble can come to you and feel soothed." This isn't flattery, it's information.

Accurate, perceptive praise is a rarity in our society. It shouldn't be. We all need it, and we'd all love to give it—it's just that nobody ever told us it was OK. Well, I'm telling you now. Everybody needs practice at being both the praiser and the praisee, so after your partner has told you what's right about you, switch roles. There are just a couple of simple rules to follow.

For the praiser: Don't let any criticism sneak in, even if it's "constructive" or compassionate. (This rule is especially important for husbands, wives, and lovers; friends are less likely to want to improve each other.) That means you may not say, "If you just took your glasses off and let your hair down, you'd be really beautiful," or "Some people might say you're opinionated and stubborn, but I think you're definite and strong." The person being praised already knows all that negative stuff by heart and doesn't need to hear it again. Be honestly positive. You'll be amazed how it enhances your appreciation of someone you love to put your perceptions of him or her into words.

For the praisee: As difficult—and delicious—as you will find it, for three minutes you are allowed to do nothing but sit and listen and take dictation like a very conscientious secretary. Don't interrupt. Don't argue. And don't inwardly discount every word your partner says. You're always ready and waiting for criticism, but praise will sneak right up and sock you in your tummy. If you just sit and take it, it can give you gooseflesh, it can even make you cry. So you may try to wiggle out of it. If your partner says, "You're very sensitive," you'll think, "Ah hah. Weepy, weak, hysterical." If s/he says "Sensuous," you'll go, "Fat." Don't do that. Take your partner at his or her word—and get those words down on paper, so you can't revise, edit, and qualify them in memory.

There are a couple of variations on this theme if you find it hard to take your praise right between the eyes. One is to have your partner put it in writing. Another, even better, is to get together with two friends, turn your back on them, and listen while they discuss your good qualities with each other. Then switch around and put somebody else in the "warm seat."

But if you'd really rather not have to ask someone else to tell you the good news, there's a way that you can find out for yourself.

VERSION NO. 2: CREATING YOUR CHEERING SECTION

The truth is, you already know what your own assets are. Whenever you get the chance to talk about yourself in a safe disguise—like astrology—that knowledge pops out. It's there. The color exercise was one of those disguises. When you spoke for your color, I'll bet you declared all its powerful and beautiful and tender qualities. You didn't choose that color in the first place for being ugly or drab, did you? And that color is *you*—a vital part of you.

It's time to come out of all the disguises and start admitting that your positive qualities really do belong to you. But that's hard to do without help. Like every human being, you need *positive feedback* from someone who's on your side before it becomes safe to feel openly good about yourself. Your own family may not have known how to give you that kind of feedback when you were growing up, but now that you are grown up, you can get it for yourself. You can create an imaginary ideal family to be your private cheering section. They will tell you all the good things about you that you really know—but aren't allowed to tell yourself!

The imagination is a very powerful tool, and we'll be using it a lot in this book. We think that only novelists and storytellers have the ability to create characters and give them life. It's not true. That's a human power, and everybody has it—we use it in our dreams! I'm going to show you how to use it consciously, to help you realize your life dreams.

The imaginative technique we're going to use in this exercise is called role-playing. If you pretend that you're someone else—your mother, your father, a famous baseball player, an Eskimo, a beagle—you tap into a deeper source of knowledge, and you'll discover that you know all kinds of things you didn't know you knew. In this case, you're going to pretend you are some very special people who are taking a loving look at you and saying what they see.

Take a few minutes now to think of the four or five people you would choose if you could have anyone in the world—anyone in all history and literature—as your family. I mean your *ideal* family, the kind I described as "the environment that creates winners": a group of people who cherish what's special about you, encourage you to explore all your own talents, and help you keep going when you're down. Give this some thought and care, because you will be meeting these people again as we go along. When you start working toward an actual goal they'll be there to help you feel that you're not alone—that you have the best and most select company in the world.

Choose people you feel a special kinship with: people whose ideas or activities strongly appeal to you, people whose life experience or temperament would make them sympathetic to you (Katharine Hepburn might say, "I know how it is to have a hot temper"), people whose faces you love. Choosing your "family" is like choosing your color: you're asserting your style to select and shape the world around you. You will pick each of your "family" members for a very good reason.

I chose Albert Einstein because he looked as kind as my grandfather, and because he had done badly in math and had a trivial job as a patent clerk, but was so wrapped up in his interests that it never stopped him. And I chose Bette Davis because she is both tough and vulnerable, self-sufficient, witty and smart, and I'd like to have her on my side in a fight! Other favorites of mine are Margaret Mead and Alice's waitress friend in the movie, "Alice Doesn't Live Here Any More."

A writer I know chose the great Austrian poet Rainer Maria Rilke because he'd traveled disconsolately all over Europe bumming off his aristocratic friends, worrying about money, waiting for inspiration, and deploring his own lack of self-discipline. The other members of her family are John Keats, Glenda Jackson, Colette, and Pelé—because she likes his smile!

Write the names of your "family" members down on one or two sheets of paper, with a good paragraph's worth of space under each one. Now close your eyes and imagine that you are one of those people, *and you are watching yourself come through the door.* From the point of view of your "family" member, notice how you move, how you talk to people, the way you use words, the expressions on your face. Watch kindly, with curiosity, interest, and fondness, as if you were watching your favorite child. Write down all the *positive* qualities you see. *Only the positive ones! (Same rule as in Version No. 1, and for the same reason: you don't need to hear all the negative stuff for the umpteenth time.)*

For example:

Einstein: "I can see that Barbara has a good mind—quick, eager, varied. She has a lot of original ideas, and she knows how to make herself understood. She speaks clearly and chooses words well. She's warm and interested in other people. I like the way she responds to everything that is going on around her. She's involved. And she has a lot of energy."

When your first family member has said all she or he has to say, move on and become the next. Each one has a very different point of view and will notice different positive qualities about you. Like this:

Bette Davis: "She's tough, she's got a sense of humor and a great belly laugh. She's not afraid of life. And she sings well, too, with a wistful quality that contradicts the toughness." (Describing myself as myself, I'd be likely to say, "I'm disorganized, impulsive, and probably talk too much." It was a shock to me the first time I saw myself through others' eyes!)

I've told you about my past record, so if *I* can do this, believe me, *you* can.

When you have role-played each member of your "family" in turn, go back and read through their answers. You will have a comprehensive portrait of what's right with you.

Surprised?

There's just one more exercise in your Stylesearch proper—one more useful thing to know about yourself before you take the next step: designing a whole life for yourself in imagination.

YOUR PERSONAL STYLE IN ACTION

Remember that one of the things I asked you to have your "family" members notice about you was *how you move?* Your style is not only a way of seeing the world, but also a unique way of moving through it. If the colors and belongings you surround yourself with reveal your style of *vision,* the activities you enjoy reveal your style of *action.* Sid Simon, author of *Values Clarification* (Hart Publishers) has developed a way of classifying your favorite activities to come up with a *life quality profile:* a concise portrait of *how you like to live.* Fast or slow-paced? More physical or mental activity? With constant company or more by yourself? With what unique balance of these and other factors?

If someone asked you these questions directly, you might be able to give an approximate answer. But after doing this exercise you'll even be able to put it into percentages if you're mathematically inclined

("60–40 in favor of physical"). And again, you may find some surprises, because you'll be looking at your actual preference pattern rather than the often inaccurate image of yourself you've been carrying around in your head.

EXERCISE 7: Twenty Things You Like to Do

Twenty?? Yes. You have to come up with twenty. That's the only rule. I don't care how trivial some of them seem to you—like "eating ice cream"—and I don't care why you like to do them. If you get down to nineteen and you're really desperate and can't think of one more, put "Scratching when it itches." Anything.

Make a simple chart. In the "down" column on the left-hand side, write the things you like to do, one through twenty, in whatever order they come into your head. Don't bother trying to rank them in order of preference, because that's impossible—it's roses and oranges again.

In the "across" column along the top, write the following questions (if you turn the paper sideways and write them vertically, you'll have room):

How long since last done?
Costs money or free?
Alone or with someone?
Planned or spontaneous?
Job related?
Physical risk?
Fast or slow-paced?
Mind, body or spiritual?

You can add any other intriguing categories that occur to you. (For instance: On my list five years ago? Mother/father likes also? City or country? At home/out in the world?) Everything we've done in this section has been to show you that you have the power and the right to reshape the world to fit you. And that includes the exercises in this book! If you can improve on them, or tailor them to your own needs and insights, do it!

When you have filled out your chart, see what patterns you can find.

What did you learn about yourself . . . the kind of life you're living now . . . and the kind of life you'd love to live?

Here's how some other people answered:

Marianne, 32, wife and mother: "I was surprised to find out that there really are easily twenty things I like to do!"

Doris, 45, nurse: "First I got depressed. I said, 'There's no way I could ever do them all.' And then I thought, 'Why not?' "

Ellen, 28, medical student: "I was surprised by the variety. My life has become so single-minded . . . there are a lot of dimensions of me that aren't getting much expression right now."

Jim, 43, lawyer: "It's been altogether too long since I've felt I had time to do about 90 percent of the things I enjoy!"

Lucille, 25, secretary: "It's more important to me than I realized to be physically active and spontaneous. I really shouldn't be spending eight hours a day at a desk."

Allen, 19, student: "Most of the activities I love best really require very little money. This was a revelation to me, because my father had convinced me that I should go into a profession or business where I could earn a six-figure salary. After doing this exercise, I thought, 'What for?' "

Judy, 35, writer: "I'm going to need to earn more to live the kind of life I really want. Travel, skiing, going to concerts and theater and restaurants are all important to me, and they all cost money. Maybe I'd better give some serious thought to trying for a bestseller."

Maurice, 68, retired restaurateur: "I like to be surrounded by lots of busy, noisy people! What am I doing in this goddamned Golden Age condominium?"

Dolores, 24, bookstore cashier: "I'm happiest when I can spend most of my time by myself or with the person I love."

A good look at your own style can tell you many things you never realized about who you really are and what you want. And it can give you a new confidence in yourself. Once you see that every move and choice you make puts your unique stamp on the world, you realize that *you already have the power to shape your life.* Now you're ready for some fantasy practice at expanding that power into wider realms.

LIFE DESIGN REHEARSAL

Using the information you've gained about yourself through your Stylesearch, you're going to play at shaping space and time to fit your needs. First you're going to design an environment so perfectly tailored to *you* that in it all your best qualities would emerge. And then you are going to imagine your ideal day.

Your total environment is often shaped less by your needs and preferences than by whom you live with and what you can afford. How you spend your days is largely determined by your responsibilities. We assume that these factors are pretty much unchangeable—"hard realities." Sure, we could live exactly as we pleased—if we won the lottery, or deserted our families! And the first is improbable and the second is unthinkable. So we may sometimes daydream about a life cut and measured to our desires, but we know those dreams are "self-indulgent" and "unrealistic." Life's just not like that.

And yet that kind of daydreaming is extremely important. You should be doing more of it—and taking it seriously—because it's trying to tell you something. It's your genius itching to get its hands on some of that big-time, space-time clay and start making worlds. All right, let's turn it loose and find out what kind of world it wants to make!

There's only one rule for the kind of imagining you'll be doing in these next two exercises, and that is *no reality considerations!* In the world of play, like the world of dreams, there is no law of gravity, no death or taxes—and no irreconcilable conflicts. So if you want two things that seem to contradict each other, don't worry about it. Put them both in. If you love two people, you get to have two lovers. If you want to be in the country *and* in the city, or you need to be alone *and* live with people, or you want to have two beautiful children *and* a full-time career, say so. In these fantasies you don't have to do what you were told to do at age 5: "Make up your mind." You get everything.

EXERCISE 8: Your Ideal Environment

In one paragraph—or more, if you like—answer this question:
In what imaginary environment would your best self emerge?
Most of us have never asked ourselves that question because it's not

considered askable. What we've been trained to ask is, "How can I fit into some preexisting environment? How can I change myself to fit the world?" When we go to the store, we hope we'll fit into the clothes on the racks. If the jeans are too long or too narrow, it's we who are too short or too fat. If we happened to have three arms, we'd cut one off rather than politely but firmly insist on a jacket with three sleeves!

Just in fantasy, I'd like you to try shaping the world to your needs for a change. Imagine an environment that is perfect for someone with all your present characteristics—a world so tailored to your nature that you'd be at your best in it without changing yourself one bit. Let the environment do all the work for you.

I'm going to stop right here and define my terms a little bit. By "environment," I don't just mean your physical surroundings. Sure, it would be nice to have a house with a patio and a swimming pool and a huge fireplace, and it might be even nicer to be in the Bahamas under a palm tree. But I don't want you to spend too much time on the color of your walls or the climate and the vegetation, unless that is vital to your best state of mind. It may be. But "environment" is also, very importantly, your *human* environment: the kinds of people you'd like to be surrounded by; how much privacy you need, and how much interaction; what kinds of help you'd like; what kinds of responses you'd want to your ideas.

You might need to be challenged . . . or just really listened to. (You will certainly need to be respected.) You might want to be a teacher, with the opportunity to inspire your students; or you might like to be a learner, surrounded by people who could teach you all kinds of fascinating things. You might want to be in charge of a large operation staffed by totally cooperative, efficient, loyal people who are dying to do whatever you tell them to. Or you might prefer to be a member of an egalitarian group effort. It's entirely up to you.

And "Let the environment do the work for you" means *don't change yourself* in this fantasy. Above all, don't improve yourself. Improve the world, so that your characteristics stop being problems. If you hate doing the housework, don't imagine *you* being more self-disciplined or patient. Imagine eight little gremlins following you around cleaning up after you! (Be as whimsical as you like—this is fantasy, so anything goes.) If you're disorganized, or you need a lot of love, or you're shy, or you tend to procrastinate, don't think of those characteristics as "weaknesses" that need changing. Think of them as *design problems*—challenges to your ingenuity as a world-maker. Create an environment that fits and supports you as you are, so that you are comfortable, secure, and free to turn in your best performance.

Gerry, a 38-year-old accountant, said, "One feature of my ideal environment is that everyone around me would be clumsy—because I'm clumsy, and I'm sick of being noticed for it!" Soft-spoken Miriam said, "No one can ever hear me. I'm always struggling to speak up. In my ideal environment, I'd live in a big, spacious house in the middle of a forest with my family and my best friends, and no one would speak above a whisper. I'd be the loudest one there!" Personally, as an old pro at procrastination, I'd like my ideal environment to include a total boss who knew exactly what I wanted to do and would make me do it! A real tyrant who would make me toe the line of my own path.

After you've imagined your ideal environment, I'd like you to do one more thing: list a few adjectives telling what *positive* qualities in you—intellectual, emotional, creative—would emerge if you were in that environment. ("Loving," "assertive," "playful," "productive," "serene," "independent," "sexy," etc.) In EXERCISE 6: *Seeing Yourself as Others See You,* you discovered the good qualities you have right now. This time I'm inviting you to do something a little different, and even more daring: *imagine yourself in full bloom.* (If you still catch yourself feeling naughty or spoiled, or saying "Who do I think I am," just give a Bronx cheer for the incredible tenacity of those negative tapes. Give them a big hand for trying. And then go ahead and dream.)

Here's how some other people described their ideal environments—and their blossoming selves. Notice especially how specific they've been in describing the kind of *human* environment they'd flourish in.

Julia, a 32-year-old free-lance writer: "I'd like to live by myself, in the country, and near a wide variety of friends who are doing all different kinds of things. And I'd like to have a terrific lover who has work of his own he loves, and who lets me know that he loves me, but leaves me alone to work all day without making me feel either guilty or anxious. And I'd like never to quite know when he's coming over, but I'd like to be able to call him if I'm lonely, too. In short, secure, but not too secure—a little drama and suspense. The qualities that would emerge in me would be independence, lovingness, intensity, energy, sensuality, and creativity. I'd get a lot done."

Betsy, 38, mother of three: "I'd like a combination of Mary Poppins, Misterogers, Phil Donahue, and Marlo Thomas to take care of my children; a housekeeper to do that mundane pain-in-the-ass cleaning and cooking and shopping; a secretary to take care of the bills and the phone; and I'd go out and work! Qualities that would emerge: delight in being with people, sense of humor, creativity."

Tom, 55, divorced and job-hunting: "The single thing that stood out for me was how much I need love and emotional support—more than anything else. I also need an uncluttered environment where things are well-organized, because I get distracted easily. Qualities that would emerge: I'd be resourceful, kind, serene, playful, warm, and wise."

George, 43: "A cabin by a lake in the High Sierras, a small, excellent library, several good trout rods, a kerosene lantern, a bar, no telephone, the Wall Street Journal delivered to my doorstep, and my best fishing buddy on weekends. Qualities that would emerge: I'd write and think a lot. I might be the next Thoreau, instead of an investment counselor. But maybe every third month or so I'd come down into the city and work, and see a lot of movies, and be persuasive, witty, and urbane— and then go back to the mountains."

I knew George was married, and yet in his fantasy he didn't mention his wife. When I asked him about her, he said, "Of course she'd be there! I took that so for granted, I just assumed . . ." On further questioning, I learned that she'd also obligingly *not* be there on the occasions when he needed to be alone, or with his friends. George liked to cook, but he "just sort of assumed" that his wife would keep the cabin tidy for him, just as she takes responsibility for keeping their city apartment clean.

In other words, George already has—and takes for granted—a kind of emotional and practical support many of us can only write into our wildest fantasies! Another human being, a woman, provides it for him —at what cost to herself and for what real rewards, I can only guess, because I didn't meet George's wife. The changes that are taking place between men and women right now are painful and creative precisely because men like George are being forced to become conscious of how much their comfort, freedom, and productivity depend on a human support base. That there might also be a genuine pleasure in nurturing —in providing some aspects of a support base—is a discovery the

Georges of this world are just beginning to make.

Arthur, a 28-year-old educational-test designer: "I have to punch in and punch out at work, and that really goes against my nature. I like being creative, but not on order. I'd like to have a fluid situation with no fixed schedule at all—a balance of discipline and freedom. I need the support and acceptance of people who really like my work and say so; I also need occasional solitude. In that environment I'd be self-confident, abundant, creative, happy, electric, fun. I'd be good at what I do; my ideas would never end."

Vickie, 48, a novice theatrical agent: "I need energetic, supportive people around me who love and are excited about the theater. I was really surprised when I realized that I had written 'I need to be *allowed* to create and develop my own ideas.' Evidently I'm still waiting for permission! Anyway, the qualities that would emerge are: high creativity (I'm blushing!), enthusiasm, energy, drive, tenacity, leadership, communications skills, ability to organize and implement my own ideas."

Jo Ann, 36, single mother and graduate student: "Constant stimulation—learning, conversation, working on projects with other people, all kinds of physical audible tangible input and excitement. In that kind of environment my mind would be very active and alive. I'd shoot off sparks."

I think I could characterize most women accurately by saying that they are understimulated and underchallenged. Their emotions may be overused, but their minds and talents are underused. Notice that most of the environments described here include challenge and stimulation as well as comfort and support. Note also that among the qualities that would emerge, almost everyone listed "creativity." Placed in a lively, nourishing environment, the human animal is creative.

Bill, 39, artist and draftsman: "The most important thing I need in my environment is CONTINUITY—everything I'm doing relating to everything else, so that it all ties together. Right now I've got a few pieces of what I want, but they have nothing to do with anything else I'm doing. I also need ECONOMY—my life pared down to the most essential activities, not cluttered with a lot of options and distractions. Qualities that would emerge: originality, productivity, and steadiness."

What did you learn about yourself and what you would need to become all you could be?

This exercise is an important rehearsal for real-world life design. Because even at its most playful and fantastic, it is very revealing of what you really do need to function at your best. The optimum environment for you will be one that provides real equivalents for all the major features of your fantasy. *And this book is going to help you create that environment*—because you have a right to it.

Of course the actual process of creating that environment will be a little different from just shutting your eyes and dreaming. It's going to involve dealing with stubborn, resistant substances like time and money, habit and fear—and stubbornest of all, other people! But believe it or not, all these inner and outer obstacles can be overcome. That's purely a matter of strategy. And *fantasy comes before strategy*.

Unless you can dream, how do you know where you want to go? And until you know where you want to go, how can you sit down and plan how to get there? I'm going to show you how to get there; the whole second half of this book is packed with practical strategies for tackling "hard reality." But *you* have to imagine the "where."

SHAPING TIME

Suppose you lived in a real-life version of your ideal environment, and all your best qualities were in full bloom. How would you spend your time? What activities and people would fill your day? (EXERCISE 7: *Twenty Things You Like to Do* should give you plenty of material!)

In this next exercise, you're going to do a very special kind of imagining. I call it *real daydreaming*. It is one of the most important techniques you'll be using in this book.

If someone asked you what it would be like if you had a million dollars, you'd probably answer something like, "It would be terrific. I'd have a house by the sea, and a sailboat, and an airplane, and I would . . ."

Stop right there! *Any response with the word "would" in it is not real daydreaming*.

When you have a dream at night, do you lie there thinking in your sleep, "Wouldn't it be interesting if this were really happening?" No. It *is* happening. It's *real*. You are experiencing it. When you were a child, your daydreams were just as vivid and present as your night dreams, simply because you hadn't been taught to label them "unreal." What you're going to do now is deliberately revive that power of visualization and belief.

"Real daydreaming" is *present-tense, first-person, visual,* and *sequential.* In other words, it's *happening.* You see, feel, and experience everything that's going on around you; time passes just as it does in real life, only faster. Like this: "This is fantastic! I'm sitting here with a million dollars. Let's see. What shall I do first? . . . OK. I'm in a mansion on a hill above the sea in Maine. My airplane is in a little hangar behind the house. I can see my sailboat rocking down at the dock. It's a cool, sunny morning, and the whole day stretches ahead of me. . . ."

EXERCISE 9: Your Ideal Day

With pen in hand and as much paper as you need (or a tape recorder if you prefer to dream out loud), take a leisurely walk through a day that would be perfect if it represented your usual days—not a vacation day, not a compromise day, but the very substance of your life as you'd love it to be. Live through that day *in the present tense* and *in detail,* from getting up in the morning to going to sleep at night. What's the first thing you do when you wake up? What do you have for breakfast? Do you make it yourself—or is it brought to you in bed, with a single rose and the morning paper? Do you take a long, hot bath? a bracing cold shower? What kinds of clothes do you put on? How do you spend the morning? the afternoon? At each time of day, are you indoors or outdoors, quiet or active, alone or with people?

As you go through the hours of your fantasy day, there are three helpful categories to keep in mind: *what, where,* and *who.*

What are you doing—what kind of work, what kind of play? Imagine yourself at the full stretch of your capacities. If you'd like to sing or sail, and you don't know how, in this fantasy you do know how.

Where—in what kind of place, space, situation? A London flat, an Oregon farm, a fully equipped workshop, an elegant hotel room, a houseboat?

Who do you work with, eat with, laugh and talk with, sleep with? You will undoubtedly want to write some of your favorite real people into your fantasy; you might also want to include some types of people you'd like to be surrounded by—writers, musicians, children, people your own age, people of all different ages, athletes, Frenchmen, financiers, simple country people, celebrities.

Just as you did with your ideal environment, turn your imagination loose. Don't put down what you think is possible—put down the kind of day you'd live if you had absolute freedom, unlimited means, and all the powers and skills you've ever wished for.

Most people put a lot of loving care into this exercise. It's one of my favorites, and I enjoy finding out about other people's ideal days almost as much as I like making up my own. As you read the following responses, notice the kinds of details each of these very different people has found important in each of the three categories: what, where, and who.

Julia, 32, the free-lance writer we've already heard about: "I wake up at 6 A.M. I'm living in a cool, spacious adobe house in New Mexico, with Navajo rugs on the floor and red peppers strung from the rafters. I get out of bed without disturbing my husband or the three cats who are still asleep on and around him. I go out to the stable, with the two beautiful salukis bounding beside me, feed the Arabian mare, and let her out to pasture. Then I do a little jogging in the cool morning air.

"I go back in and have coffee and a light breakfast with my husband. By 7 A.M. I go into my study, which has a big window looking out over the mesas and a big wooden desk with a broad top and lots of drawers. I write at least until noon, and two or three hours longer if I feel like it. I write whatever I please—no deadlines, no space limits, no editors' requirements. That's all over for me. I've made my reputation—and a very modest fortune that's producing interest in the bank. I've got land and a vegetable garden. I can write for myself and my friends, and if somebody wants to publish it too, fine.

"It's very important that I get lots of mail from friends all over the country and even the world!

"I meet a friend for a late lunch in town, and browse for an hour in the bookstore. In the afternoon I practice guitar and write songs; or I set type on my old hand press for a friend's book, while bread bakes in the oven and Bach plays on the stereo. Before sunset I go for a ride on the mare—gently, because I'm pregnant!

"Friends—writers, carpenters, teachers, potters, farmers, and their kids—come over for dinner, which my husband cooks. After dinner, I play guitar, and we sing, laugh, and talk around the fire. When the guests have left, we read for an hour or two, take a walk with the dogs in the starlight, and then go to bed."

Aline, 45, executive secretary to a Chicago magazine publisher and mother of three teen-agers: "I wake up, slowly, at about 7:30. That's important. I don't have to worry about getting everybody's breakfast, because John and the kids not only make their own—they bring me mine on a tray. After all, I am an important executive with weightier matters on my mind than who likes his or her eggs over easy!

"The kids wash the dishes and get ready for school while I put on my makeup and dress in the gray Chanel suit I selected the night before. (I'm twenty pounds thinner, of course.) We live in a high-rise coop with a picture window overlooking Lake Michigan, and there's time for us all to have a cup of coffee by the window and discuss what each of us is going to do today.

"Unless the weather's really miserable, I walk the ten blocks to work. It clears my head and gives me a chance to organize my thoughts for the day. When I walk into my big corner office, with the blue rug that matches the lake, I'm greeted by my secretary, who hands me a sheaf of urgent memos and letters awaiting my signature. The working day is a lot like my present boss's—phone calls to both coasts, difficult decisions, lunch with Muhammad Ali and his agent to negotiate for his memoirs, a boardroom meeting on a possible merger, the private screening of a film by our production affiliate—except that *I'm* the boss. I'm the general. And it taxes every bit of my intelligence, courage, and charm!

"I take a taxi home at 7:30. Whoever's had time has made dinner— or if the kids were all too involved in their own activities, they've ordered a pizza! I take off stockings, earrings, all the lady-executive trappings, and get into jeans. After dinner, I sit on the rug and play a ferocious game of Scrabble with my son, or help the twins with their homework. Before bed, I look over the next day's schedule in the office and decide what I'm going to wear. And then John and I share a precious half hour of jazz and brandy."

Peter, 25, a truck driver for an oil company: "I wake up late—around 9—because I've been up all night helping one of my cows deliver a calf.

It's OK because I have a staff that got the milking machines out at 6 this morning. They've gone away and won't be back until this evening. I walk downstairs into the kitchen. It's a big room with a table in the middle, and my wife is sitting there feeding our baby. The coffee is on and smells great. They both give me a big smile, and the baby stops eating and insists I pick him up. I have him on one arm, the coffee in my hand, and my wife is standing beside me with her arm around my waist, and we're all looking out the window at the beautiful farm we own, with a three-story red barn and the cows grazing up on the hills. It's a sunny, beautiful day.

"I have to go out to the other building and work on one of our trucks. They're big trucks, for transporting cattle, but they're in beautiful condition and I keep the motors in perfect shape. I'm so good at that that the neighbors are often coming over to have me help them with their engine work, and we sit around and drink beer, and work on the trucks sometimes. I arrange with my wife that I'll come down and get her and the baby at lunchtime and we'll go up to the pond and have lunch there.

"All morning I check the trucks out, tuning up a little here, adjusting there. I have a perfectly equipped garage, which is clean and organized, and every tool is in place. I do a little painting on one of the trucks— bright red—and neaten things up, and then I go outside.

"I go for a walk up on the hill to cut down a stand of briar that's getting into the coats of my cattle, and into their mouths too. Oh yes, I have a dog running after me. A nice big one, who likes to play, but can be very quiet too, when I feel like being quiet. We get to the briar patch and hack it down. It's good, hard work. Then we burn it while he keeps the cows away.

"The whole day is great. The work is steady and sometimes hard, but it's outdoors and I love it. I go to the barn when it starts to get dark, and pull the hay down for the cows, and the staff gets the milkers hooked up. The baby's asleep or something, because my wife is up in the loft with me, helping me throw the hay down. She's small, but she's strong, and funny. Makes me laugh all the time, because I can get too serious. Finally she starts tripping me so I fall down in the hay and she gives me a big hug and we're laughing a lot.

"Dinner is good and big, and some friends come over to eat. After-wards we sit around and talk for a couple of hours, and then they go home. I go around, tighten things up. Check out the doors, and the boiler, and the barn. Listen to everything, and everything is quiet and all right. We go up to bed early—maybe 10 or 11 o'clock because we're getting up early tomorrow and going into town to do some shopping. We fall asleep with our arms around each other."

Now let's take a closer look at your ideal day. By asking seven simple questions about it, you can learn a great deal about what you really need to be happy . . . how much of it you've already got . . . and what's preventing you from getting the rest of it.

FANTASY ANALYSIS: GETTING DOWN TO BASICS

I invited you to embellish your fantasy day with everything you could think of that would make that day perfect for you. But some of the things you put in may be much more important to you than others. Let's find out what they are.

Question No. 1: In each of the three categories—what, where, who —*what elements of your ideal day are absolutely indispensable to your happiness?* That is, if you never had them, you'd always be dissatisfied and long for them?

Question No. 2: What elements are *optional, but still very desirable?*

Question No. 3: What elements are *pure frills*—they'd be nice, but you could do without them and never really be unhappy?

You may find it helpful to make a little chart, like Julia did:

INDISPENSABLE

What:	writing
	music to listen to
	physical exercise
	animals
Where:	a private study with a big desk
	a fairly spacious place to live
Who:	my husband
	lots of friends near and far

OPTIONAL BUT DESIRABLE

What: learn to play guitar

Where: live in beautiful country near a culturally lively town

Who: a baby (strange as it may sound, I *could* be content
without having a child—but I'd rather have one!)

FRILLS

What: the horse
the printing press

Where: my own adobe house in New Mexico
(I'd be thrilled if I had these things, but I wouldn't
pine away if I didn't.)

That doesn't mean you shouldn't get them! I don't want you to think for a minute that this breakdown to basics is the first step toward a craven compromise with "reality." It is not. I firmly believe that you are entitled to *everything* you want—including all the frills. All we're doing here is zeroing in on your *priorities:* the things you really can't live without, the things you must therefore concentrate on getting into your life first and soonest, so that you will have the abundant energy to go for the rest.

Julia, for instance, has identified writing as the center of her life. If she doesn't have adequate space and time to write, learning to play the guitar won't be much of a consolation. In fact, she won't feel like doing it. But if her writing and living are in order, her energy and confidence will overflow naturally into the "optional but desirable" category. Her horizons will expand outward in widening circles from a happy center. And so will yours.

Not every fantasy day can be broken down as neatly as Julia's. Aline said her only indispensable element (apart from her family in the "who" category) was a "what": the executive job. And yet the high-rise apartment and designer clothes, which could be classified as "optional but desirable," would follow naturally from the kind of position and salary she wanted. Peter insisted that virtually all the elements of his fantasy day—having a dairy farm—were indispensable. Nothing less than the full scenario would satisfy him. Fine—more power to him! However your fantasy breaks down, our next task is to *measure the distance* between your life as you now live it and the minimum ideal day that would make you happy.

Question No. 4: What happens when you walk through an adjusted fantasy day with only the indispensable elements in it?

Obviously if you feel the way Peter does, your adjusted ideal day isn't going to look much different from your full-fledged fantasy. Julia, on the other hand, was able to describe a day like this:

"I'm living in New York City, where I live now—but in a bigger apartment. I get up early, have coffee with my husband, feed the cats, and walk to my study a few blocks away. It's a top floor room I've rented in a brownstone that overlooks a pretty courtyard. I write until noon, or longer if I feel like it. Then I pick up the mail, go to a health club, work out and swim.

"The rest of the day is basically the same: lunch with a friend . . . browsing in a bookstore . . . baking bread . . . listening to music . . . dinner with friends. Just take out the house, the horse, the printing press, and the guitar—for now."

Once you've got your adjusted ideal day clearly in your sights, there are three more important questions to ask about it.

Question No. 5: What—if any—elements of that day *do you already have?*

Very few of us are totally discontented with the status quo. Some of our wishes and choices have managed to find their way into reality. This question shows you what's *right* with your life; it makes you aware of the sources of satisfaction you already have. Those will be your base and your energy source as you start moving and adding more of what you want to your life. Knowing what you've got also helps you to localize and focus your discontent—the subject of the next question.

Question No. 6: What elements of the adjusted ideal day are conspicuously absent from your life right now? Use the three categories—what, where, who—to help you pinpoint what's missing.

These two questions really work together—and the results may surprise you. Julia realized that her adjusted ideal day really isn't all that different from the way she's living now. She has all the "what" and "who" elements—her work, four cats, a husband and friends, music and exercise. The big hole in her life is "where." Her apartment is small and cramped, and she hasn't got proper space to work. Aline already has the basic pattern of the life she wants—a family she loves, a responsible paying job—but she wants them on a grander scale, in brighter, bolder colors. She wants to be an executive, not an executive secretary. She wants to go all the way. And at home, she'd like more cooperation from her family.

Peter, on the other hand, said, "I really don't have any of the elements of my ideal day—what, where, or who. I'm driving a truck and living in a damn small apartment. But wait a minute, I am a good mechanic, and I keep the trucks in top shape, when I can. If I had some money, or could save some, I could probably buy one of the trucks from my boss. But it's not for cattle, really. Anyway, the farm is the point. How could I ever get my hands on a farm? I am lucky, though. I know that lady already, and I know she'd like living on a farm."

Now you've got fantasy and reality matched up so you can compare them. You may have learned that your present life isn't as far off the mark as you thought it was; or, like Peter, you may have confirmed that you really are light years from where you want to be. But in either case, you now know more precisely what's missing . . . and you know what you've got to work with. Dream and reality are in focus. *Now let's try focusing in on the gap—or the barrier—between them.* For the first time since we began, I'm going to ask you to take a good look at "hard reality."

Question No. 7: What stands between you and having your adjusted ideal day tomorrow? That is, what would it take to get all the missing elements? What problems or obstacles are presently stopping you from getting them?

For Julia, it's money. A bigger apartment would cost her twice the rent she's paying now, and she'd have to pay at least $100 a month more for a separate study.

Aline realized that all she's really lacking is self-confidence, or a belief in herself. She said, "I think I have the experience and the knowledge for an executive job in magazine publishing. In fact, I know I do! But I'm scared to stand up and make my move. Same thing with my family. I could ask for—or demand—more help, but I don't want them to be mad at me!"

Peter said he needed so many things—a farm, money, some experience with cows and the business of running a dairy farm—that he tended to get overwhelmed and give up before he started. He was able to sum up his feelings of futility in two major obstacles. "One: I don't really believe it's possible to save the money to buy a farm from a workingman's salary. Two: even if it is possible, I wouldn't know where to start with all the details."

What stands between you and your modified dream day—the minimum "what," "where," and "who" that would make you happy?

I want you to know that you are certainly going to need what Aline needs. Not courage . . . not self-confidence . . . but *support*. You'll find it in the last section of this book. And you are certainly going to need what Peter needs. Not a pep talk (You can do it, kid!) . . . not an inheritance from an obscure rich uncle . . . but a *game plan* that tells you what to do first, and then what to do next after that, and so on, all the way to the goal. You'll find that in Section III. As you saw in Chapter 2, everybody needs structure, and everybody needs support. The ones who don't need 'em have already got 'em! So those are universal problems.

But then come all the specific, personal, circumstantial obstacles that keep us from having what we want. For you, it may be money . . . or a school degree that's required to do the kind of work you want to do . . . or a new job . . . or the contacts to get one . . . or a skill you don't have . . . or the time to learn it . . . or twenty extra pounds that are cramping your style with the opposite sex . . . or several of the above . . . or something else I haven't even mentioned.

I'd like you to do a very simple thing—so simple that you won't believe it's the first step to overcoming those obstacles. But it is. Take a sheet of paper. Write the word "Problems" across the top. And then just list them—all the real-world reasons why you can't have your dream.

You have now begun to see "hard reality" for what it really is: not an all-pervasive nerve gas that poisons hope and paralyzes will, just a couple of concrete and clearly-defined problems. At this point, I know those barriers to your dream may look insurmountable. Don't worry about it. Just write them down. As we work on clearly defining your goals in the next chapter, more problems, obstacles, and objections will probably occur to you. Add them to the list. I want you to keep that Problems List with care—because a little later on it's going to turn out to be a gold mine.

When you're choosing a concrete goal to go for—and that's going to be your next task—it's more important than ever to get reality considerations out of the way, so that they don't dim or diminish your vision. I want your goal to be larger than life (our lives are too small!) and in living color, so that it's worthy of the real you—and something you can fall totally in love with. But that doesn't mean we're not going to come back and deal with reality. On the contrary! We're going to tackle it with relish—and technique. When I show you how to convert insurmountable obstacles into solvable problems, and how to liberate the inborn problem-solving capacity of your mind, your Problems List will yield all the raw materials you need to build a good, solid road to your goal. But first, let's get a good sharp fix on where you're going.

You've discovered that you know how you want your days to be, just as clearly as you know what clothes you want in your closet. Now it's time to start shaping fantasy and style into something you can actually get your hands on.

–4–
Goalsearch

What is a goal?

A goal is the basic unit of life design. It's easy to dream; with just a little encouragement you can close your eyes and conjure up a whole new life for yourself. But if you want to make that life come true, you will have to start by choosing one piece of it and deciding that that's the one you're going to go for first. Then you may still have to do a little work on that piece to turn it into something that's really reachable— not a mirage that keeps on receding ahead of you. A true goal—the kind that will hold still and let you catch it—lives up to two basic rules.

Rule No. 1: A goal is *concrete*. It is a matter of facts, not feelings. You will know beyond a doubt when you've arrived, because you will have something in your hands that you can look at, touch, and show off to other people. I'll give you an example.

Suppose you think your goal is "to be a doctor." In fact, that's still a dream. Your *actual* goal is, "To get my M.D. degree." Why? Because on the day when they hand you that piece of paper, you and society will agree that you are now a doctor. You may not feel much like a doctor. Or you may feel like a doctor one day and a terrified fake in a white coat the next. The process of growing into the healer's role is gradual, complex, and uncertain; you cannot predict the exact date when you will at last feel unshakably sure that "I am a doctor." But there's nothing uncertain about an M.D. Either you've got it or you haven't —and you can take concrete steps to get it by a specific date.

That's a key point. Your true goal, or *target*, has to be a *concrete action or event,* not only so you'll know for sure when you get there, but so that you can make that date with success in advance! Setting a *target date* is the beginning of all effective planning—the antidote to both procrastination ("Oh, I'll get there someday") and despair ("I'll *never* get there"). If you know you've committed yourself to write three short stories by April, or to get your M.D. degree by June, 1985, then *time* suddenly becomes a quantity you can work with—and had better start working with right now if you don't want to miss that deadline. I'll have more to say about target dates later on. Right now it's enough simply to recognize that you won't be able to set a target date unless you have a target. Nobody has ever succeeded in designing and building a bridge to a cloud.

Becoming a doctor is an easy example, because the target—getting an M.D.—is ready-made. But suppose your goal—like the goal of two young actresses I worked with—is something like "To be a movie star"? That's still a dream, of course, because how are you going to know when you're a movie star? The answer is, *only you can decide.* You can make your target any concrete, specific action or event that will satisfy you that you've arrived—but you must choose one, or you'll never get on the road at all.

What would have to happen for you to be able to say, "Now I am a movie star" (or the best literary agent in New York, or a successful racing yacht designer, or famous, or rich)? Your answer won't be the same as anybody else's answer, because the "same" goal can mean completely different things to different people. (Remember how two people could look at the same color and call it "rust" and "rose"?) I know I'll be rich when I have $100,000 free and clear—and I know millionaires who aren't there yet! For Carol, a Minneapolis secretary and part-time model, being a movie star means glamour and publicity —her name in all the gossip columns, her face in all the poster stores, furs, limousines, flashbulbs. June, an undergraduate student of theater, sees stardom as getting the best parts and the highest accolades for her acting. So when Carol and June both sit down to make a *target* out of "being a movie star," Carol might say, "A poster of me in every poster store," and June might say "Getting my first Oscar." And they'd both be right. *The only person you have to satisfy is yourself.*

There are two guidelines you can use in the actual process of goal choice that will help you zero in on the right target for you. I call them your *touchstone* and your *role model.*

Your *touchstone* is *the emotional core of your goal*—what you want and need from it, what you love best about it. It's the sweet center of that goal for you. Creative fulfillment . . . fame . . . money . . . the chance to help people . . . closeness to nature . . . love—if you can put *your* touchstone into one or a few words, it will not only help you pick a target that's loaded with the kind of sweets that nourish *you,* it will also show you how to design the shortest, most direct and gratifying route to that goal, and it will get you to the essence of any goal that looks impossible.

A *role model* is someone you'd like to be, someone who's actually done what you want to do—or the closest thing to it. You probably already have at least one role model. Whom do you particularly admire? Whose life and achievements do you covet? Role models are not only good for goal definition, but for inspiration, encouragement —and practical guidance. If anyone anywhere on Planet Earth has done what you want to do, it means that you can do it too. Put that person's picture up on your wall. Go to the library, read about his or her life, and find out how s/he did it! You might get some ideas. Remember Peter, who wanted to be a dairy farmer, starting from scratch, but didn't believe it was possible? I suggested he pick up local newspapers from the towns he drove through in dairy country, until he got to know something about the local people and saw how a lot of them made it through the yearly business of farming on sheer determination—not because they had a lot of money. He found an interesting role model. A young man from a nearby city who had never been on a farm, and moved into the area—onto a dairy farm which also served as an inn or hotel for hunters in hunting season—and who ran a snowmobile and "all-terrain vehicle" dealership from his garage.

Here's how touchstone and role model can help you draw a bead on your target:

Carol	Dream:	movie or TV star
	Touchstone:	glamour and publicity

Role Model:	Farrah Fawcett-Majors
Target:	my face in every poster store

June	Dream:	movie star
	Touchstone:	acclaim for fine acting
	Role Model:	Anne Bancroft
	Target:	Get an Oscar

This process should give you a target that passes the second test for goals:

Rule No. 2: When you say "This is what I want," *you're not fooling.* If I could wave a magic wand and POOF! you'd have that goal right now, you honestly think you'd be delighted.

The purpose of this rule is to distinguish real, gut dreams from passing fancies. Many of us have daydreamed at one time or another of being a movie star, or a mountain climber, or even President of the United States. But if I waved my magic wand and POOF! you were halfway up Everest, would you be in your element—or would you long desperately to be home in your nice warm armchair daydreaming about it? There's an easy way to find out. Use your own built-in magic wand —"real daydreaming"! Remember? First person, present tense, visual, and sequential. Like this:

"POOF! I am the President of the United States. I am sitting at my desk in the Oval Office. It is 9:30 in the morning. On my left is a stack of paper about two feet high, urgently requiring my decision on such matters as the energy crisis, the Middle East peace negotiations, the SALT talks, and the diplomatic status of the People's Republic of China. On my right is a red telephone, ominously silent. I . . . I . . . Agghh!! Let me out of here!"

That, my friend, is the acid test for any goal. Try living it in imagination. How does it feel? Love it? Great. Hate it? Change the target. Not just whims, but also "shoulds"—the things you think you ought to want because your father, grandmother, wife, husband, or favorite teacher wanted them for you—will be unmasked by this "magic wand" test. When I say that you must have what you want, it's equally important for you to know that *you must not work hard to get what you don't want.* It will only give you indigestion—and you won't be any good at it anyway. So try to rule it out from the start.

"But what if I'm not sure?" you may be saying. "I've come up with something I think I'd love, but supposing I get there—or even halfway there—and discover that I've made a terrible mistake and it's not what I want after all?"

Simple. You will take the piece of paper on which you wrote down that goal, tear it up into little pieces, and throw it out the window. And then you will take another piece of paper and write down another one. *No goal is written in blood.*

One of the most harmful misconceptions in our society is that you've got to figure out what you want and then you've got to *stick* to it. This attitude is one of the things that makes it so hard to get into action. We hesitate to commit ourselves to our choices because we're afraid they will be life sentences! That's nonsense. Goals exist only to serve you and make you happy. You don't exist to serve *them*. If a goal isn't serving you, you are free to change it. It's just that sometimes there's no way to find out whether or not a particular goal really suits you except by trying it. If it doesn't suit you, you will still have gained something priceless: *the experience of making real progress toward a goal—and the practical skills for doing it.* Those skills can be applied to any goal—just as your hands, once they've actually built a bookcase, can easily craft a kitchen cabinet.

CHOOSING A TARGET

The way you go about actually choosing your target will depend on what kind of dreams you cherish—and that in turn depends on who you are and where you are in your life right now. You may be a single-minded achiever with one burning ambition, or you may be an "artist of living" to whom the total quality of life is all-important. You may be basically happy with your life as it is, yet have one or more long-dormant interests you'd like to work into it for your own pleasure. You may be in one of the adolescences of life (I think there are at least two), when everything is up in the air and you aren't really sure what you want. You may be a "Renaissance person" who isn't happy unless you have two or three irons in the fire at a time. And *you may be any or all of the above at different times in your life.*

Wherever you start, you'll have a different set of design problems to grapple with. Your goal may seem too vague, too distant, or too broad to fit neatly into target form; you may feel you have no goal at all—or too many goals altogether. But in each case you can arrive at a target that is *carefully tailored to you* and *realizable in time.* Here's how some real people have done it.

The Naked Touchstone: Andrea

It took quite a bit of coaxing before Andrea, a 26-year-old New York secretary, admitted with embarrassment that what she really wanted was *to be famous*—she wasn't even sure what for. "I think it's really kind of sick that I feel this way," she said. "It keeps me from being able to just do things and enjoy doing them."

The first thing I did was give Andrea a friendly little lecture to get her off the hook of her own guilt. I'll give it to you too, because this kind of apologetic attitude is so common and so crippling. *What you want is what you need—and you must have it.* I don't care what it is —short of blatantly destructive or self-destructive acts—and "Why do you want it?" is one question I never ask. If what you want is to marry a millionaire, fine! I've actually helped someone do that. If it's fame, great! Andrea doesn't have a guilty secret, she has *a touchstone in search of a goal.* Before it can find one, though, it needs to be more clearly defined.

I asked Andrea whether any kind of fame at all would satisfy her. What if she designed a new kind of shoelace, made five million dollars, and got written up in *Time* as one of "The New Millionaires"? Would that do it? She said, "No, money isn't that important to me." Well, then how about going over Niagara Falls in a barrel? Another decisive "No." So we were *not* simply talking about fame. I asked Andrea whether she could name some of the things she thought she might enjoy being famous for.

"Well . . . movie star or director, singer, photographer, fashion

designer. It's fame for performance, for a kind of continual performance
—not a one-shot deal. The trouble is, I don't know whether I'd really
like to do those things, or whether I'd just like to be famous for them!"

I asked her whether she would like to be *respected* for what she did
—for the quality of her work. She said yes, that would be important.
So Andrea's touchstone could now be defined: "Fame for continual,
quality performance."

Now we had to figure out how she could get some of that flavor of
fame into her life as quickly as possible.

That's a point I'm going to be driving home for the rest of this
chapter—and the rest of this book. *The sooner you start getting some
of what you really want, the more energy you'll have to go for the rest
of it!* You'll also be happier, healthier, and nicer to be around. That's
why it's so important to identify your touchstone—and to pick a target
that gets at least a shining chip of it into your hands right away. I'm
not a believer in "delayed gratification." Never take the long way
around if you can get the essence of your goal by a shorter route.

Since fame itself was more important to Andrea than the field she got
famous in, it would speed things along if she picked a field where she
didn't have to start from scratch. So I asked her if she already had skills
and experience in any of the things she thought she'd like to be famous
for—filmmaking, photography, fashion design. She said she'd done
some photography, and had even gotten so involved that she'd stayed
up all night developing prints in a friend's darkroom! So photography
it was. Now we needed to find out what kind of photography would
bring Andrea the celebrity she wanted by the speediest route.

Fine art photography was out. Andrea would undoubtedly find the
artist's route to fame far too slow, hard, and chancy; she'd give up in
frustration long before she got her first taste. That's what I mean by not
going the long way around. Both fashion photography and photojour-
nalism looked more promising, but Andrea thought fashion was too
technical and competitive and news photography too anonymous and
dull. At this point, I told her to try naming a *role model;* it might jell
the process of goalsearch for her.

Andrea chose two: Richard Avedon, the controversial portrait artist
who started out as a fashion photographer, and Annie Leibowitz, the
young *Rolling Stone* photojournalist whose pictures of rock stars have
been collected in two books. Her choices were inspired—because *celeb-*

rity is contagious! Celebrities are vain. They *love* to have their pictures taken. And some of their stardust is bound to rub off on anyone who makes it her business to take their pictures. Andrea's quickest route to fame with quality might very well be taking good pictures of famous people.

From there it was a short step to defining Andrea's *target:* "To have one or more photographs of celebrities published in a quality national magazine." It was beautifully tailored to Andrea's needs, it could be planned for a target date—and she knew she'd love it. Of course, she came up with all kinds of problems. I told her to put them down on her Problems List:

"I can't afford to quit my job—too little time to work on this

"Big magazines won't take unknown photographers

"I'm afraid I'm not good enough

"I'm too shy to approach famous people."

Don't forget to compile a Problems List of your own as you define *your* target.

The Long Haul: June

What had always stopped Andrea from thinking clearly about her goals before was the feeling, "I know what I want, but I think I shouldn't want it!" For June, the theater student whose target was "Getting my first Oscar," the problem was different: "I know exactly what I want, but it's so far away—how will I ever get there?"

June was a senior at a large state university who had fallen in love with acting in student productions and had gotten rave reviews in the school paper. She was bravely aiming high, but she didn't even know whether to move to New York or Los Angeles after graduation, much less how to put her new ambition on the shortest road to success.

When you have a long-range target like June's, it's still, in a way, a dream. You can and should set a date to it—that will help to make it real—but it isn't a goal you can plot your path to, reach out and grab . . . at least not soon enough to give you joy and hope. So you will need to set yourself a *first target:* a smaller goal that's both a step on the road to your ultimate destination and a little triumph in its own right. And once again, the most important factor to keep in mind is your touchstone. Since June's touchstone was "recognition for fine acting," it would make little sense for her to move to L.A. and try to get her first TV commercial—a first target that might be perfect for Carol, the other aspiring star I knew whose touchstone was "glamour and publicity." June will get more of her kind of satisfaction sooner if she makes her first target something like, "To star in my first Off-Off-Broadway workshop." Once she's reached that, she might make it her next target to land a major part in a low-budget or student movie.

Touchstone planning is high-energy planning. By designing her path so that she gets the kind of experience and recognition she wants right up front, June may find that she reaches her goal—that Oscar—much sooner than she ever dreamt possible. On the other hand, she'll also have plenty of chances to decide on the basis of *experience, not fantasy,* that yes, this flavor of success really is for her . . . or it really isn't . . . or it was, but she's had enough now and is ready for something else —like teaching or painting or a year in Spain.

Remember: long-term goals especially are never written in blood. Because we change. And one of the things that changes us most is getting what we want. Sometimes your touchstone is like a stone in the middle of the road: until you get it, you can't get past it. When you do get it, it may whet your appetite for more of the same . . . or a part of you may be at peace for the first time, so that you can suddenly hear the voices of your other loves. So if you think you have a long-range goal, a first target is a handy *unit of commitment*—a sort of trial marriage! It's also just the right size for learning and practicing the planning techniques in the second half of this book.

The Ideal Day: Peter, Aline, and Julia

You may have another kind of trouble arriving at a first target if the goal you want is a broad one—a vision of a total lifestyle. Suppose you're a city mouse with a tidy little apartment and a tidy little salary, and what you really long to be is a country squire living on a vast estate? Or suppose that like Peter, the would-be dairy-farmer, you've made your actual target "To live my ideal day in every detail"? (That, by the way, is something you *can* put a date on.) When you look at the gap between where you are and where you want to be and the thousand things that have to be done to cross it, your question is going to be, "Where on earth do I start?"

Again, setting a first target—one that both makes you happy *now* and leads toward the rest of your dream—is the key to action and the antidote to despair. But in this case the process of choosing that first target is a little different. Instead of using your touchstone, you'll use the breakdown of your ideal day.

In each of the three categories—*what, where,* and *who*—you decided which elements of your fantasy day you've really got to have, which are optional but desirable, and which ones are just the sugar roses on the cake. The most important question you can ask yourself now is: *What is the highest-priority item that is missing from my life right now?* If you can give a single resounding answer to this question, you've got your first target.

For example, if you live in the city and you've just got to be down on the farm, your first target is a "where": to get yourself into a house with at least a few acres and a few chickens around it. (If you think that's impossible, just write down all the reasons why it's impossible on your Problems List and put them aside for later.) If you're like Aline, the executive secretary who wanted to be an executive, then a "what" —a promotion or change of job—will be your first target. Or you may be like my 32-year-old lawyer friend Miriam, who has "everything but" —she has a good job with an insurance law firm, a beautiful apartment, nice clothes, friends she loves—and has calmly decided to find the one piece that's missing for her: a husband.

But what if more than one crucial piece of your dream is missing? You may remember that Peter had almost none of the elements of his ideal day—and he wanted all of them! If you're in that bind, there's a second question that will help you get out of it: *Of the essential elements that are missing, which one can I get most quickly, cheaply, and easily?* That's where you'll start—because my objective is to get you on your path without more delay. That first target will lead you toward the next element of your dream . . . and the next . . . and the next.

Julia, the free-lance writer, needed *space:* living space and working space. If she had both, she'd already be living her stripped-down ideal day—and making progress toward the full scenario. But she didn't think she could afford both. Which should she make her first target? To move to a bigger apartment with an extra room to write in could solve the problem in one stroke, but it would more than double the rent of Julia's little rent-controlled studio, and moving would take at least two months away from her work. She realized that the quickest, cheapest, and easiest alternative was to keep her apartment and rent a separate work space for about $100 a month. With a good place to work in, she'd get more done, earn more money—and be better able to afford an apartment she really loved.

One thing Peter could do right away, at no expense, was to pull his fiancée into the project and spend some time researching the whole project. That would get him on his path by providing two of the pleasures of his ideal day: working on solving problems that had to do with being a farmer, and doing it with someone he loved. Once the two of them find some likely locations and start visiting some of the farms, they'll be ready to think about the money details. In fact, it may very well be that some of the situations they want could be available without huge down payments or the need for Peter to give up his present job right away. Peter might even find a job as driver and mechanic in a farm-equipment dealership in the area of his choice. He could repair tractors and combines and get to know the local farmers and their farms, so although he won't be living on a farm, he'll be doing what he loves—and surrounding himself with country life, country thinking, and learning actual facts about the requirements of his dream. (By the way, if there's a lot of "who" missing from *your* life, I'll tell you a secret: *there's nothing like doing what you love to attract the people you need.* Get your show on the road, and you'll find that a lot of people want parts in it.)

Impossible Dreams: Adele

It happens at least once in every Success Teams seminar, when I make the outrageous statement that everyone—regardless of age, sex, income, or education—can get what she or he really wants. Somebody always raises a hand and says, "Oh, yeah? Not me." Adele, a handsome woman in her early 50s, said, "What *I* want is to be prima diva in the Metropolitan Opera. And I've never sung a note in my life. Let's face it . . . there's no way."

Some people say things like that just to prove that I'm wrong, that you *can't* get what you want in life. Those people usually flunk the magic-wand test. They don't really want to be President of the United States or the next Beverly Sills; they just want to protect their real dreams against hope and the pain of disappointment. But sometimes we're dealing with something much more serious: an old childhood dream that's refused to die. Remember the exercise where you thought about "What You Might Have Been" if your childhood environment had been different? Well, what if you still secretly long to be that concert pianist, ballerina, heart surgeon, Chairman of the Board, astronaut, or famous novelist—and you're 30, 40, 50 or 60 years old?

I stick by my statement. If you really, really want that dream, *you can still have it*—unless it's a dream like Adele's. She really does have a problem, because she has chosen the pinnacle of one of the few professions—there are only a few—in which it's truly impossible to make it to the top from a late start. These are the physically demanding arts and sports in which the youthful capacities of the body, plus early training, are a must. A 45-year-old insurance salesman, however physically fit he is, cannot make it his goal to become a major-league ballplayer, a professional boxer, a principal tenor at the Met, or Rudolf Nureyev. (That's not to say he couldn't take up dance or singing or boxing or baseball and achieve considerable skill and pleasure.) And Adele cannot be Beverly Sills. She's right about that. But that doesn't mean she should give up her dream. She should take it very, very seriously, because it's telling her what she needs to be happy. And that is something she can and must get—*her touchstone.*

If you're deeply in love with a goal you're sure is impossible, don't become bitter about "what might have been" and consider your life wasted. Ask yourself, *what is the touchstone?* Why do I want this goal? If you came to me with Adele's dream, I'd try to find out what it is about being Beverly Sills that you'd love so much. Is it stardom—being rich, famous, adored? Or do you just love to sing and long to be able to make those wonderful sounds? Is it opera in particular that you love to sing? Have you always wanted to get on stage and sing in an operatic production? Or are you so crazy about professional opera that you'd do anything just to be around a top-flight opera company, even if you can't sing a note?

Now take that touchstone and design a goal around it!

If what you want is to be a star and get interviewed on every talk show from coast to coast, you can do it. I promise you, there is something unique in your style or your experience that you can parlay into stardom. People have achieved celebrity for everything from bridge to gardening, from a love of cats to the experience of motherhood. And everybody knows that once you are a star, you get the chance to do all kinds of things—even get up in front of people and sing!

If what you love is to sing . . . sing! In the shower, in the morning, at the top of your lungs, at the drop of a hat. I love to sing. I do it in my kitchen all the time. I don't need good reviews, and I can wear whatever I want! Seriously, take voice lessons. Why not? You can get good enough to please yourself, good enough to sing *Lieder* with the accompanist from your local music society, even good enough, if opera is your passion, to star in an amateur production . . . and if you can't find one, start one. You might just wake up one day and find yourself the local Beverly Sills.

If you want to get next to a professional opera company, there are a dozen ways to do that. You can march straight to the production office and tell them they need a crack secretary who knows opera from A to Z. (It's OK to use your skills to get through a door.) You can start an Introduction to Opera course for adults or children, and arrange to take them backstage after performances. You can organize charity benefits. You can write program notes. You can interview company members on public-access cable TV. The list could go on and on—and it should include *every idea that comes into your head,* no matter how silly, far-fetched, or half-baked it seems. "Take off all my clothes and streak across the stage during Act I of *Aïda*" would be a perfectly legitimate item on your list.

This is *basic brainstorming*—the simplest form of a proven technique for liberating the ingenuity to solve problems. It's a way of casting your net as wide as possible before you haul it in and examine your catch. If you're afraid to let your thoughts go beyond the limits of "reality" and "good sense," you may never catch that one fugitive idea shining on the margins of possibility that holds the answer for you.

When you've put down all the ideas you can think of, you go down the list and look at each one. No matter how absurd or impractical that idea is, *you must find something useful in it.* Then note problems; *what I learned about myself* (the goofiest idea that pops into your head can give you clues to your own talents and needs); and finally, *suggestions and lessons.* That way, even if you throw that idea out, you're only throwing out the shell; you've saved the meat, and you can get new ideas from it.

For example:

Idea:	Streaking
Useful:	It gets lots of attention *fast*
Problems:	Wrong kind of attention—too anonymous, short-lived, embarrassing, and you wind up in jail
What I learned about myself:	There's a little voice in me saying "Look at me —see me"
Suggestions and lessons:	A more dignified kind of publicity stunt? Street theater? Singing in the park? Speechmaking?

Then you go on from there. And sooner or later you're going to find a target that will get you the core satisfactions of your "impossible" dream in eminently possible form.

But I want you to know that most dreams are not impossible. We've just been brainwashed into thinking they are. A few limits to possibility are in the human body. A few. *The rest are in the mind, and those can be changed.* Look how drastically the rules about what women can and can't do have changed in the last ten years! We've got female executives, astronauts, truck drivers, West Point cadets, and jockeys. It's about time for another cruel set of myths to get their comeuppance—the myths of ageism, the ones that say "It's too late." Those myths don't only hurt "senior citizens" facing forced retirement. They do violence to our whole life cycle, lopping off another set of possibilities at each decade. If you're not studying ballet at 10, if you're not a concert pianist by 20, a promising scientist or novelist by 30, an up-and-coming young executive by 35, and at the top of your field by 45 . . . forget it!

It's just not true—not a word of it. A former concert pianist in her 60s has told me that some of her best and most serious pupils are people in their 40s. What they may have lost in agility, they more than make up in drive and concentration. Unlike so many young people, they know what they want, they know how to work, and they know the value of time. And the same is true of older people in pursuit of any goal. There are examples all around us of people who've started a whole new activity or career in the second half of life and been resoundingly successful—like English professor Norman MacLean, who published his first book to rave reviews at the age of 72. Or like Grace Bloom, who got her Master's degree at the age of 86. Or like Catherine Zirpolo, who "always wanted to be in the theater. 'When I was about nine, I wanted to be like Theda Bara or someone like that. I would practice in front of the mirror.' Although Zirpolo's family discouraged her theatrical ambitions, and marriage at eighteen and children soon after further postponed her plans, she never lost her love for the theater. . . . 'And at the age of seventy-five I began!' she marvels." She is a featured player with the New Wrinkle Theater of Greater Boston, a performing troupe made up entirely of players over 60.* So it's hardly "too late" for a 28-year-old to take up the cello, or a 54-year-old to get into politics!

Short of total impossibility, there's only one question to ask yourself about an ambitious goal like "What You Might Have Been." And that is: *Am I willing to work for it?* Are you willing to spend the ten or fifteen years building a political career that it would take to run for the Senate? Do you have the competitive passion for the corporate climb? Are you willing to be the only 40-year-old woman in your medical school class, and to be 45 before you start your practice?

I don't mean, "Are you too scared to do it?" If your goal is worthy of you, if it really challenges you, you're bound to be scared. That fear is natural, and it's no reason to give up on a dream you crave. The real question here is, *How badly do I want it?* If the answer is, "Badly enough to go all the way," then more power to you, and I'll show you how to deal with the fear. But what if you decide that the price in time and work simply outweighs the satisfactions of the goal?

You have an alternative—an alternative both to giving up that dream and to enslaving yourself to it. *Find the touchstone and design another goal around it*—one you would be willing to work for. Get the same

*Nancy DuVergne Smith, "New Wrinkle Theater," *New Age* 4 (February 1979): 48.

satisfactions in quicker, simpler form. If the heart of doctoring for you is helping people, you might choose nursing, physical therapy, counseling, midwifery, massage, dance-exercise, or nutrition. If your touchstone is fascination with the scientific aspects of health and disease, you could go into medical pathology, scientific writing, or medical illustration. It's up to you. The real kicker is that you may come up with something better suited to you than the original goal!

When we think about what we want to do and be, our imaginations often get stuck with the standard roles available in society's costume closet: doctor, lawyer, merchant, chief. We choose one that sort of vaguely approximately fits us, and then we try to fit ourselves into *it* —instead of finding or making up something that's perfect for who *we* are. For example, when I was a little girl I wanted to grow up and star in Broadway musicals. My role model was Judy Garland. I couldn't have told you why, but I can tell you now: I craved attention and admiration and love. I wanted to get up on stage and sing my heart out for an audience and have them pour their love out for me.

As it happened, what I grabbed and got was being a therapist. And every time I walked into Group Laboratories, of which I was the president, I got looked at as if I were important. I was very famous on Ninety-first Street and Broadway. Nobody else had ever heard of me, but I felt like a star. I was giving everything I had, and I was getting all the love and respect I'd ever needed—not from a far-off audience, but from people I could love and touch. It gave me the strength to go on and invent the Women's Success Teams Seminars, where I can get up and perform in front of forty to three hundred people—and even go on TV.

The reason it all happened is that life tricked me into discovering my touchstone. If I *had* become a Broadway star, I might have loved it, but I doubt it. I think I would have hated it. I tried acting, when I was thirty and divorced and alone in New York with my kids. I scraped together a little money, enrolled in acting classes at HB Studio, and got a few parts in small showcases. And you know what? The only thing I liked about it was getting up onstage, turning people on, and basking in their love. I didn't like acting classes, I didn't like rehearsals, I didn't like theaters, I didn't like other actors—and I didn't much care for pretending to be someone other than myself. (That's how I'm different from a born actor.) If I hadn't had my kids, who kept me from traveling in summer stock productions, I might have gone on with it anyway, but I like to think that by now I'd have gotten tired of it and gone on to do exactly what I'm doing!

I designed the touchstone concept to encourage you to be just as inventive on purpose as I was by necessity and inspired accident. You can have the most fun of all designing a goal if you're in one of those "adolescences" I mentioned—the periods of change and self-discovery when you aren't at all sure what you want, and the world is wide open.

There are two "official" adolescences. One is the late teens and early twenties, when so many kids knock around trying out different jobs in different places in an unhurried search for something that feels right. The other is mid-life, when a man or woman has met the goals of the first half of life—raising kids, economic security, success in a profession —and may be free and ready for something totally new. But you really reenter adolescence whenever you go through a major life transition, like marriage, divorce, widowhood, your kids starting school—or meeting a long-held goal! Even losing a job, with its financial anxieties, can give you an opportunity to reexamine and redesign your life. Even early motherhood, with its heavy demands on time and restricted freedom of movement, changes your image of yourself and opens up new possibilities. Just reading this book may have pitched you headlong into an adolescence! (The root meaning of the word is "being nourished to grow.") If so, you may be having a lot of fascinating but confusing second thoughts about what you want in life. You may not even be able to define your touchstone—or to choose one out of all the possibilities that are calling to you.

You're in luck. The genius child in you is getting a fresh chance. You get to play around with *all* the talents and qualities you discovered in your Stylesearch, combining and recombining them like pieces of a puzzle until they click into a goal design that's uniquely yours.

Starting From Style: Alan and Victoria

The most important exercises to work with here are "The Private-Eye Game" and "Twenty Things You Like to Do." Your Detective's Report and Life Quality Profile give you a rich and compact portrait of your own genius. Is there a unifying theme running through that portrait that you could call your touchstone? Do different aspects of your style suggest some possible goal ideas? Can you invent ingenious combinations that get several of your qualities and interests into one package? Remember to use *basic brainstorming* to free your imagination. The wildest idea you come up with may be the one that gives you your goal.

Alan's Detective's Report revealed that he liked plenty of space, the textures of wood and stone, and natural foods. He lived in a small apartment in Chicago, but he'd taken the plaster off one wall to expose the brick, and painted the rest of his walls white to get as much light and spaciousness into the apartment as possible. He had lots of plants, and a big poster of a mountain view that was almost like a window into another world. The books on his shelves ran heavily to things like Thoreau and Rachel Carson and the Whole Earth Catalog.

Alan's Life Quality Profile told him first and foremost that, at 29, he wasn't living the kind of life he loved best. He lived in Chicago because he had gone to school there, and after school he'd gotten a job with an educational publisher, which he enjoyed. But he loved to be outdoors; he liked mountain climbing, though he hadn't done much of it (there isn't a decent-sized hill within 1000 miles of Chicago); he enjoyed doing things with his hands, but as a busy city person he hadn't had much time for that either. He liked to be alone. He loved to read. He didn't need a lot of money to be happy—and he'd *save* money on vacations if he lived out West. After looking over this portrait of himself, he summed up his touchstone as "Closeness to nature—in particular, the Rocky Mountains."

That didn't tell Alan anything he didn't already know—*but he'd never considered it a legitimate basis for designing his life!* Like so many of us, he'd assumed that the serious business of earning a living ruled out having what he loved most in the world for more than two or three weeks out of each year. He'd always figured he was lucky enough to have an interesting job. His Success Teams seminar convinced him of the importance of living a total life more in line with his genius. Challenged to design a goal, Alan said he thought he'd be happy as a national park ranger, fire lookout, forester, or tree planter. Even better, since it would work in his love for books, he could open a bookstore in a small mountain town—or start a small publishing firm specializing in field guides, backpacking manuals, and nature philosophy. Or, since he liked his job, he could explore the possibility of opening an office of his company in Denver, or transferring to the sales department and asking for the western territory.

Of course, no matter which of these potential goals Alan chose, there would be problems. He knew he'd have to face his father's disappointment if he chose a field like forest rangering that didn't make use of his education. Starting a bookstore or publishing firm required risk capital and entrepreneurial know-how he didn't have. And moving west for his own firm meant persuading his boss of the move's business value. But problems are not a reason to give up on having the life you want. *Choose the goal that sounds most exciting to you—even if it's the most "impossible."* Alan decided to start a small specialty publishing house. He made his target the incorporation of the venture with enough backing capital to survive for two years. (Always remember to state your goal in the form of a *target* that can be reached by a specific date.)

Victoria, the divorced, 42-year-old mother of four, loved to get her hands on fine antiques—which she couldn't afford. She'd inherited one beautiful old table from her aunt; otherwise, she'd decorated her house with the best things she could find in junk shops, a couple of which she had stripped and refinished herself. She loved to spend Sundays prowling around those shops among dusty old things that might turn out to be treasures. She was fascinated by the feel of living history old things gave her. Her favorite books were historical romances. She enjoyed giving parties with gourmet cooking, beautiful table settings, and good conversation—when she could get the younger kids into bed and find three matching plates that weren't chipped. She remembered her college years with nostalgia, because that was the only time in her life when she'd been surrounded by people active in the arts. She loved going to the theater.

Victoria had a lot of trouble and fun defining her touchstone. She finally expressed it as "Authentic historical atmosphere—the drama of the past in things, especially elegant things." But she didn't have any trouble coming up with goal ideas—she found about fifteen! Some of them were: become an antique dealer or interior decorator; open her own second-hand shop so the dust-covered treasures would come to *her;* become an auctioneer and run estate sales; do professional refinishing in her garage; design "period" sets for productions in a local theater; lead tours of the great castles of Europe—or of the historic homes in her own town; start a local historical society.

Victoria's problems were time and money, and they loomed large. She supported her kids by working as personnel manager for a large insurance company. Her job was fairly routine but secure, and she couldn't afford to give it up. But she realized that an occasional wistful ramble through the antique shops near Hartford was just not enough of what she loved. So I advised her to make her first target something she could start doing or learning *now*, in the time she had free— weekends and an occasional evening.

Victoria happily set herself not one but two targets: to start doing refinishing jobs for friends and neighbors on weekends (which would bring her both pleasure and extra income), and to enroll in an interior-decorating course in the city one evening a week, with an eye to a possible future change of career. On top of that, she's volunteering to design the set for her daughter's high-school Shakespeare play!

Victoria's situation brings up a problem you're likely to run into, too. What if, after doing the exercises in the first half of this book, you've got *too many* things you want to do? You can't possibly fit them into one lifetime; you'd need at least five.

Congratulations! You haven't got a problem, you've got an embarrassment of riches. I'm not going to tell you to make up your mind and leave the lost possibilities for your next incarnation, because nobody's ever succeeded in proving to me that there's going to be one. What I'm going to do is *give* you five lives—in imagination—as a guide to getting the most out of the one you've got.

FIVE LIVES—AND HOW TO LIVE THEM ALL

Think about it: if you had five lives, what would you do with each one?

I don't mean if you were five different people. I mean if you could be *you* five times over, and explore a different talent, interest, or lifestyle to the fullest each time.

This is an exercise, and like all the exercises in this book, it's flexible —you're supposed to tailor it to you. If you could manage nicely with three lives, take three. If you need ten, help yourself. I just picked five because it's a nice round number.

In one of my lives, I'd be exactly what I am. In one I'd be a nineteenth-century botanist and spend all my time painting flowers. In another I'd be a theoretical physicist. In my fourth, I'd still be Judy Garland—no, something a little less intense and tragic: a musical-comedy star! In my fifth, I'd be a hermit and live alone on an island and write.

My writer friend Julia says that she would be:

1. A writer
2. A professional musician (this was "What She Might Have Been")
3. A linguist and world traveler
4. A naturalist or marine biologist
5. A wife/mother/farmer

Gene, a 47-year-old mortgage banker in a real estate firm, wanted four lives:

1. Head of the Department of Housing and Urban Development
2. A fishing guide
3. A novelist ("What He Might Have Been")
4. A radio announcer for major league baseball

Harriet dropped out of college twenty years ago to marry Gene and have five kids. She said if she had it to do all over again five times, she'd be:

1. The mother of five
2. A scholar of English literature
3. A painter
4. A dancer ("What She Might Have Been")
5. The boss of some large project or enterprise

Amanda, my editor, said she'd only need *two* lives. In one, she'd spend a lot of her time outdoors, riding, biking, gardening and "putting up," surrounded by animals of all kinds. (As a little girl she wanted to be a racehorse trainer.) In the other life she'd live in New York City, go to museums, concerts, and theater, give wonderful parties, study ballet—and be an editor. "The only trouble is," Amanda said, "whichever life I was in, I'd miss the other one!"

That's just it. If you have to choose just one of your "lives," even if it's the one you love best, you're going to long for all the rest of them. Because *they are all vital parts of you.* The saddest phrase we ever got drummed into our heads was "Make up your mind!" There are people in this world who seem to be born for one single purpose, but they're the rare exceptions. Most genius is multifaceted. Even Einstein loved music as much as he loved physics. To ask him to choose between Bach and relativity would have been like asking, "Would you rather cut off your right hand or your left?" And it's the same with you. In each of your "lives" is something you love very, very dearly and need to get into your one life—*and you can.*

I have not decided yet what I'm going to be when I grow up, and I promise you that when I'm 80 I still won't have decided. What I plan to do is as many things as I can. What I plan to get is whatever I can get my hands on. As far as I'm concerned, there's only one answer to the question, "What do you want?" and that is, "Everything!"

In Mexico they have a wonderful saying: *"La vida es corta, pero ancha."* "Life is short, but it's wide." I'm not even so sure about the "short" part; have you really grasped the fact that you'll probably have twenty or thirty or forty more years to fill? In any case, there's a lot more room in your life than you think—room for everything in your "five lives" and then some. Finding that room is simply a matter of *making effective use of time,* and that means *planning*—the skills and techniques you'll learn in the second half of this book. Once you know how to use your days and weeks as the stepping stones to a goal, you will realize that time doesn't have to be a boat you're adrift in, or a treadmill you're running on. It's a raw material you can use the way a sculptor uses clay, and out of it you can shape not just one goal, but many.

So the first target you've chosen for yourself in this chapter is just that: the first. As your total life design unfolds, it will include *many* goals of different kinds, sizes, and shapes—from losing ten pounds by next month to traveling around the world ten years from now; from building your own dream house to block-printing this year's Christmas cards. *Anything you want can come true if you cast it in the form of a concrete goal.* And since the ultimate goal is a wonderful life, one that includes some of everything you love, I'd like you to try your hand at designing a *life plan*—a larger pattern of multiple goals that works in everything in your five (or three, or ten) "lives."

Before I show you some of the ways you can fit many goals into one life plan, I want to remind you again that you're not signing any contracts in blood. As you move through life, your perspective and priorities will change; new interests will appear on your horizon, and some of the old ones may fade. Your life plan five or ten years from now may not bear much resemblance to the one you draw up today. But it's always a good idea to have one. It's a way of reminding yourself that the time ahead of you is yours to create in your own image, however that image may change.

Sequential Goals: Switching Horses in Midstream

The most obvious way to fit more than one major interest into your life is to concentrate on one at a time and do them one after the other. People who change careers in mid-life—say, giving up an executive job to open a bookstore in Vermont—are following this kind of life plan. We are surprised and impressed when someone does that only because we've bought the fool notion that it is "normal" for people to make up their minds once and for a lifetime. There are many people for whom switching horses in midstream comes much more naturally. Like me: my lifestyle is to change goals every five or ten years. I can't think of a better way to live than to do something till I'm satisfied or bored with it and then do something else.

Sequential planning is a good way for a woman or man to combine intense involvements with family and career, or for a couple to alternate breadwinning and nurturing responsibilities and periods of study or creative work. A woman might decide to have her children early, and go back to work or school when they have reached school age—like Harriet, the mother of five, who finished college and entered a master's program in English when her youngest child was in junior high. Or, she might decide to achieve a certain level in her career before having her first child in her 30s. Travel is another goal it often makes sense to plan for after a professional or financial goal has been met. Julia's life plan for the next ten years includes all three: to write a book of her own, travel for a year or two and learn languages (one of her five lives was "linguist and world traveler"), then settle in the country and have a child ("wife/mother/farmer").

The advantage of sequential goals is that knowing the next juicy one is there and waiting spurs you on to meet the target date for your first goal. The pitfall of this kind of planning is that it can be used to postpone the goal you want—and fear—the most. And if you use it that way, it won't work, because you can put that goal off indefinitely. So it's a good rule of thumb to rank your Five Lives in order of importance to you—and then go for the most important one first, even if it's not the one you're living now.

Simultaneous Goals: Moonlighting

But what if two or more of your "lives" are equally important to you? Suppose you're a happily split personality like Amanda, who is half Kentucky bluegrass racehorse breeder and half cosmopolitan New York editor? Then you go for both at once! You become an editor moonlighting as a racehorse breeder, and vice versa.

Amanda has pictures of thoroughbreds all over her office bulletin board, including one of her "godchild"—a young filly owned by friends. She spends vacations and frequent weekends at the races in Saratoga or at Belmont. Like Clark Kent shucking his business suit for Superman leotards, she can switch from stockings and earrings to jeans and boots and back again with equal agility. The only way she feels she could improve on her double life is "more of both"—permanent dwellings in both city and country and an even deeper involvement in both her worlds.

My guess is that simultaneous goals work best when the two (or more) "lives" you're living are very different—because then each provides a refreshing change from the other. The "moonlighting" plan can also be a way of resolving the conflict between two touchstones that are notoriously hard to get together: financial security and creative satisfaction. In New York City there's a group of excellent jazz musicians who play club dates weekends and some evenings. On weekdays, they are . . . Wall Street stockbrokers!

Alternating Goals: The Patchwork Quilt

A variation on the "simultaneous" plan is to arrange your life so that you can devote alternating blocks of time to the pursuit of different goals. This comes very naturally to teachers, who have long summer vacations for traveling or mountain-climbing or creative projects or leading student tours; university types even get a whole sabbatical year off for research or writing. But you don't have to be an academic to plan your life in this pleasant patchwork fashion. Margaret, a nurse-midwife, works and saves money for two years at a stretch and then spends six months traveling through Europe or Asia. And Gene, the mortgage banker whose four lives included fishing, writing, and baseball, has invented what he calls a "businessman's sabbatical." Every few years he takes off from two to five months without pay and spends them tracking down fish in a quiet Florida backwater.

Multimedia Goals

Another way to have all your "lives" in one is to combine two or three interests into one goal. Amanda has published books on horseracing; Julia, who would have given one of her lives to marine biology, writes about whales; Gene plans to devote his next sabbatical to writing (life No. 3) about baseball (life No. 4); and Margaret could combine her profession with her love for travel by offering her much-needed nursing skills in different parts of the world. A multimedia goal can make you extra happy, because two or more of your talents are active at once, and no really important part of you has to wait on the sidelines.

I'll go further, and say that if you want to get the maximum joy and energy out of your life, *nothing you love should ever be left sitting on the shelf.* Everything you put down in your imaginary "lives" should be actively present in your life at all times, because you put it on that list for a reason. A talent or interest is a living part of you—like a hand or an ear or an eye. It needs to be used, it needs to be fed, or it will atrophy—and you'll be less than you're meant to be.

But how is it possible to keep five or six interests going at once? Many of us haven't even managed to develop one talent yet. We're fascinated and appalled by the spectacle of a "Renaissance person" like Buckminster Fuller or Margaret Mead—that's one of our definitions of "genius" as somebody different from the rest of us. What if you are the kind of person who needs to do one thing at a time? How on earth can you keep a love for horses alive while you're in law school, or learn to play the violin while you raise a child *and* write a novel? There just isn't that much time and energy to go around.

Main Meals and Side Dishes

The answer to the dilemma is: whichever interests are not included in your current main goal (or goals), make them "side dishes"—things you do every now and then just for pleasure. This is especially important when you're working toward a single goal that's a long haul. Don't say, "Oh, I'll own a horse someday when I'm a successful lawyer," or "I'll immerse myself in music *after* I finish writing this book." There will come moments when you just can't write or study or whatever any more—official or self-made vacations. Some of that time you are going to spend slumped in front of the TV set, or playing frisbee with the dog. All of us need time just to goof off. But some of it you can use to go horseback riding, or to sit and listen to music—whatever you've discovered you need in your life, even though it can't take first priority right now.

I'll give you an example: me. I'm operating at a very high energy level right now, going eighteen hours a day. I'm meeting my No. 1 goal with Success Teams; I have drive, designs, plans, and I love it. But I start crashing from dream deprivation if I don't also get some of the sweets in my other, secret "lives." So whenever I have some free time, I draw pictures of flowers! My walls are covered with them. I also like to read books about physics. I've found an island I can go to by myself when I really need to get away (my "hermit" life). And it is in my life plan within the next three years to be in an amateur musical comedy—something really silly, like *The Boy Friend.* I'm going to get up onstage and I'm going to tap dance and sing. There's no way to stop me, because I know it will make me happy.

An old childhood dream you've decided you don't want any more is almost always an indicator of something you still need in your life, because it goes very deep. Julia, for instance, said that under different circumstances she might have been a professional musician. As a small child she had a very exact musical ear, but nothing in her environment connected that talent with the fact that real, flesh-and-blood people make music. As a grown-up she would still like to learn to play the violin; she knows that with enough time and work she could get good enough to enjoy it. But full-time writing doesn't permit it.

What she can learn from this is that *she must have music in her life* —even if it's just to listen to. She'll feel happier and more alive if she listens to it a lot. She can always make it a future goal to study the violin when her current writing goals are met—but in the meantime, the musical part of her can be alive and singing even without an instrument.

"Side dishes" are delicious in their own right. They can also be the seeds of future goals, a way to keep something gently simmering on the back burner until you can move it up front. There's always room for them in your life, because they can be things you do once a week, once a month, once a year, or even just once. A "side dish" might be a weekly dance class, the history books you read in the evenings, a picture of a horse on your bulletin board, or even just the promise of a month on the beach compressed into one beautiful shell on your desk. It's a living reminder that life is not a miser, and you have the right to *everything* you love.

—5—
Hard Times, or The Power of Negative Thinking

All right—so you've found out what you want. To be perfectly honest, you want to own the world . . . or at least a nice big slice of it. Now let's be realistic. Can you get your house cleaned tomorrow?

Up to now we've been having nothing but fun. But now it's time to take a look at your Problems List. I invited you to postpone all the real-world difficulties so that you'd feel free to aim high; the only trouble with soaring in fantasy is that it's an awfully long way down to earth. Of course, you saw it coming. You're no dummy; you know there's a real world out there, and that high hopes and a great idea aren't enough. You need a track record, connections, know-how, money, guts—all kinds of things you may not have at all in the field you've chosen. To design your goal without taking this into account may have seemed to you a little like shoving everything under the bed to make your room look clean when you were a kid: the moment had to come when you (or your mother) lifted the bedspread, peered underneath, and groaned because the mess was still there.

OK. Let's take a good look at the mess. "I'll never get the money." "My husband won't like it." "I've got a wife and four kids to support." "I was always a lousy student." "I have absolutely no self-discipline." "I've never picked up a camera in my life." "Women don't advance in my company." "My children need me."

Whatever the problems on your list are, they're very real—and looking them in the eye can be overwhelming. This is the moment when you may crash. You may get depressed. And you may start to hate me for conning you into believing your most extravagent dreams could happen. That's OK. In fact, if you're down, I'm glad to hear about it. Not because I'm a sadist—but because if you aren't having some of those feelings *now*, I promise you they are going to hit you a day or a week after you close this book. And that would be worse, because then you'd have to cope with them alone. So this is the moment to confront "hard reality" and find out just what's making it so hard.

Glance through your Problems List once more. I can tell you without looking that some of them are real and perplexing problems that will take some energetic thinking to solve. And now I'm going to tell you something that will surprise you. *Those are the easy ones!* Those are the fun ones. They're purely a matter of strategy and game plans.

Suppose you want to get from point A to point B, and there's a river in between. What do you do? Well, you get a boat. You can't afford to buy one? You borrow one. You don't know how to row? You get a friend to row it for you. OK? OK. You've got a solution. It's as simple as that.

That is a *strategic problem*—the kind where you're asking, "How can I do it?" and you really want an answer. Strategic problems are hardly any trouble at all. They're discouraging right now only because you don't know how to find the answers. But there are answers. *There is no strategic problem that cannot be solved,* as you'll begin to find out in the next chapter. In fact, the whole second half of this book is designed to give you techniques and resources for solving strategic problems of every conceivable kind: time, money, know-how, contacts, credentials, space, equipment, and how to balance family responsibilities with your right to your own goals.

But there's another kind of problem hiding in your list that *can't* be solved by all the strategies and good ideas in the world. And unless we find out what that is right now, you won't even be able to tell what the real problems are, much less do any constructive thinking about them. Because this other kind of problem disguises itself as a strategic problem—and then that strategic problem mysteriously refuses to be solved.

Like this:

You want to get across a river, and you're brainstorming on it. You say, "Well, I could take a boat."

Then you say to yourself (or to anyone else who's trying to be helpful), "Yes, but I don't have a boat."

And then you say, "Mary has one. I'll borrow hers."

And then you say, "Yes, but I don't know how to row."

And then you say, "Well, I'll ask Mary to row it for me."

And then you say, "Yes, but Mary's very busy, and anyway I don't like to ask for favors."

And then you say, "I know Bill would do it. I drove him to the tree nursery last week, and anyway, he's in love with me. He'd help."

And then you say, "Yes, but I get seasick. I don't want Bill to see me that way."

I call this the "Yes-but" game. It is a sure-fire sign that what's really going on is *not* a simple attempt to solve a problem. You will reject every useful idea you or anyone else comes up with, "yes-butting" until you are purple with frustration and furious at whoever's trying to help you—and they'll be furious with you because you won't let them help!

The truth is, *you are not looking for an answer at all.*

And that's because the real problem isn't how to get across a river. You're no idiot; you can figure that one out as well as anybody. You just keep on saying, "Yes, but it's not that simple!" And you're right. It isn't. The real problem is very deep and painful and complex, and it has nothing to do with boats or rowing or seasickness. What it does have to do with is the *negative feelings* that come up every time you start thinking about going for your dreams.

That's where the hard part of "hard reality" really is. It's not in "reality." It's in your feelings. Half the time, when you say "I can't," or "It's impossible," or "I don't have this or that," all you're really trying to do is something very natural and healthy that has been forbidden by our culture.

You're trying to *complain.*

THE POWER OF NEGATIVE THINKING

Complaining—bitching, moaning, *kvetching,* griping, and carrying on—is a terrific and constructive thing to do. You've just got to learn how to do it *right.*

That sounds funny, doesn't it? You were brought up to believe that complaining is not nice and you should never do it. Of course, you do it anyway, but you don't like yourself when you do. Every one of us would like to be able to say, "I'm not a complainer." We're supposed to be able to pull in our belts, put off our pleasures, bear our disappointments, and face our fears without a squeak of pain or protest.

Hemingway called that kind of behavior "grace under pressure." I happen to consider it mildly psychotic.

The truth is that it just isn't human nature to feel good all the time. And when you're feeling bad or hurt or angry or frightened, you should be allowed to make a fuss and your body knows it!

I happen to believe in the efficacy of complaining the way some people believe in the efficacy of prayer. It's good for you. There are lots of times when you need it. And one of those times may be right now. Because the first half of this book has done something that's almost guaranteed to make you hurt and mad and scared—it's gotten your hopes up. Again. And now you're feeling pain for all the times you tried and it didn't work. For how hard it's been. For the lack of support. For all that lost time. You're feeling fear that you're going to get duped or disappointed again—that this book is just another hype and it won't work for you either. And pain and fear can make you fighting mad— at the forces that made you give up your dreams in the first place, and at me for reviving the hurt along with the hope. Who the hell do I think I am, to tell you you can have what you want?

Uncomfortable as they are, these are healthy feelings. I'd worry about you if you said meekly, "Thank you for turning me on to my fantasies." You'd have been turned on to them all along if you hadn't gotten slugged in the jaw a hundred times. The pain and anger you feel about that memory is a sign of life! After all, what you gave up was everything you loved best. And if *that* doesn't hurt, it's only because you're numb! The reawakening of hope is never painless. It's like running warm water over a frozen hand: your fingers hurt as feeling comes back to them. But do you say, "The hell with this. It felt better when they were numb. Let frostbite set in. Let them amputate."? Of course not! What you do is, you stomp around and cry and curse and swear. You start out in tears and end up laughing. And it *helps!*

Your dreams are just as important a part of you as your fingers. And you shouldn't have to put them back on ice just because it hurts to thaw them out. You ought to be allowed to stomp and holler and cry and swear—and have a good time doing it. That's what I call *Hard Times.*

But the hurt of old disappointments and the fear of new ones isn't necessarily the only kind of negative feeling lurking in your Problems List. There's another kind that comes up not because you're afraid to believe me, but because you're afraid you *do!* It's beginning to look like maybe this time you're really going to get your bluff called. And that means you're going to have to get out there and start doing some things that will make you very nervous. Like making phone calls to intimidating people. Like sticking a blank sheet of paper in the typewriter, or a blank canvas on the easel. Like walking in and asking politely but firmly for that raise. Like—maybe even—winning.

If you think you're nervous *now,* just wait till the next chapter, when you find out that you can—and should—start working toward your goal, not next week, not next month, not "someday," but *tomorrow.* Wait till all those too, too solid obstacles—the million bucks you'll never have, the family who will surely throw you out or die of malnutrition—start melting away, and you realize, too late, how safe you felt hiding behind them. A lot of times when you start reciting all the reasons why you can't get your goal, it's not because you really think you can't. It's because you'd really just as soon not. It's because you sort of hope you won't have to.

What you really are is *scared.* You're probably embarrassed to admit it, even to yourself, because you're a grown-up and you're not supposed to be afraid of anything. But there are a few thousand reasons to be scared when you start going for what you want. Some of them are part of the high cost of success in our society, especially for women. We got a look at those when we talked about the environment that creates winners—and the environment that doesn't: negative tapes . . . ignorance of ways and means . . . lack of support . . . guilt at leaving people in the lurch . . . fear of being left alone. It's murder trying to achieve your goals while you're carrying all those fears on your back, and with the help of this book, you won't have to. You're going to learn how to prepare for difficult situations like interviews. You'll find out that it's OK to fall on your behind and get back up again just as often as you need to. You'll learn to provide yourself with all the support you need: a team of real and imaginary winners who will help you out and cheer you on. And you know what?

You'll still be scared.

There is nothing in this world that's worth doing that isn't going to scare you. The moment you make the commitment to going for your dreams, you've begun to venture into the unknown. And the human organism's natural response to novelty and risk is adrenalin. Butterflies in the stomach. Wobbly knees. Pounding heart. It's commonly called stage fright, and it's just nerves, but it feels like a heart attack. Comfort is one of the things you can forget about right now. You're not going to have it any more. Excitement, company, help, and support, yes. Comfort, no.

So what do you do?

You do what every actress worth her salt does before she goes out on stage on opening night: you have a fit. You kick, stomp, and cry, "The lights are ghastly, the lines are awful, the playwright should be shot, the director's an idiot—I'm not ready, I *cannot* go on, I *will* not go on, I'm *leaving!*" And then you walk onstage under those lights . . . and you're fine.

That's Hard Times, too.

Hard Times is nothing but a good old-fashioned gripe session raised to the dignity and status of a ritual. Other cultures have made an art form of complaining. Look at the Flamenco gypsy's howl. Listen to the blues! The universal peasant poem is a string of curses directed at heaven . . . and what do you think the Bible means by "lamentation," anyway? A fancy word for bitching and moaning, in my book. All those people obviously knew something we don't. But we can learn to recognize and honor the need to complain—and then to be as openly, vividly, and *creatively* obnoxious as we can. It takes a little practice, because we've all been conditioned to be sweet and polite even when we're feeling like an alligator with a hangover. But you'll be surprised at how quickly your inhibitions vanish.

You can try it right now, in the privacy of your own mind. Take any item on your Problems List—it can be a perfectly serious obstacle to getting your goal, like a lack of money or schooling or too many family responsibilities. Sit down and really think about why that problem makes the whole idea totally impossible. You can take a sheet of paper and write down your thoughts if you like; title it "It Can't Be Done." It's a good idea to start out earnest, depressed, and a little whiny: "Even if I did get into school, I'd probably flunk out the first semester. I've always been a lousy student, I get headaches at the thought of sitting down to study."

Now, little by little, if you can—and you almost always can—start having fun with your negative feelings. Exaggeration, self-parody, melodrama, defiance, and obscenity are all useful weapons, and anything is a fair target: yourself, me, your goal, mother, flag, and country. "The truth is, I hate studying. It bores me and I can't concentrate and I hate *you* for suggesting it. I like things fine just the way they are. I'm too lazy to bother with all this. I think I'll eat a lot of chocolate and get fat." Say anything, as long as it's a mean, miserable complaint with some punch to it.

Did you notice that your energy level went up? Does your goal suddenly look a little less impossible? You haven't solved anything yet. The strategic problem is still there. Your doubts are still there. So why are you laughing?

Because you've dug down through all those heavy layers of "I can't," and struck a defiant gusher of "I don't want to and I *won't.*" Depression is an energy crisis, and *negativity is energy*—pure, ornery, high-octane energy. It's just been so repressed and tabooed that we've forgotten something every 2-year-old knows: how good it is for us to throw a tantrum. We're all such good little girls, such brave, stalwart little boys, such polite little children—and inside every one of us is an obnoxious, exuberant little brat, just squirming to be let out. I've got one. So do you. That brat is your baby, and you'd better love her, because you ignore her at your peril.

If you had a child who was bursting with energy, and you dressed that child up in white and took her to church and tried to make her (or him) sit still and be quiet, that child would wreck the whole service. But if you put him (or her) in a pair of old Levis and let him run amok in the fields, roll in the mud, tease the dog, kick the cow, scream and holler, and take a nap, when he got up he might just go to church and behave himself.

Somewhere along the line our culture has sold us the absurd idea that we've got to have a positive attitude to succeed. We're afraid to be negative because we think it means we won't *do* anything. And yet the evidence to the contrary is overwhelming. A quick look at your own experience will show you how powerless positive thinking really is. Oh, it feels good—while it lasts. The first morning you get out of bed saying,

"I know I can do it, I know I can do it," it makes a whole new day for you. You walk around whistling to yourself, thinking, "God, I could run the world with this idea!" The second morning you know you're lying. You not only can't do it, you can't even get out of bed.

Trying to force a positive attitude is the surest way in the world not to get something done. A *negative* attitude, on the other hand, will get you to do it.

I call this The Power of Negative Thinking.

You can demonstrate it very easily if you have kids who hate to do their homework. (I've never met a normal, healthy child who loved it.) If you say "You've got to do it! Long division is good for you. Look, if you don't do your long division you're not going to get good grades, and then you won't get into college, and then what will happen to you?" I guarantee that your kids will lock themselves in the bedroom and read comic books. So next time, try saying this instead: "You're so right. Long division is repulsive. It's awful. So why don't you put your homework on the floor and jump on it? Hate it. Kick it around the room. Curse and swear at it. Use the dirtiest words you know. I'll go in the next room. And when you're all through, put it back on the table and do it." You'll find your kids will be laughing—and their long division will get done.

Of course they have to do it. They know they have to do it. *But they don't have to like it.* And neither do you.

The operative principle of Hard Times is, "Get it off . . . and then get on with it." *You've got to let negative attitudes and feelings happen.* Only then will you be ready for positive problem-solving, planning, and action.

Of course, there's only one little hitch I haven't mentioned yet. Throwing a tantrum isn't nice. Complaining isn't socially acceptable. Indulging in your grouches and fears may make *you* feel better, but what about the innocent bystanders around you? Their feelings may be hurt if they happen to get in the way of a stray expletive. "I hate this thesis, and I hate the goddam typewriter, and I hate you too!" They may worry that you really are going to have a nervous breakdown, or leave for Bermuda, or whatever threats you happen to fire off in the heat of the moment. They may think you're a little odd, if not certifiably crazy. What should you do about them?

Simple. Tell them exactly what you're doing—and invite them to be your audience and cheering section. Say, "This is Hard Times. I'm mad, nervous, fed up, and for the next five minutes I'm going to go totally bananas. Don't pay any attention to anything I say. You can stick your fingers in your ears if you like. It will all be over in five minutes." And then you run amok—and instead of ending in emotional wreckage, apologies, and tears, everybody ends up laughing. Once you learn this, you'll never forget it, and as soon as the people around you catch on, they'll start doing it too.

When you feel a Hard Times session coming on, you can tell your audience that there are three possible responses that will help you:

1. APPLAUSE. We should all develop artistic appreciation for each other's brats. Every really inventive complaint deserves cheers, laughter, and such comments as, "That's a beaut," or "That's a stinker." If several people get going together, a spirit of competition can develop. It's fun to see who can come up with the nastiest gripes, and such contests invariably end in laughter and really clear the air.

2. PARTICIPATION. The last thing anyone should do is argue with you or try to help you look at the sunny side. You don't need to be talked out of your negative feelings—if anything, you need urging on! Tell your audience if they want to say anything at all, for God's sake don't make it constructive. If they can pitch in and say something *de*structive, they're more than welcome. It's nice to hear yourself backed up by a friendly chorus of snarls and moans. Makes you feel less alone.

3. ADMIRATION. There's another reason why we sometimes complain that's a really subtle one. I used to do it, and it took me quite a while to understand why.

When my sons were small, it seemed like I spent half my life working my brains out and the other half griping about it. I'd march up to my kids and say, "Look at all the work I did. I got up at six, I made the beds, I did the dishes, I vacuumed and dusted the whole house . . . I'm exhausted!" And they'd feel terrible. They'd say, "Look, do you want us to do the dishes?" And I'd say, "No! I'm not mad! I just want . . . I don't know what I want!" I didn't mean to make them feel guilty and miserable. None of us knew what was going on.

And then one day it hit me. I didn't want them to do a thing. All I wanted was for them to say, "You know, you're really fabulous. How did you do all that?" And then I'd beam and say, "Oh, it was nothing."

The truth is, I was very proud of myself. But I didn't dare come right out and say so, because I was afraid I'd get shot down for being so conceited. None of us knows how to say, "Sit down. I want to tell you what I did all by myself against very tough odds. I want you to know I was Herculean." We're not allowed to brag, so we whine instead.

This kind of complaining is an appeal for admiring recognition. When you've had a hard row to hoe and you've hoed it, you deserve sympathy and praise. If this were the American frontier and you were Paul Bunyan or Wild Bill Hickok, you could boast about your heroic deeds and make a poem of it. But a Hard Times session will serve just as well. And if you tell your audience what you're after, they'll probably say, "Is that all? Why didn't you ask? I've been secretly admiring you all along—I just thought you were so strong you didn't need to hear it!"

So much of what we need just boils down to *permission.* Permission to feel what we feel—and say it. To let each other know. And to find out that what we feel isn't freakish, or destructive, or wrong. It's just human—and shared.

THE PRIVATE GRIPE

There will be times and places, however, when you won't be able to complain out loud. I don't recommend doing it with your boss, for instance—unless he or she is also a close personal friend. Many professional and business situations are what I call "on stage" situations, the kind where you have to keep up appearances even when you're quaking inside. You'll find some handy First Aid for those in Chapters 9 and 10. But meanwhile, you should know that the fact that you sometimes have to act like a Spartan doesn't mean you have to *feel* like one. If you can't bitch out loud, or there's nobody listening, or you've just got an incurable case of good manners, you can still let your brat out in private —and provide a sympathetic audience for yourself.

You can keep a Hard Times Notebook.

A small spiral notebook of the type secretaries use is ideal, because you can carry it in your pocket or purse. To set the tone, you might want to draw a nice negative face on the cover. Or find a picture of a lugubrious basset hound or somebody with a bad hangover, and paste that on. But this is optional. What really counts is the words you write inside.

As you proceed with the problem-solving and planning sections of this book, there will be many times when you feel like giving up the whole thing. Whenever that happens, get out your Hard Times Notebook and write down all the nastiest complaints you can think of. Let the brat, rebel, and cop-out in yourself have a field day. Record curses, confess fears, revel in all your own worst qualities, and plot fantasy escapes. The same rules apply as for complaining out loud—and for listening. Accept your own complaints with sympathy and relish. Have a good time, if you possibly can. Don't rationalize, apologize, explain, or argue with yourself. Above all, *never try to solve problems in your Hard Times Notebook.* This is the place for 100 percent unadulterated negativity. It will make entertaining reading when the fit is past and you're feeling good again—or the next time you're feeling rotten and need inspiration.

WHEN IT HURTS TOO MUCH TO LAUGH

But what about the times when you're hurting so bad you can't be funny? In some moods, past defeats and present problems seem overwhelming. It's no joke. And there are some life situations, like the loss of a job or a love, that are so hard that you can't be a brat about them. You'll laugh again later. Right now your only concern is to get through the rough time in one piece.

When you're in that state, suffering in silence is the worst thing you can do. You need the relief of complaining now most of all. And there's only one thing you need from whomever is listening to you: to be heard.

Real listening—quiet, sympathetic, and totally attentive—is one of the rarest commodities in our society. None of us knows how to ask for it, and very few of us know how to give it. You know there are plenty of times when all you need is to tell somebody how hard it's been, how you felt when s/he left you, when the kids were sick, when there was no heat. You don't want your problems solved. All you want is to see that click of recognition in another person's eyes that says your pain is valid and what you've lived through is real. Then you know you could go on. But for that to happen, someone has to listen with ears and feelings open—and mouth closed. How often have you really gotten that? More often, you either get well-meaning good advice—which you angrily and guiltily reject without knowing why ("If George is such a bastard, why don't you leave him?" "No, no, you don't understand!")

—or, if the other person can't think of any way to help you, her attention wanders out the window, up to the ceiling, anyplace but on you. I say "her attention" because most women are like this: if we can't cure another person's ills, we don't want to hear about them. And that's because we don't know that *listening is enough.*

Funny thing: men are better at it. They've always known about the healing power of that most ancient of psychotherapists, the bartender. He doesn't do anything but polish glasses and given an occasional grunt while his customer works his way deeper into his second double Scotch and his tale of woe. So when one man walks up to another and says, "Sam, I'm an alcoholic, my wife is leaving me, I've lost my job," Sam says sincerely, "Geez, Joe, that's rough"—which is precisely what Joe needs to hear. But I know perfectly well that if Joe walked up to me and began, "Barbara, I'm an alcoholic . . ." I'd go, "Oh my God. What do I do now? Let me talk to your wife. You can live in my house. I'll take you to the steam bath. I'll find you a job." Women are *fixers.* I've got to fix. Most of you have got to fix. We do it in the name of compassion—and it's heartless. What's more, it makes us feel, "Oh no, another person on my back!" And then we make the other person pay in subtle ways for help that she or he never asked for in the first place.

So when someone tells you a Hard Times story, it's much kinder not to say or do anything at all except show that person with your eyes that you are reliving the rough times with him or her, using all the resources of your imagination and feelings. If you have to say anything at all, you can say, "That sounds awful," or "Ouch." *That's all.* Otherwise, don't interrupt. She or he will be finished, really finished, in five or ten or at the most fifteen minutes. Real listening is the cure for chronic complaining. You know from your own experience that when you see in someone's face that your words have registered, you don't need to go on and on.

So make it a point to ask for this kind of healing attention when you need it. There are three little words that have been missing from our vocabulary: "Please just listen." (Note: tell your listener not to fake it, because then it won't work. If s/he is distracted, or just not in the mood, s/he should simply be honest about it: "Sorry, I just can't listen today." And the same goes for you when you're the listener.)

Can you use your Hard Times notebook for this kind of serious complaining if there's no one around to listen? Definitely—but you still need somebody to talk to. And sometimes the very best listeners are the ones you talk to just in your mind.

Some people still feel comfortable—and comforted—talking to God, Jesus, or a saint for whom they feel a special personal affection. But since religion has lost its central place in our lives, many of us don't have this source of comfort any more. It's too bad, because it was such a good one. I'm not suggesting that you do your complaining to a Supreme Being unless that really comes naturally to you. But I think those of us who aren't religious ought to have our "saints," too: kindly figures who loved and battled life, who lived through hard times of their own, who can give us their wisdom, humor, and understanding. Children often have imaginary friends they talk to, sharing their secrets and their sorrows. I know a painter who used to pray to Cézanne and Matisse when she was a girl! I think that's a skill we grown-ups ought to recover.

Is there one member of the "ideal family" you selected for yourself in Chapter 4 who is your favorite, or who lived through and triumphed over troubles not so different from yours? That person can be your personal "saint." You can probably guess who mine is, since I've already told you that Albert Einstein reminds me of my grandfather! If you don't already have pictures of your "family" members, at least get one of your "saint." Put it up on the wall above your desk, or wherever you'll be working on your goals. (If you don't already have a work space of your own, you should start thinking about finding one.) If your "saint" is an imaginary character from literature, find a photo or painting that looks the way you imagine he or she would look.

Now, when you're low and alone and need somebody to talk to, you can tell your troubles to Marlene Dietrich or Henry Thoreau. You'll be amazed at how much good it does. That's because your own private "saint" will never try to fix your problems, stare out the window in embarrassment, or tell you to cheer up. She or he will just listen, like God or a good bartender, looking back at you with that steady, warm, sad-merry gaze that says, "I know. I've been there. It's rough."

UP, DOWN—AND FORWARD

If your personal "saint" is a real or historical person, there's one more thing you can do that will help you over any rough spots on the journey to your goal. Read his or her biography—or even better, letters and journals, if they are available. You'll learn a fact that will surprise you—and encourage you. Famous people have suffered the same ups and downs as the rest of us. The only way they are at all different from you and me is that they didn't take the low moods as signals to give up. They sometimes felt like giving up, of course. And do you know what they did then? They complained. The private writings of accomplished people reveal that they did one hell of a lot of complaining. And I think it's one of the ways they got where they did. Because they kept going. And so they made the great discovery that you are also going to make: *success does not depend on how you feel.* Human moods have remarkably little to do with effective action—and it's a good thing, or we'd still be living in caves.

This is terribly important to realize, because deeply ingrained in our culture and our past experience is *the mistaken notion that you can only do well when you're feeling good.* You've had highs—those periods in your life when you just couldn't roll the dice wrong. You felt unafraid, self-confident, articulate, creative, and you knew you could do anything —for a day, a week, or even a month. Right? Well, that was just about the worst thing that has ever happened to you. Because then, as sure as night follows day, a low rolled in and wiped out your sense of progress, leaving you feeling like you were right back at zero. And ever since, you've been sitting around waiting for that high to come back so you could do it again. You probably assumed that famous people feel that way all the time—otherwise how could they have done what they did?—and that there's just something wrong with *you.* And publicly at least, famous people aren't telling, because they're afraid people will find out that there's something secretly wrong with them!

A peek into their private lives and feelings explodes the myth. If anything, the great souls and high achievers have had more emotional highs and lows than the rest of us. That's not because they were born with extra helpings of passion and drive (another myth)—it's because they're committed to realizing their life designs. That means they're out there in that high-risk area you're heading for. When you get there, you will not need antidepressant pills, bottled courage, or Norman Vincent Peale. You'll just need *structure* and *support.* That's what all true winners have had in one form or another, and it, not elation, is what keeps them moving forward. It's only because you haven't had that external support system that your low moods have been able to stop you before. And so we're going to spend the rest of this book constructing it for you.

But before we start, I'm going to equip you with one more useful tool for your success survival kit. It's a brief, simple notation you will put down at the end of each day, called an *Actions & Feelings Journal.* In it, you will trace the line of your own forward progress through all your ups and downs, and accumulate unshakable proof in your own handwriting that your progress does not depend on your moods.

You can keep this journal in another spiral notebook like the one you use for Hard Times, but a plain pad of paper will do. At the top of each page, write the following column headings:

DATE   WHAT I DID   HOW I FELT

Starting today, as you work with this book, make a brief note each evening of what you've done that day—no matter how small or unimportant it may seem to you. You might start with "Decided on my goal," or "Started Hard Times Notebook." As you draw up your game plan and start moving toward your goal, you'll be recording things like phone calls you made, letters you've written, visits to the library or employment agency, a helpful conversation with a friend, a page or a paragraph or even just a sentence toward the article or thesis you have to write. Just buying a pad of paper, some stamps, or a pair of new shoes for an interview is enough.

If you think you haven't done anything that led toward your goal, put down whatever you did do that day. Never write "Nothing." Write "Paid bills" or "Cleaned house" or "Went to the movies" or "Stayed in bed and ate a whole pizza all by myself." You need to begin to realize that *now that you have a goal, your whole life is heading toward it.* Even what look to you like backward steps are positive actions of another kind. They express some real and valid part of you, and they serve a purpose. Maybe you were pushing yourself too hard and needed a rest. Maybe you were feeling scared. Maybe your brat needed a whole day to him- or herself. Maybe you needed to give yourself a reward. That's OK. Just write down what you did. Don't judge it.

Under "How I felt," you might put "Great," or "Hopeless," or "I feel like I'm getting somewhere," or "Scared," or "Bored," or "Angry at all the time I wasted before," or even "Fed up with the whole thing."

Again, don't judge your feelings. Just record them as honestly as you can.

Even if you've never kept a journal before, this one is a cinch to keep —it just takes a few minutes and a few words each night. But try to make it a regular habit. The more faithfully you keep it, the more revealing it will be.

One purpose of your Actions & Feelings Journal is to keep a simple record of what you accomplish day by day. You can't imagine how important this is. Most of us have a very distorted notion of how things actually get done in this world. *We think that accomplishment only comes from great deeds.* We imagine our heroes striding toward their goals in seven-league boots—writing best-selling novels in three months, building business empires overnight, soaring to stardom out of nowhere—and this gives rise to painfully unrealistic expectations of ourselves. And yet nothing could be further from the truth. *Great deeds are made up of small, steady actions, and it is these that you must learn to value and sustain.*

Often you feel you've done nothing when you've actually done a lot. That's because what you did do seemed beneath notice—it was so small that it didn't "count." But it did—just as each stitch counts toward a finished dress, each brick or nail toward a house you can live in, each mistake toward knowing how to do things right. Directed action, no matter how small, moves toward its point. When you write down what you've done, you will have to realize you've done it—and you'll begin to see how small steps add up.

The second purpose of the Actions & Feelings Journal is to let you discover for yourself how your feelings and actions are related—or unrelated. You will find that they don't match up in any consistent, predictable, cause-and-effect way. You can often do as much when you're feeling negative as when you're sparkling. When I started keeping my Journal, I discovered that I often make the least substantial progress on my high days—I'm too busy celebrating, knocking on wood, wondering how long it will last, and so on. I also found that a really abysmal low often precedes a burst of growth or inspiration. When you *are* low, it's harder to appreciate what you've done. You may not have the jubilant sensation of progress even when you have the fact of it. That's why an objective record of your actions is so important. The daily entries in your Actions & Feelings Journal will represent *gained ground:* real progress you can see and savor, whatever your mood of the moment may be.

Being human, you can't always have a positive attitude—and you don't have to. You cannot be consistently self-disciplined—and you don't have to. You can get where you're going anyway, and have fun doing it. Are you feeling scared or mad? Get scared. Get mad. Is your self-esteem non-existent today? Don't worry about it. It's irrelevant. Look in the mirror and say, "I'm horrible, I'm a failure, I'm ugly. I'll never make anything out of myself." Applaud yourself. Enjoy your negative attitude. And then roll up your sleeves and get down to business.

Three

Crafting I: Plotting the Path to Your Goal

Hard Times clears the mind the way a thunderstorm clears the air. After a good gripe session the oppressive haze is gone, far things look near, and you're in the mood to come up with practical strategies for getting there. When you start plotting the actual steps to your goal, you'll understand why it was so important first to discover your emotional investment in "It can't be done." Because here's where you find out that it *can*.

I'm a down-to-earth woman, and this is a down-to-earth book. It's not about castles in the air—it's about the nuts and bolts and plans and principles of engineering that get castles built here on earth. But if there's one section of this book that comes close to being about miracles, this is it.

Down-to-earth miracles, that is.

Right now what you've got is a clearly-defined target and a list of the strategic problems that stand in your way. By the end of this section, you will have a step-by-step *plan* for getting to your goal—a bridge of actions connecting that distant dream to your doorstep. In other words, we're going to start turning obstacles into stepping stones.

What accomplishes this transformation? There are no magic wands, it's true. But you have two perfectly ordinary, absolutely priceless resources in your possession right now that can do as much as any magic wand in any fairy tale you care to name. One of them is in your head. The other is in your address book.

They are called *human ingenuity* and *human community*—or in plain English, a head full of brains and a room full of friends.

These two between them really have the power to move mountains. They can get you a million dollars, or they can get you what you want for $5,000 or $500—or for free. They can get you an introduction to Mikhail Baryshnikov. They can get you a working farm with six holstein dairy cows. They can get you a job in a new field without having to go back to school; they can get you into school and through it without a dime. They can get you the capital and know-how to start your own business. They can get you unstuck from a low rung on the corporate ladder. They can get you married. And I'll be showing you exactly how in the course of this section.

The technique for liberating ingenuity is called *brainstorming*. The technique for mobilizing community is called *barn-raising*. They are specific antidotes to the two mainstays of "hard reality": *conventional "wisdom"* and *pathological individualism*.

Conventional "wisdom" is the attitude that says, "It'll never fly." Then it goes on to say things like, "Only rich people can travel around the world first-class." Or, "You have to have an M.B.A. to get a good job in business these days." Or, "You can't make a living in the arts unless you're already famous." Or, "You can't make a successful business out of what you love." *All true winners are people who have taken conventional "wisdom" as a sporting challenge, instead of a pronouncement of defeat.* They assume that its rules were made to be broken, so they don't even stop to ask, "Can it be done?" They just ask, "How?"

Answers to that question start turning up as soon as you suspend all rules of conventional "wisdom" and look at each problem with pure, playful creativity, as if it had never been seen on earth before. That's brainstorming, and with its help you'll discover that some of the things you thought you needed to reach your goal—the really tough ones, like a lot of money, or a Ph.D.—may not even be necessary. You can invent alternative routes that are not only quicker and more direct, but closer to your path and a lot more fun.

Brainstorming will give you a wealth of ideas for the steps to your goal. But if a page full of good ideas were enough, everyone who's ever had a fit of inspiration—and that means everybody—would be rich and famous. So once you've pitted your native wit against conventional "wisdom," you will have to do the second thing enterprising people have always done: get help.

If this book has one single most important purpose, it is to mount a full-scale attack on the most destructive piece of conventional "wisdom" there is: "You've got to make it on your own." Nobody can. Nobody does. And yet we often hesitate to ask anyone for help, advice, or even instructions to the corner store for fear that it means we're "dependent." I know a grown woman, the mother of three children, who wanted to go back to college but couldn't sign up, because when she got to the campus she didn't know which building the registration office was in! She wouldn't ask anyone, because she thought she should know how by herself and was afraid she'd look like a fool.

That's what I call *pathological individualism*. I don't mean the marvelous *individuality* that makes each of us unique. I mean the cultural disease of extreme "self-reliance" that has cut us off from the most potent resource we have for achieving our goals: each other. The best ideas, the ones that really work magic, are the ones that draw on the knowledge, skills, and contacts of other people. I'm going to show you how you can mobilize your human resources to help you meet your goal. I call the technique "barn-raising," after the way people in pioneer communities pitched in to get each other's barns built in a day. A barn-raising is the closest thing I know to a magic wand. It turns the most "ordinary" group of people—friends, family members, co-workers, even strangers—into a gold mine of helping hands and minds.

Brainstorming and barn-raising together will give you the steps to your goal—steps you can start taking *tomorrow*. But you also need a way of organizing those steps into a map of your path you can actually follow. As you work through Chapters 6 and 7, you will learn to draw a special kind of visual plan called a *flow chart*—the heart of your Portable Success Support System. It is the tool that turns the dream in your head into *a structure outside yourself* that will guide your actions step by step and keep you on the track. Once that's been done, it takes only one more step to bring you to the threshold of action: setting *target dates* and putting your plan into a *time frame*. We'll be doing that in Chapter 8.

–6–
Brainstorming

You need three items before you're ready to start brainstorming: a pad of paper, a couple of pencils—and a problem.

Right now the problems on your list are probably stated in a form something like this: "I can't because I don't have X." For instance, Jill, 30, wants to move up to a management position in the accounting firm where she's worked as a secretary for four years. But she can't see any way to take that step without going back to school and getting an M.B.A.—which would take another two years she doesn't want to wait and $8,000 she hasn't got. Alan, a 28-year-old Chicago editor, wants to start his own small publishing firm, but he doesn't have the capital. Joyce, a 43-year-old mother, wants a paying job as a fund-raiser, but she has no previous job credits to put on her resumé—just one experience as a volunteer.

Credentials, experience, and money are among the most common obstacles conventional "wisdom" places in our paths—and often enough, when we look at the world around us, conventional "wisdom" just seems like common sense. But now that we've gotten the negativity out in Hard Times, you're ready to look at each of those obstacles in a more positive light: as a challenge to your ingenuity. And that change in attitude is as simple as a change in gra nmar.

"I can't because I don't have X" is a dead end. Your brain can't work with it. To turn it into a form your brain just loves to work with, take that one flat statement and turn it into a pair of leading questions:

1. How can I get it without *X*?
2. How can I get *X*?

Either of those questions can be the takeoff point for brainstorming. But it's almost always a good idea to start with question No. 1. Because the point isn't just to get to your goal by any means at all. It's to get you there by the quickest, most direct, most personalized route—one that will get some of the rewards of your goal into your life right away. When we talked about choosing a first target in terms of your touchstone, I told you that I want you to start doing what you love tomorrow —not five years from now, when you've made a pile of money or finished your Ph.D. This is the operative principle to keep in mind throughout your planning. Never take the long road if you can find a shorter one that will get you to the same place.

In the language of goals, this means that the only time to go straight into brainstorming with question No. 2—"How can I get *X*?"—is: one, if you're 150 percent sure that *X* is the only way to your goal (there's really no alternative to medical school if you want to become a doctor); or two, if *X* itself is something you love for its own sake, like wealth or scholarship or professional standing. Then it's not really an obstacle at all—it's one of your touchstones! With those two exceptions, never assume that conventional "wisdom" is correct until you've tried question No. 1.

For example, you may be depressingly certain that you have to have an M.B.A. to get a good job in business . . . or an M.S.W. or Ph.D. to do responsible therapy . . . or an M.A. in education to teach. In our ever more credential-happy society, there appear to be fewer and fewer doors you can walk through without a piece of paper, which will cost you thousands of dollars and thousands of hours. Well, I'll tell you something. At a conservative estimate, 75 percent of the conventional "wisdom" about credentials is pure gobbledygook.

In case you didn't know it, school is a big business. It's also a safe haven for those of us who just love to be in rehearsal. We can go to school until we're ready, and then go to school some more until we're *really* ready, instead of jumping in the water and starting to swim. Don't get me wrong. I'm not against higher education. I think everybody should go to college and study art and philosophy as an end in itself—like sending your mind to summer camp. But if you are heading for a specific goal and you're considering school as a means to that end, check your situation out carefully.

Is a degree an integral part of what you want to do—like becoming a research scientist or a history professor? Or is it an absolute necessity to get where you want to go? If you're in any doubt about this second question, do a little role-model research on the careers of the most interesting people in your field. Did the journalists you admire most go to journalism school? (Not likely.) Did all the male executives in your office or your business get hired with M.B.A.'s? (Ask around discreetly —and remember that nothing that's not required of a man can now be legally required of a woman.) Does your favorite poet or painter have a Master's in Fine Arts? If the answer is "no," the chances are excellent that you don't need a piece of paper to do what you want to do, either, and that you shouldn't waste your time and money getting one. Instead, grab yourself a plain old piece of blank paper and ask yourself, "How can I get it without *X?*"—*X* being more school.

Just this once, I'm going to give you some ideas to get the juices flowing. There are ways that I and people I know have achieved our goals outside the academy, and they all revolve around the idea that the best, directest, most exciting way to learn most things is *by doing them.*

CREATIVE HOOKY, OR: FIVE WAYS TO LEARN—AND EARN—BY STAYING OUT OF SCHOOL

1. Nerve. Otherwise known as talking your way through a door with nothing going for you but talent, cheek, and desperation. If you *know* what you'd be good at, there's nothing lost—and often much to gain —by just walking into wherever you want to be and presenting yourself. It's a little hard on the nerves, but you'll get plenty of help with that problem in the last section of this book.

This is the way my own career got started. When I came to New York, I had a B.A. in anthropology. Now there is nothing on earth more useless for getting a job than anthropology. You find me an ad that says "Wanted: B.A. in anthropology." I'd like to see it. I was what you might call highly unemployable. But I had to find a job that would feed my kids, and I was naive enough to hope for one that wouldn't starve my soul. I had the intuitive feeling that I would probably be good at working with people. So I screwed up my small supply of courage and answered one of those ads that said "Experience preferred." I noticed that it didn't say "Required," and anyway I figured that the experience of walking around on earth for thirty years ought to count for something. The job was as a counselor in a drug program, and I talked my way into it—probably because they needed manpower as badly as I needed the job.

I walked in there at nine the first morning with my knees shaking. By 5:00 P.M. I knew I hadn't been wrong. I might be green, but I was in my element. From there, one thing led to another. While I was still working at that job, I started group therapy. Within a year I had become an assistant-trainee of the head therapist. And then four of us split off from him and started Group Laboratories. Over the next eleven years I made a tidy living doing group and individual counseling; I was a consultant at three medical schools, teaching their psychiatrists and psychologists; and I got invited to speak and give creativity workshops all over the country. None of this happened because I had a piece of paper. It happened because I found the right swimming pool, squeezed my eyes shut, and jumped in. To this day, I have never gotten one unit of academic credit over the 108 units required for that B.A. in anthropology.

2. *Volunteering.* In a world of professionalism, where money is the measure of seriousness, volunteering has gotten something of a bad name. It's supposed to be amateurish, dilettantish, the sort of half-committed playing-at-work that society matrons do on alternate Tuesdays. I want to set the record straight right now. Volunteer work is one of the best ways there is to get your feet wet and gain experience in a new field—whether it's in a zoo, a hospital, a school, a museum, a neighborhood newspaper, a political campaign office, or a family farm. You don't need credentials or prior experience. You don't have to pay them a cent for your training. But what's best is that volunteering gets you started doing what you love right away, even if it's only once a week. Or—if you're trying out a tentative goal—it lets you get the living feel of a profession before you commit yourself to full-time work or training. And it equips you with experience, contacts, and references that will be useful if and when you do decide to make that commitment.

Volunteer work is the great cure for the classic vicious cycle, "Can't get experience without a job; can't get a job without experience." If you think unpaid experience doesn't count on a resumé, think again. If Joyce has done volunteer fund-raising while her kids were in school, then she's been a fund-raiser—and she should neither hide nor overemphasize the "volunteer" part when she applies for a paying job. *Experience is experience.* If you're like 22-year-old Jack, who spent a year of Saturdays and a summer vacation working with handicapped kids and had letters of reference to show for it, then you've got something at least as valuable to offer as an M.A. fresh from the books.

True, the M.A. may get paid a higher starting salary than you do—*if* she or he gets hired. On the other hand, you may get hired where an M.A. may not! Jack did. With a B.A. in English, he is now working as a resident counselor at a school for special children. Pieces of paper are a dime a dozen these days. People who've cared enough to get firsthand experience aren't. If the time comes when Jack decides he does want that piece of paper, his track record will make him a first-rank candidate for graduate school admission and financial aid.

Three years ago, Diane was a 24-year-old secretary with a B.A. in nothing special. Her secret dream was to be a city planner. She was totally unqualified; all she had going for her was a passionate love for New York City. She loved to walk around and savor the flavors of different neighborhoods, and she wished everyone could see and appreciate the city the way she did. But that special quality of vision wasn't going to get her into graduate school, and in any case, she couldn't afford to quit her job and study full-time. Even night-school classes were beyond her pocketbook. For the clincher, New York City happened to be going broke just then, and the city planning department was firing people, not hiring them.

That's a pretty staggering list of obstacles. Nonetheless, today Diane has an M.A. in city planning and a high-paying job with a major corporation. She works for the relocation office, introducing recently transferred executives and their families to the resources and delights of their new home. How did she do it?

In a brainstorming session, Diane came up with something she could do right away, and for free: take part in local planning-board meetings. She was so outspoken and enthusiastic in those meetings that within a few months everyone from block association leaders to city councilmen was calling her for ideas and advice. By the time she felt ready to apply for school, she knew most of the people who really make things happen in the city, and they all wrote her recommendations. She was awarded a full-tuition scholarship to Hunter College!

Diane's boyfriend was so thrilled for her that he offered to pay her rent so she could quit her job. But after one semester, she was hired into a teaching assistantship that paid her way. Diane was now not only studying *and* teaching city planning—she was already *doing* it every week on those local committees. And by the time she finished her Master's, her contacts and reputation were so widespread that she was offered a job in the first corporation she walked into.

That's how you take what you love most in the world and turn it into a career. Diane isn't "exceptional." She made a hit with local pols, professors, and potential employers simply because she was in her element. Her energy and imagination were irresistible, and yours will be too as soon as you're on your path. Volunteering is one of the best ways to get out there *now*.

3. *The Sorcerer's Apprentice.* The most ancient and natural way to acquire skills and knowledge is by hanging out with someone who's got them—watching, asking, helping. Before schools were invented, doctors, lawyers, and great painters all learned their trades this way. Psychoanalysts and carpenters still do. It's how I learned to be a therapist. There's an element of apprenticeship in any good education—but in many fields you can set up an apprenticeship for yourself.

My feeling is that there's hardly a person on this planet you couldn't walk up to and say, "I've followed your work for a long time, and I'd really like to learn from you. I won't cause you any trouble. I'll empty your wastebaskets, I'll clean up your workshop, I'll carry your gear. I just want to be near your mind." It's a rare curmudgeon who wouldn't be flattered and receptive. Most highly accomplished people want to share what they know with other eager minds. Seriousness of interest and a willingness to help out are the only real qualifications. A young potter named Juan Hamilton has become the assistant and close companion of the great painter Georgia O'Keeffe. Agnes Nixon, reigning queen of the soaps and creator of (among others) "All My Children" and "Another World," got her start sharpening pencils for Irna Phillips, who pioneered the soap opera form with classics like "Love of Life" and "Guiding Light." Young writers send their work for criticism to established writers they admire, and sometimes a close mentor-protégé relationship develops.

There are formal programs that have been set up to connect willing "masters" with would-be apprentices. The architect Paolo Soleri always has a staff of young paying guests who help him cast wind bells and build his "arcologies," or experimental desert cities. Writer May Sarton and others took part in a Union Graduate School program in which they acted as advisors for independent student projects. (For further information about apprenticeships see the "Resources" appendix at the end of this book.)

But you don't need a formal program to put you in touch with someone whose work you love. You don't even have to go in cold with a letter that may or may not be answered. In the next chapter you'll learn how you can get an introduction to just about anyone on earth you want to meet.

4. Starting from Scratch: The Independent Alternative. Another way to start out on your path without a degree is simply to sit down, draw up a plan for a mime class, political seminar, walking tour, art-therapy group, or editing service, and put ads in your local paper. That's the wonderful thing about doing what you love: you can do it wherever you are, because your resources are really inside yourself. All you need is talent, personal experience, love—and a carefully worked-out idea, or *program design.* How do you think *Weight Watchers* got started? Jean Nidetch wasn't a doctor or a nutritionist. She was a lady who wanted to be thin. She designed a package for other people like herself and turned it into a multimillion-dollar business.

Whether what you want is to be rich and nationally known or just to hold a weekly discussion group in your living room, remember that the key to survival and success for any independent program is *an angle.* What you've got to do is find and fill a specific need that nobody else has thought of filling. That's what Jean Nidetch did. That's what I've done with Success Teams. A therapist I know designed a series of seminars called "Who Takes Care of the Caretakers?" for therapists, counselors—and mothers! Two of the most successful small bookstores I know specialize in children's books and murder mysteries. Jake, a marine biology freak who didn't want to go to grad school, started a seaside nature museum for kids and got a grant from his city.

Just starting from scratch, you can develop involvement, competence, and authority in your field without one extra day of school. That's how it worked out for me. But once again, if you decide to go to school later on, you'll go in with two great advantages: a track record and hands-on experience.

5. *The Generalist/Popularizer.* I wish I could think of a better name for this one—maybe "the go-between." It's a strategy for anyone who's fascinated by the poetry of a technical field but hasn't got the knack or the patience for technical training.

Many professional people can use help communicating their ideas to the public. They're specialists in physics or nutrition or international law, not in the graceful use of the English language. And sometimes they're even too specialized to talk to each other. If you can write, or even just organize ideas, you can get up to your ears in any field without a degree. I know a man who spent ten years putting together the first textbook to coordinate psychology with brain physiology. Until he came along, the mind-and-behavior people had barely been speaking to the brain people, and vice versa. And I know a woman who got a large foundation grant to pull together all the far-flung branches of research on the learning disability called dyslexia. Her only qualification was that she was dyslexic herself, and cared desperately about finding a solution. A 20-year-old college English major who wanted to be a member of the first space colony decided to start by doing magazine interviews with scientists like Carl Sagan and Gerard O'Neill. A housewife interested in nutrition developed a newsletter for the food industry on federal labeling regulations. Writing, editing, interviewing, starting a specialized newsletter or a cable-TV talk show with a theme—any of these could be a wonderful way to gain admission to a world you love without the expensive ticket of a Ph.D.

Those are just a few examples of the kind of direct, ingenious route to your goal you can dream up if you take conventional "wisdom" as a challenge instead of a finality. We've been talking about credentials and schooling, but the same goes for any obstacle that looms large on your Problems List. I can't brainstorm every kind of goal and problem for you, or this book would go on for two thousand pages. But I don't have to. You have the prime source of all the ideas you'll ever need right between your ears. All you need is a tool for getting them out and putting them into organized form.

BRAINSTORMING TECHNIQUE

The brainstorming technique I'm about to teach you is a two-stage process. The first stage will be familiar to you from Chapter 5. You suspend reality and bat the problem around from here to the land of Oz, accepting every idea with uncritical delight, until you've come up with some really fresh thinking. I call Stage 1 "Woolgathering," and the wilder and woolier the better. This time you'll have the option of doing it either alone or with a little help from your friends—imaginary and real.

The second stage is something new. It brings the best of your windfall of wild ideas down to earth and puts them into practical, do-able form. You could call Stage 2 "Bridge-building," because that's exactly what it does: bridges the Grand Canyon between dream and reality, inspiration and action.

As a working example, I'm going to take what is probably the single most universal and exasperating obstacle conventional "wisdom" places in our paths. A woman in one of my seminars put it succinctly: "I just see a mountain in front of me, and its name is Money."

Now, money is a very peculiar substance. It doesn't behave according to the laws of physics. Any amount you *don't* have—whether it's $5,000 or $500,000—will appear to be a mountain. Almost any amount you do have will not appear to be enough to pay next month's bills! Money often seems to be an emotional substance—the very incarnation of "I can't." So, just to take a properly defiant attitude toward this obstacle of obstacles, let's start with a really big mountain—a million dollars. It will be a good warm-up exercise for your own brainstorming, because if you can stretch your mind around this one, your own money problem isn't going to give you too much trouble no matter how big it is.

Just suppose your goal happened to be to sail around the world on your own yacht. That would be a pretty far-fetched fantasy for most of us, and a natural item on your Problems List might be, "Only millionaires can afford yachts." ("I can't because I don't have X—I'm not rich.") So your question No. 1 would be, "How can I get a yacht (or access to one that would satisfy me) without a million dollars?" And question No. 2 would be: "How can I get a million dollars?"

Now, should you go into brainstorming with question No. 1 or question No. 2? That depends on only one thing: the *touchstone* hidden in your goal. I see three possible touchstones here:

1. Being rich for rich's sake
2. Owning your own yacht
3. Sailing around the world in style

Only if actually being rich is your touchstone should you start your brainstorming on Question No. 2!

I'm not saying you wouldn't like to be rich, mind you. Who wouldn't? But if what you're saying is, "If only I were rich, I could do this, and this, and that"—if, in other words, you want to be rich *as a means to the end* of doing what you really love—it's a much better idea just to go ahead and do it. Once you're in action, you'll have so much energy and imagination that you'll turn up one hundred ways to get rich by doing what you love—if you still care. (You may not, once you've found out that you don't need lots of money to live your good life.) But if you decide you've got to get rich first, it's a good bet you won't get rich—and you won't get what you want, either.

Obviously, a million dollars can be made. Plenty of "ordinary geniuses" like you and me have done it, and you can use brainstorming to figure out a way. But nontouchstone dreams, "means-to-an-end" dreams, have a funny way of never coming true. That's because they don't tap into the one real power source you've got: your heart's desire. People who really want to make money *make* it, because making money turns them on. The rest of us just let it turn us off to what we do care about.* But we don't have to. Human ingenuity invented money in the first place. Human ingenuity can find a way around it.

So let's assume in our hypothetical example that your touchstone is either "owning your own yacht" or "sailing around the world in style." We'll start with Question No. 1, and see how you could get that goal for very much less than a million dollars.

---

*Very often, we also let it shelter us when we're scared. Being poor is one of the best excuses not to go for your dreams. It gets you much more sympathy than being fat. Nobody knows how to argue with poverty. We're all much too bamboozled by money in this society.

STAGE 1: WOOLGATHERING

The different brainstorming techniques differ only at this stage in how you get your ideas, not in what you do with them once you've got them. There are three different ways to do "Woolgathering."

Brainstorming alone

Sit down with pencil and paper in a quiet place, where you can daydream undistracted. Across the top of the first sheet of paper, write the problem—for example, "How to get a yacht/sail around the world in style without $1,000,000?"

Now start writing down every idea that pops into your head, and I mean *every* idea. Don't rule out anything, no matter how far-fetched or frivolous it seems. If you wanted a yacht, "Go down to the boat basin at night and steal one" would be just fine. At this stage, don't edit or judge your ideas. It could inhibit your imagination, and you might miss a good one. Take as long as you like; keep going till you run dry.

If you have trouble shaking off the habitual limitations on your thought, first check and see whether a little Hard Times is called for. Discouragement or apprehension may be weighing you down. If not— and you just seem to need a spur to fresh thinking—there's a second technique for brainstorming alone that can really turn your mind loose.

Role-play brainstorming

In the "Seeing Yourself as Others See You" exercise in Chapter 4, you discovered that playing the part of another person can open up unsuspected stores of knowledge in your own brain. Besides being great fun, this is one of the best ways in the world to get fresh ideas.

Your everyday identity is itself a role you've been cast in by time and place and culture. It doesn't express your total human potential. You were born with the same basic equipment in your head as a Stone Age hunter, an eighteenth-century duchess, a Mississippi riverboat gambler, or a Japanese monk. You have the capacity to assume any of those points of view in imagination—and it's like looking at the world with new eyes.

You can use your imaginary "ideal family" as a cast of characters for role-play brainstorming, or you can try playing the roles of some diverse and far-out characters, like these:

1. an old mule driver
2. the queen of a foreign country
3. a mad genius
4. a Martian
5. a fool
6. the president of a giant corporation
7. a Samoan fisherman (Eskimo hunter, Watusi warrior, etc.)
8. an engineer who builds bridges in the Andes
9. a Texas oilman
10. a 5-year-old girl

To get into any role, just close your eyes and spend a few moments imagining yourself into the life and mind and environment of that character. Then look at your problem from his or her point of view and write down whatever solutions come to mind.

For example:

Albert Einstein: "Intelligent conversation is a very rare commodity. Perhaps there is someone who owns a yacht who would simply like to have you on board for stimulating company. Or perhaps there is something you can teach—about the stars, or the Greek Islands, or the Galápagos. What about a floating university or seminar? Surely someone would provide the boat and the funds for that."

Bette Davis: "Hell, I'd stow away and then charm them into letting me stay on board."

Samoan fisherman: "Whenever we need something, we make it ourselves. Of course, a dugout canoe is easier to build than one of your strange and foolish boats. I know, because they get wrecked on our coral reef from time to time. You could have one of those if you want. They're no use to us. You'd have to do some patching up, though."

You get the idea.

Role-play brainstorming will come to your rescue when you get stuck for ideas alone. But if you can get a bunch of *real* people to toss ideas around with you, all the better! Brainstorming is always done in groups in business, industry, and creativity workshops, and for a good reason:

each mind brings a different angle of vision to bear on the same problem. You've probably had the experience of effortlessly solving a dilemma for a friend who was totally blocked on it—or having a friend to do that for you. That effect will be multiplied if you can get four or five people to pitch in. Group brainstorming has the added advantage of being a natural takeoff point for a barn-raising, as you'll see a little later on.

Brainstorming with a group

The people you call in to brainstorm don't need to know the first thing about the area you've got the problem in. In fact, the less they know the better! On a brainstorming team, you want *inexperienced* people, because the experts in any field only know what *can't* be done. Naive people come up with the best ideas in the world. That means children too. Kids above the age of four are astonishingly creative, because they have no restrictions on their thinking at all. When 6-year-olds were asked to design a vehicle that could drive over rough terrain with big ditches in it, they reinvented the tank.

Older people are terrific too. They've known a world without television or jet planes or superplastics, and their minds are often slower, deeper, more resourceful. But anyone can play: your husband, your wife, your mother, your friends, the TV repairman. And they'll love it. Playing with ideas is the world's best party game. You can invite people over, serve wine and cheese, and make an evening of it.

The one rule you must be sure to establish is that at this stage of the game there are no rules. No holds barred—the weirdest idea is a welcome guest. Once you've put the problem on the table, your job is to sit there with your pencil and write every idea down. Don't let one of them escape. It might be the one you are looking for.

After a good brainstorming session of any of these three kinds, your list of ideas might look something like this:

OWN YACHT
1. steal a yacht
2. marry somebody who has a yacht
3. win a yacht in a contest
4. win a yacht in a poker game

5. buy shares in a yacht with a group of people
6. get an old hulk and fix it up

SAIL AROUND THE WORLD

7. stow away
8. make friends with somebody who has a yacht and get invited aboard as a guest
9. rent a yacht
10. trade the use of a yacht for something I have (living loft, country cabin, etc.)
11. get hired on a yacht as a:
    captain
    engineer
    crew member
    waiter/waitress
    bartender
    gourmet cook
    masseur/masseuse
    companion to elderly or handicapped person
    tutor to young children
    lifeguard/swimming teacher
    entertainer—musician, magician, singer, comedian, court jester, etc., depending on your talents and on what you're willing to do (Everyone —but everyone—has something to offer: a sense of humor, a great recipe for chocolate cake. . . .)
12. design a private educational tour for rich people
13. design a promotional voyage for a boat company
14. design an around-the-world goodwill mission for ecology or peace or an end to hunger
15. design a scientific expedition or "floating seminar": for instance, re-trace the voyage of Darwin's *Beagle* for a travel agency or group

If it really was your heart's desire to sail around the world on a yacht, somewhere on this list you would find an idea that appealed to you— and one you could do without becoming a millionaire first. Of course, at this point you'd still have no idea how you were going to "get an old hulk and fix it up," or "retrace the voyage of Darwin's *Beagle.*" Those ideas look almost as far-fetched as the original million dollars! But it's going to be the whole purpose of Stage 2 brainstorming to provide answers to the question: *"How?"* So don't worry if the most intriguing ideas on your Stage I list still look pretty far out. Just take it from me: if you really want it, it can be done. For instance, before you dismiss my yacht example as fairy-tale stuff, take a look at this:

> "*Sofia,* an 89-foot, three-masted schooner and floating cooperative, is looking for crew members. Since being restored from very battered condition in 1969 . . . *Sofia* has hauled cargo in the Caribbean, fished in New Zealand, sunk in the Galápagos, and in nine years, sailed around the world. She's had 50 or 60 crew members, about ten at a time . . . Past members have usually put $1,500–$3,500 into the boat and become part owners."
>
> *CoEvolution Quarterly, Spring 1978*

I found that clipping *after* I'd made up the example . . . and at about the same time, there was a news story on TV about a mysterious series of yacht hijackings! While I don't recommend piracy on the high seas, it does go to show that no idea is impossible.

The sample list of ideas above also shows you some of the general types of strategies you can devise for getting around the money obstacle —or drastically reducing its size:

1. There are plenty of ways to get things, even big things, without buying them:

    a.   beg
    b.   borrow
    c.   steal
    d.   trade
    e.   win
    f.   rent
    g.   make

2. Sell yourself. Swap something you can do—gardening, magic, talking with old people or kids, telling jokes—for free admission to a world you want into. Two friends of mine longed to live in the country, but could see no way they'd ever have enough money to buy or rent the kind of place they dreamed of. So they advertised their services as caretakers—and are now living year round on a famous rock singer's farm!

3. Even if money is required for your project, it doesn't have to be

your money. Be the idea man or woman. Design a package and sell it to somebody who is a millionaire.

4. Share the cost of your dream with people you'd like to share your dream with. Basia, a textile designer in her 30s, confessed that she harbored a hopeless million-dollar fantasy of her own: to start an artists' community in her own villa in the south of France. Once I got her to drop her assumption that it was impossible, brainstorming quickly produced a solution: get together with several like-minded friends and share the rental of a villa. (Cost to each: about $2,000.)

See? Being poor is no excuse not to go for your dreams, no matter how big they are.

TRANSITION: EDITING YOUR LIST

OK. You've got a list of ideas for "How to get my goal without X" (or "How to get X"). You wrote down every idea that came along, so some of them are strictly whimsical. Some of them are workable ways of getting to your goal, but not things you think you'd particularly like to do. Then there will be a few ideas that look promising. I don't mean the most "possible" ones, I mean the ones that make your heart beat faster. They may still look pretty pie-in-the-sky. Your next job is to pick the one or two best ideas and then start bringing them down to earth.

Let's take a look at how a real-life person did it.

Mary, 27, the divorced mother of a 2-year-old daughter, had decided her first target was to go to medical school. Mary had been a premed major in college and had gotten good grades, but then she had fallen in love with a cellist who spent a good part of the year traveling with a professional string quartet. Since music was Mary's other great love, she had made the difficult decision to marry her musician and travel with him instead of going on in medicine. When the marriage didn't work (her husband fell in love with the new second violinist), she moved back home to her upstate New York town, where her married sister could take care of her daughter while she worked for an electronics company.

Mary felt that she'd chosen the wrong fork in the road and that, with no money and a small child to support, it was too late to go back. But she obviously still wanted very much to be a doctor! I urged her to make entering medical school her first target, and to put all the reasons for discouragement on a PROBLEMS list. They were formidable:

1. no money
2. my college science is very rusty
3. older women and mothers have trouble getting into med school
4. child care (if I have to leave this area)

I told Mary to take those problems through brainstorming one at a time. She picked "money" to work on first, because she was going to need money for everything: premed refresher courses, tuition, food, rent, child care. She did her brainstorming with her sister and a friend while their kids played under the dining room table. Her first list of ideas looked like this:

Problem: How to get through medical school without a dime of my own
1. get a scholarship
2. get a loan
3. win the New York State lottery
4. marry a rich man who will send me through school
5. join the Armed Forces and let them send me through school
6. get my story in the local papers and attract a wealthy patron
7. stand on the streets of New York City with a sign saying, SEND THIS MOTHER TO MEDICAL SCHOOL

That's how brainstorming often works. You think of all the staid, sensible, obvious ideas first, like scholarships and loans. Then come the "rescue fantasies": someone is going to come riding along in a white Cadillac and carry you away, or appear mysteriously on your doorstep with a check for a million dollars. Being free to give those fantasies a legitimate place on your list brings liberating laughter—and only then do the really audacious, original ideas begin to flow.

In fact, they'll look *too* original. When Mary first glanced over her list, she said, "Maybe I can get a loan, but I'm afraid it won't cover living expenses. Ideas No. 3 and No. 4 are just silly. As for No. 5—me, join the Army? No way. I'd go nuts in a week. I kind of like No. 6, but frankly it doesn't seem to have much chance of working, and besides, I've got too little nerve and too much pride to go begging. That really rules out No. 7."

Stop right there! When you reach this point with your list, *don't cross anything off.* Like Mary, you probably think you could throw out about nine-tenths of your ideas without further ado, but there are two very good reasons why you shouldn't do that yet. One is that even the craziest idea has something to give you before you abandon it. The other is that *pessimism about an idea's workability can masquerade as lack of interest in it.* And until you've probed a little deeper into each idea with the magic question "How?", you won't really know what the word "possible" means.

The first rule of transition brainstorming, either alone or in a group, is: *Never throw out any idea* until you have asked three questions about it:

1. What is the useful element (or elements) in this idea? (You must find something of value in each one.)
2. How can I (we) get around the impractical elements of this idea? (In other words, instead of being reasons to junk the idea, any snags would become a *miniproblems list* calling for a new round of Stage 1 "Woolgathering.")
3. What further ideas does this idea suggest?

Let's see how Mary did it—and what surprises she turned up.

IDEA NO. 1: GET A SCHOLARSHIP

1. *Useful elements:*	No debts
2. *Problems:*	a. must have super-good grades and test scores
	b. I'm not sure there are scholarships to med school
How to solve:	a. go to night school and study like mad

                                    b. do some research on financial
                                    aid to med students

3. *Further ideas:*   Create a scholarship! Write to
                                    large corporations offering to let
                                    them do good for society and the
                                    cause of women and get great
                                    publicity by sending me through
                                    medical school!

Now that's an exciting idea, one that really set off fireworks in Mary's
brain—and if she had just thrown out "Get a scholarship," she would
never have thought of it! Mary didn't know whether anything like it had
ever been done before, and she had no idea how corporations would
respond to her approach. But the very fact that you're bold enough to
try something brand new can impress the right people. And the time
certainly looked ripe to offer big companies favorable publicity for their
enlightened attitude toward women. So Mary set this idea aside as a
promising one and continued with her original list.

IDEA NO. 2: GET A LOAN

1. *Useful elements:*   standard procedure, channels exist

2. *Problems:*   a. good grades, as above
                                    b. might not cover living expenses
                                    c. years of debt

   How to solve: a. & b. same as above
                                    c. unavoidable

3. *Further ideas:*   get a private loan, rather than an
                                    outright gift, from a wealthy
                                    individual (as in Idea No. 6 on
                                    list)

Ideas No. 3 and No. 4—winning the lottery and marrying a rich man
—Mary recognized as outright "rescue fantasies," which had done

their job of uncorking her imagination, and which she wouldn't really want if they *did* happen. She didn't want luck *or* love to solve her problem—she wanted it to come from her own ability and deserving.

IDEA NO. 5: JOIN THE ARMED FORCES

1. *Useful elements:*	training free
	living expenses provided
2. *Problems:*	I'd hate it!
How to solve:	no way
3. *Further ideas:*	Is there some other organization that would train me in exchange for service? Peace Corps? Government? Foreign government? Australia? Investigate

IDEA NO. 6: FIND WEALTHY PERSON VIA LOCAL PAPERS

1. *Useful elements:*	appeals to local pride
2. *Problems:*	a. unlikely to find a taker
	b. feels like asking for charity
How to solve:	a. try and see
	b. swallow pride—or decide I'm worth it
3. *Further ideas:*	Do "create a scholarship" idea and get a newspaper article written about that—send clippings to corporations—& even to national magazines!

IDEA NO. 7: STAND ON STREET WITH SIGN . . .

This idea may sound outlandish, but Mary's sister, who gave her the idea, told her the true story of a young man who staked out a corner of Fifth Avenue in a sandwich board that said, "Send This Nice Jewish Boy to College." He got enough money to go! (Of course, he had nerve —and an angle.) Mary had to admit it was enterprising and would have the advantage of not indebting her to one person, but it just wasn't her style. The further idea she got from it was, "Put an ad in MS. and other magazines asking for $1 contributions."

When you reach this point, you're ready to go into Stage 2 brainstorming with the idea or ideas you like best. Mary chose the "Create a scholarship" idea. (She decided that she'd also investigate the more conventional sources of financial aid.)

STAGE 2: BRIDGE BUILDING

Before you did any brainstorming at all, your situation looked like this:

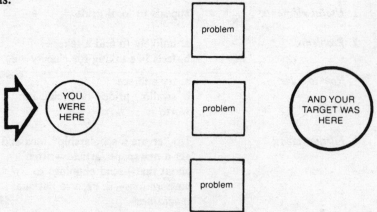

In Stage 1 brainstorming you transformed one of the problems into a *subgoal:* a specific way of getting one of the things you'll need for your goal. In Mary's example (her other problems, getting admitted to medical school and finding child care, can wait for now):

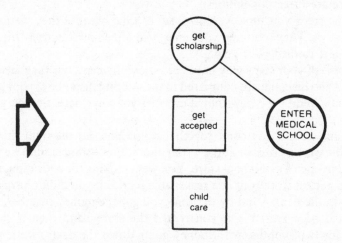

A subgoal is a first break in the wall of problems and the first link in your plan. *But it's almost as far away as your goal itself.* Mary wanted to win a kind of scholarship that didn't even exist yet except in her own imagination. You may have decided to get financial backing for your small business from an investor or "angel" you don't know how to find . . . or to sell a screenplay you haven't written yet . . . or to take an advanced painting class when you haven't made so much as a sketch in twenty years. There's still a big gap to get across before you reach that subgoal. What we've got to do now is build a solid bridge of actions over that gap, from the subgoal right to your doorstep. You'll be able to take your first step on that bridge *tomorrow,* confident that it will lead you step by step all the way to your goal.

There's only one way to build that kind of bridge, and that's the way you're going to do it in Stage 2 brainstorming: by *planning backwards* from your goal. If you've ever tried for your dreams before and been frustrated, the chances are good that you started out like this:

and then wondered why your best efforts petered out somewhere in the middle. You had energy and guts to spare, and even some excellent ideas. What went wrong?

There are three possibilities:

1. The steps you took were a waste of time because they were the wrong steps. They scattered your energy in fifteen directions instead of focusing it toward your goal.

2. Some of your steps may have been the right steps, but they seemed so small and insignificant compared to the size and distance of your goal that you couldn't see how they'd ever get you anywhere. So you gave up.

3. Your steps didn't come together right. You did the right things, but in the wrong order or at the wrong times. For instance, suppose you wanted to open a small bookstore. You went looking for a location, and found a perfect storefront at a reasonable rent. But you didn't have any money in the bank—and by the time you got the money together, the store had been rented. Or: you rented the store—and then it stood empty for two months, with money going down the drain, while you tried frantically to learn all you needed to know about the retail book business.

If that has happened to you, your basic mistake was thinking that just because *action* goes forward, from the present to the future, *planning* has to go forward too. It can't. Planning has got to go *backwards:* from the distant future to tomorrow . . . from the intimidatingly large to the reassuringly small . . . from the whole vision of your goal to its component parts, little things you can do one by one. "In reality, great deeds are made up of small, steady actions"—remember? But before you can put great deeds together in reality, you have to take them apart on paper to discover *what* small, steady actions, *in what order,* will really get you there. Here's how you do it.

Two questions are your tools for breaking down subgoals into the smaller and smaller steps that lead up to them. The first is, "Can I do this tomorrow?" If the answer is "No," the next question is, "OK, what would I have to get done first?" For instance, Mary's subgoal is to get a scholarship from a large corporation. Could she have that money in her hands tomorrow? Of course not. Well, what would she have to do first? She'd have to send letters to a whole bunch of corporations:

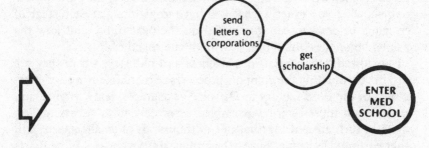

Can she mail those letters tomorrow? No. What would she have to do first? Draft a letter, and compile a list of promising corporations and their addresses. If she wants to use another idea she got out of her Stage I list—to have an article about her plan appear in the local paper and enclose clippings with her letter—she'll also have to arrange to get such an article published:

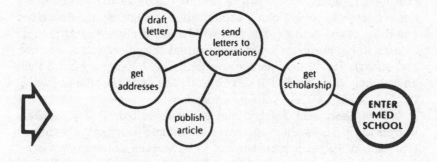

YOUR FLOW CHART

I'd like to stop for a moment and explain that this kind of visual framework for brainstorming—where you write the steps down in funny little circles, working from right to left—is called a *flow chart*. The one you will draw as you do your Stage II brainstorming is probably the single most important item in your Portable Success Support System, because it will not only help you think—it's also going to help you *act*. When it's finished, it will be a detailed map of the path to your goal, showing you exactly what you have to get done at each stage of the game before you can go on and do the next thing, and how the various "branches" of action have to come together.

I borrowed flow charts from business and industry, where they are used in coordinating the complex processes of manufacturing and marketing. In the Ford factory in Detroit, for example, body, engine, and transmission must each be assembled separately from subassemblies, which in turn are put together out of thousands of smaller parts; still other parts and finishings have to be imported from abroad. Flow charts are drawn up to insure that everything comes together properly, so that on the target date for the new season, a finished Ford rolls sparkling off the assembly line.

I've been using flow charts for my own personal "business" for several years, and I've found them every bit as indispensable to my success and my sanity as they are to Ford's profits. Once you know how to use them, I promise you you'll work one out for every project you ever have in mind, right down to planning a dinner party! You won't know how you ever got along without them. Of course, the flow chart you draw of the path to your goal will be much more flexible than its cousins in big business: a highly individual design, subject to revision and change. It will look and behave more like a living organism than an assembly line. But it will serve exactly the same purpose as Ford's: to guide you in getting your goal together.

A flow chart isn't finished and ready to roll until it completely bridges the gap between the present moment and your goal. That means that each of its main branches has to be worked down to *first steps: things so small and manageable you could do them tomorrow.* So let's go back and see how Mary completed her flow chart, following her through the process step by step.

Mary has three steps to ask questions about now. One: Could she draft a letter to corporations tomorrow? Theoretically, yes, she could. But in reality, she'll want to be further along in the process of brushing up her knowledge and applying to medical schools first. And that's another major branch of her flow chart, one she hasn't even started working on yet. What she can do tomorrow, though, is make preliminary notes for that letter, as a way of getting her thinking started and making the idea real to her.

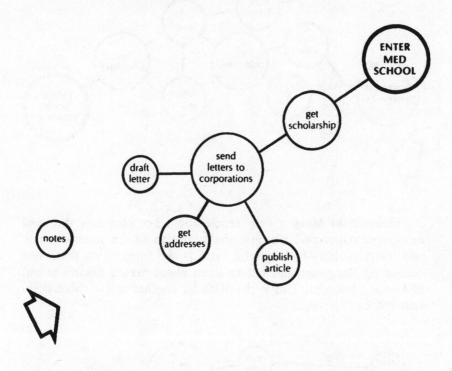

Two: Can she have a list of corporations' names and addresses tomorrow? No, she'll have to do some research first to figure out which corporations might be receptive and who would be the best person to contact in each one. Some of that research she can do in libraries, but some of it she'll have to do in another way, one we'll be talking about at length in the next chapter. (For now, I'll designate it in her flow chart by a question mark.) What Mary could do tomorrow is brainstorm on what kinds of corporations to approach: drug companies? Vitamin companies? Oil companies eager for a humanitarian image? (She felt there were ethical as well as practical questions to consider.)

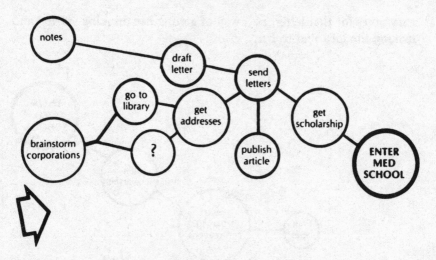

Three: Could Mary get an article about her plan into the local newspaper tomorrow? No, first she'd have to have a reporter come and interview her—and how on earth is she going to do that? Just calling up the paper and telling them about herself doesn't sound like such a hot idea. This is the place for another one of those question marks:

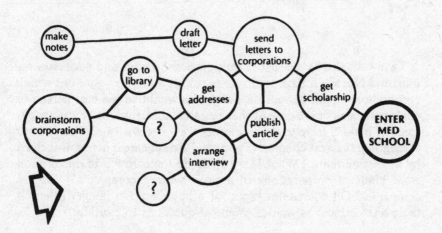

At this point, Mary has taken the "Money" branch of her flow chart as far as she can by herself. The next important branch for her to work on is "Get admitted to medical school"—and it has to be roughly coordinated with the "Money" branch so that the two come together in time. How Mary solves the child-care problem will depend on what medical school she goes to—if she stays in her own area her sister can help her out—so she can leave that problem for later.

I'm going to run quickly through the series of questions Mary asked herself, and show you how she incorporated the results into her flow chart—adding one more circle on the left for each answer she gave herself.

1. "Getting into medical school is a subgoal in its own right. Now, can I do it tomorrow?
    "Hardly.
    "What would I have to do first?
    "Well, I'd have to apply to medical schools."

2. "Can I apply tomorrow?
    "No. There are two things I'd have to do first: get high scores on the MedCATs (a general competence test for medical school admissions, like the college SAT's), and send for application forms."

3a. "Can I get high test scores tomorrow?
    Obviously not. First I have to take the tests."

3b. "Can I send for applications tomorrow?
    Not until I've decided which schools to apply to."

4a. "Can I take the MedCATs tomorrow?
    If I did, I'd flunk them! First I'd better take some kind of premed review course."

4b. "Can I decide which schools to apply to tomorrow?
    No, first I'll have to go to the library and read catalogs. (I can find out about regular loans and scholarships at the same time.) And *that* I *can* start doing tomorrow."

5. "Can I take a review course tomorrow?
    No—first I've got to find out where there is one. I can do that tomorrow, by making phone calls to all the local universities, colleges, and medical schools. Another thing I can do is dig up my old college class notes and start reviewing them on my own."

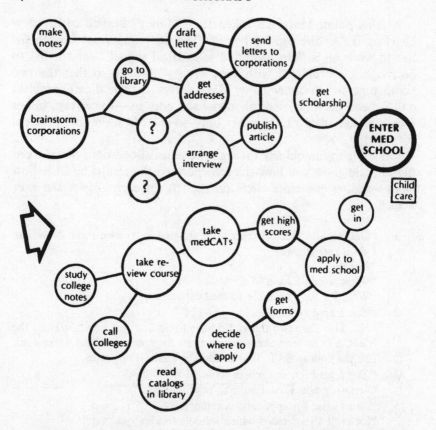

And that is an almost complete flow chart. It gave Mary five things she could start doing right away: make notes for a persuasive letter to corporations: brainstorm on what kinds of corporations to approach; make calls to ask about premed review courses; start reviewing her college science notes; and go to the library to check out med school catalogs. While she wasn't literally going to run out and do all those things the next day, they did give her plenty to do in the immediate future—small, manageable actions she could see were directly connected to her goal. If she ever had any doubts on that score, all she had to do was look at her flow chart!

Stage 2 brainstorming brings even the most unreachable goal within reach by breaking big achievements down into human-sized tasks.

There is *no* goal—I don't care if it's becoming President of the United States in twenty years—that doesn't break down to something as simple as going to the library or the newsstand or picking up the phone. Almost all goals begin with information-gathering, an act which requires no preparation and very little courage, yet sweeps you right up in the excitement and reality of your goal. Creative goals, like writing a novel or learning to paint, begin with a very modest qualitative and quantitative demand: "Write one *bad* page" or "Make 5 silly drawings of the cat." (More on this in Chapter 9, "First Aid for Fear.") Just because these first steps are so tiny, *you'll do them*. They'll get you up off your chair and out on your path where the prospect of a huge goal or subgoal would leave you sitting paralyzed.

But your flow chart isn't finished, as I said before, until all its major branches are broken down to first steps. Like Mary's chart, yours is bound to have a few holes in it—places where you get stuck short of first steps and have to write in a question mark. You may run into that kind of dead end in a much more drastic way than Mary did.

For example, Jeannette was a $150-a-week typist whose real passion was photography. Her dream was to travel through Appalachia taking pictures and to publish a book of those pictures. She knew that as an unknown photographer she didn't have a chance of getting a book advance, and that she'd have very little chance of selling a finished book even if she did find some way to finance her trip. So she went into brainstorming with a group of friends, and together they came up with a beautifully ingenious plan.

Suppose she got an old panel truck and turned it into a rolling darkroom? Jeannette could drive through Appalachia with Brownie cameras, teaching children to take pictures and develop them. As they explored and recorded their own world, she could photograph that luminous process of discovery—and put her pictures together with theirs. That would be a book with a fresh angle—and a good chance of finding a publisher. It was also the kind of project that was tailor-made to attract foundation funding.

However, this still left Jeannette stuck with a sizable money problem. Trucks, darkroom equipment, cameras, photographic paper, and just plain traveling all cost money—and getting foundation support takes time. It could be more than a year before Jeannette got her grant—or found out that she didn't get one. And she just didn't want to wait that long. She has a flow chart that isn't flowing. What can Jeannette do to break that bottleneck?

Then there's Alan, the Chicago educational-books editor whose goal was to open a small publishing house in Colorado, specializing in outdoors handbooks and literature. Alan had no capital of his own to invest in his business, and he decided to solve that problem by finding one or more investors or moneyed partners. After a great deal of thought, Alan's flow chart looked like this:

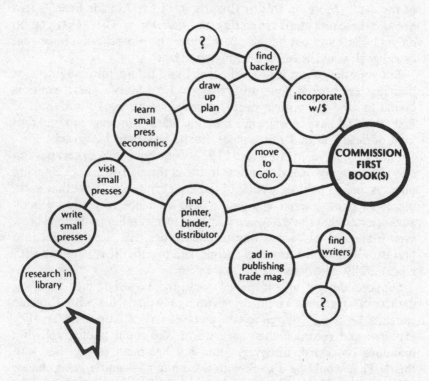

Alan was smart enough to realize that the best way to learn small-press economics was directly from the publishers who practiced them (that is, by apprenticeship), and he knew how to contact those publishers through directories that can be found in any library. But when it came to finding a backer, Alan was stumped. He didn't know anybody with that kind of money. When he brainstormed the problem, he got the wild and wonderful idea of getting an environmentally-aware celebrity like John Denver or Robert Redford to put his money and his clout behind Mountainbooks (as Alan was calling it). But that left him just as stuck as he was before, because he didn't know John Denver or Robert Redford, either, and he had no chance of meeting them.

When you come to this kind of impasse in your planning, you may get very discouraged. You may also feel embarrassed that you don't know how to pull the whole miracle off all by yourself. But I've got news for you. *You're not supposed to.*

Look at Christopher Columbus. A moment's thought will make it obvious that he did not discover America "on his own," and that there was no way he could have. There's no question that his vision, his drive, his desire was the galvanizing force of the expedition. But he was "dependent," first of all, on the brainstorming of Copernicus, who had come up with the ridiculous idea that the world was round. He was "dependent" on Ferdinand and Isabella for faith and financing, on shipbuilders for the *Niña,* the *Pinta* and the *Santa Maria,* on his crew, and on the inventors and makers of navigational instruments, the sextant and the astrolabe. If that's "dependency," then dependency is the foundation of human civilization. If you really think you should be an exception, good luck. You'll be the first.

What you have to do in this world you cannot do alone. Every successful human enterprise is a collaboration—a drawing-together of diverse resources and energies to achieve a single end. And you can and should do just that for your goal.

So when you've gone as far as you can on your own, it's time for a barn-raising.

–7–
Barn-raising

If you've done your brainstorming with a group, like Jeannette did, you're in luck. It's going to turn into a barn-raising spontaneously.

In all the years I've been working with creativity in groups, I have never once seen a brainstorming team come up with a bright strategic idea, like Jeannette's Appalachian plan, and then get up, put on their coats, and say, "OK, kid, good luck. You're on your own." That never happens. What does happen is what happened to Jeannette:

One of her friends said, "You know, a guy in my office has an old van he wants to get rid of. I'll bet he'd sell it to you for less than $200! It's in terrible shape, of course. But anyway, here's his phone number." And then somebody else said, "My best friend's brother is an auto mechanic! Maybe he'd fix the van for free if you did advertising photography for him, or portraits of his family. Let me call my friend and have her ask him." And then somebody else said, "Why don't you try to get a job in a photo store, so you can get stuff at discount? I think they even let you have the outdated film and photographic paper for free." Another friend knew a journalist who had gotten several grants, and offered to put Jeannette in touch with him for help writing up a grant proposal. The whole group agreed to ask everyone they knew to dig in their closets for old Brownies and Instamatics, and they decided to put together a list of addresses of people along Jeannette's proposed route who would be glad to let her stay overnight with them for free. Between them, Jeannette and five friends worked out a plan by which she could go ahead and set her dream in motion without waiting for a grant—

for less than a thousand dollars! And then they planned to throw a flea market to raise the money.

If you think this sounds incredible, try it. When your brainstorming team starts coming up with concrete suggestions, contacts, and offers of help, you'll find yourself scribbling as fast as you can to get down all the names and phone numbers—and within five minutes you'll have so many real and promising first steps that it takes your breath away.

When you've gotten your plan worked down to *specific needs,* that's the last moment when anyone wants to give up, go home, and forget all about it. On the contrary, that's when everybody leans forward and starts getting really involved. It suddenly looks like this fabulous thing might just happen. And it's not so much that people want a piece of the action. It's that they want to *give* you a piece of your action! Each member of your brainstorming team is realizing that she or he has something real to contribute: an idea, a contact, a skill. And each one loves the idea of being able to say, "See that house? See the third brick from the left in the third row from the bottom? I gave her that. I made it with my own hands."

In Chapter 6, we talked about the importance of identifying *emotional problems*—the hands-off kind that can only be helped by a sympathetic ear. But now we're dealing with *strategic problems,* the kind that call for helping hands. These are the problems that can be fixed—and we seem to take an uncanny delight in fixing them. You know what I'm talking about if you've ever given someone a lead that led to a job, or an apartment, or a part in a play, or a life-changing experience, or a love affair. Most of us remember and treasure every part we've ever played in someone else's survival, satisfaction, or success. And that's not because we're a bunch of altruistic saints. It's because helping each other is creative and it makes us feel good.

We're just beginning to realize that sharing skills and resources is a deep human pleasure and need, one that's wired into our survival just as much as hunger or sex. If our distant ancestors hadn't evolved an actual instinct for cooperation, they would have been eaten by sabertoothed tigers the first morning they crawled out of their caves. And the things that keep us alive always feel good. That's how nature makes sure we will do them.

Pioneer families and small farmers had to pool their labor to get their barns built, their crops plowed and harvested, their corn husked. In the process, they reaffirmed the bonds of community—and had a whale of a good time. Working together toward vital common goals strengthened their relationships as it lightened their labor. There was no split in their lives between love and work, self-interest and mutual aid. In our complex and technically advanced society, we no longer need each other's direct and personal help to survive. We're still dependent on other people, but the cooperation that keeps us alive has become abstract and impersonal. We can buy houses built by strangers. We can stand in line at the supermarket to buy our food. We can open the Yellow Pages and hire a doctor or a plumber. We exchange most goods and services for money instead of love. We've gained the freedom to pursue our individual goals—and that's a precious freedom—but we've paid a high price: the *community of purpose* that once fused work and relationship into a meaningful whole. Our most practical and satisfying way of getting things done is still *together.* And the proof is that so much of our potential stays stubbornly locked inside us as long as we try to tap it alone.

Our instinct for cooperation is still very much alive. It's looking for a job. Why not put it to work in the service of our individual goals? Sharing dreams and resources could be a wonderful way to surround ourselves with a "family" of winners—a community with a new common purpose: no longer the survival of all its members, but the fullest unfolding of each one's unique potential.

We don't have to go all the way back to pioneer days for a working model of that kind of "cooperative individualism." We have one right in front of our eyes. Our myths of "every man for himself" and "looking out for Number One" have just kept us from seeing it, because it's in the last place where we'd ever think of looking: *in the lives of successful men.* As a matter of fact, *it's the reason why they're successful!* Most of them take it so completely for granted that it doesn't occur to them to give credit where credit is due. Ask them and many will say, "Of *course* I made it on my own." But I can think of at least one high flyer from modest beginnings who's given the public lie to that Horatio Alger myth.

The popular notion is that this man single-handedly built up his family's little farm into a million-dollar business. The way he tells it, when he came home from the Armed Forces to take charge of the farm, a group of men got together with him, rolled up their sleeves, and said something like this:

"OK, son, the first thing you're going to need is a certain amount of money. Here's a loan. We figure it'll take about four years till you're in a position to pay it back. Harry here has a company that'll front you the starter seeds and fertilizer. I'm not growing anything on my lower forty, and I'll let you use it so you can get started. You can use my farm machinery too, here's the key to the shed. We've got marketing contacts in every town in the state, and old Sam has the trucks. Now if there's anything else you need, you just call on us, hear? We'll be droppin' by from time to time to see how you're doing."

And that's how Jimmy Carter, self-made man, got his start.

This system of cronies and contacts is called *the old-boy network*. It's an informal institution that many young men on the rise can call on to help themselves get established in their work. It operates both within professions—often in the form of the "mentor" relationship, where an older man takes a younger one under his wing—and between professions. It got its name from groups of men who had been classmates in school, and who kept in touch and helped each other out. The editor published the professor's book, the accountant finessed the executive's taxes, the lawyer saw the producer through his divorce, the banker got the entrepreneur a loan, the congressman threw the new Interstate to the contractor—and each man shared his ever-broadening contacts with the others.

That's how things really get done in our "individualistic" society—right at the top! Never mind the myths. *There's a network of helping hands behind every genuine success.* And do you know how Jimmy Carter ended his speech on the old-boy network?

He said, "I have never known a woman who had that."

He was only half right.

It's true that most women have been incredibly isolated in terms of our talents, dreams, and goals. Not *alone:* we'd go down to the river and beat sheets on the rocks together, or we'd meet at the laundromat, which amounts to the same thing. But until very recently, there were precious few women in a position to offer their sisters a handhold in the worlds of power, money, achievement, and adventure, and those few didn't initiate an "old-girl network"—a fact that was cited as proof of the old belief that women are competitive rivals, and that the good-buddy spirit of mutual aid is just one more piece of male equipment we were born without. Consciousness-raising groups gave the lie to the notion that women couldn't support each other, but that support rarely got beyond the emotional. We exchanged comfort and complaint, not contacts. And that gave ammunition to the belief that only the exceptional woman is built for action—and that she's not a nice person.

It's all myths. It's nonsense. Of course women will compete with each other—if two of them happen to be after the same job or in love with the same man! Men do that too, and it's as natural as when you've got two hungry people and only one cookie. Otherwise, women have always given each other, not only understanding and compassion, but enormous amounts of practical help. The fact is that *there has always been a women's network.* In the domestic and human sphere, where we felt competent and comfortable, women have shared recipes, remedies, outgrown baby clothes, tools, and techniques since time began. The traditional way to make friends in a new neighborhood was to go next door and borrow a cup of sugar!

Cooperation isn't our problem. It never has been. Women are able to share resources and skills quite efficiently, with a warmth and openness many men envy. Our only problem has been taking ourselves seriously—as full, fascinating people with dreams and gifts and goals. You've done that now. You've shaped a clearly defined goal out of the stuff your dreams are made of, and you've taken it seriously enough to work out a detailed plan for getting it. You're about to find out that that's all it takes to bring the "old-girl network" out of the kitchen and into the world—and to convince the old boys to go coed.

If you've been brainstorming by yourself, and your flow chart has some holes in it, you can call a group of people together to provide you with the missing pieces in your plan. You can throw a *resource party* —the modern equivalent of a pioneer barn-raising. And that will become the natural takeoff point for an ongoing *resource network:* an informal community of mutual aid, combining the clout and goal-orientation of the old-boy network with the versatility and comfort of the cup-of-sugar connection. In the last chapter, you learned how to build a bridge of actions from a distant goal to your doorstep. Now you're going to discover that you can build a bridge of helping hands to virtually any person, skill, or thing you need on Planet Earth.

HOW TO THROW A BARN-RAISING

To give a resource party, the first thing you need to do is sit down and ask yourself a simple question:

Who do you know?

That's another one of those tricky little questions like "Who do you think you are?" When we ask, "Who do you know?" most of the time what we're really saying is, "Are you well-connected? Do you have rich, powerful friends?" If you don't—and let's face it, most of us don't —you will probably answer, "I don't know anybody," meaning, "I don't know anybody who counts." And that's grounds for inaction.

I'd like you to forget that right now and take the question in its original, innocent sense. Who do you know? Who are your friends and relatives and acquaintances? Whose names and phone numbers are in your address book? *You've got the makings of a full-fledged, effective resource network right there.*

How many of those people should you invite to a barn-raising? In a pinch, you can just have lunch with your best friend, or even talk to her on the phone. Two heads, and two people's resources, are more than twice as good as one. But the more people you pull in, the more help and ideas you'll get, because everyone will be inspired by hearing what everyone else has to offer. Four or five is a good working number. Fifteen is about the most you can comfortably fit into your living room. (Anything over fifteen also calls for a slightly more formal procedure, so we'll talk about how to throw a large-scale barn-raising after I describe how the basic version works.) As with brainstorming, it's helpful, though not mandatory, to get people of a variety of ages, backgrounds, and occupations: someone from Montreal, someone in her sixties, someone in movies, a carpenter, a stockbroker, an encyclopedia salesman, a shrink. You can ask a few of your friends to bring along their most interesting friends—or their husbands or grandmothers. It's not necessary for everyone to know everyone else. Success Teams barn-raisings start with a roomful of total strangers.

A barn-raising not only gives fresh purpose to old friendships; it can be a great way of making new ones. I meet a lot of people who say, "I don't make friends easily. I just don't seem to attract people." I'll tell you the kind of people who do. *They're the ones who are on their own trip, who have a fabulous idea and are running with it.* They don't call people up and say, "Uh . . . whatcha doin' tonight, Marty?" They say, "I've got such and such to do, and I could use some help. Want to come over?" Everyone loves to be around them because they generate so much energy. We were taught that it was selfish to be on our own trips, much less to ask for help with them. That's nonsense. The truth is that *the most generous thing you can do for the people around you is generate energy.* So don't be shy about inviting people over to help you out. There will be plenty in it for them. You're not only going to give them the chance to share in your goal, you're going to give them inspiration and help with theirs. If there's anything *they* want or need in their lives right now—a piano teacher, a tenants-rights lawyer, a set of kitchen cabinets, a ride to Vancouver—a barn-raising is the place to ask for it.

Your get-together can begin and end with socializing, but in the middle it's got to be a business meeting, with everyone's attention focused on the problem at hand. You start things off by telling everyone, first, all about your goal, and second, everything you've figured out you need in order to get it. For instance: "My dream is to start a horse ranch and riding stable. I've already got my first horse, and she didn't cost me a fraction of what I expected. What costs is the tack! I need leads to second-hand saddles, bridles, and blankets that I can buy cheap or trade for riding lessons. I also need customers—people who would like to take private riding instruction for ten dollars an hour." Or: "I'm going to move out to Colorado and start a small publishing house called Mountainbooks. I've got to find a partner or investor with enough money to back the enterprise for two years. This is a shot in the dark, but does anybody know anybody who might have a personal contact to John Denver or Robert Redford? I also need personal contacts to small-press publishers and to writers who specialize in the outdoors and nature field." Be ready with pencil and paper, because the ideas will really start flowing.

There are two rules you've got to follow if you want your barn-raising to be effective. The first is: *Be as specific as possible about what you need.* (Unless you've gotten stuck for ideas and you want some group brainstorming, working with your flow chart should have helped you reach this point.) Asking for "help" doesn't work. It may get you sympathy, or some well-meaning suggestions that miss the mark, but eventually you'll just get a helpless shrug. But if you ask for a second-hand piano, a contact in the music business, or lessons in auto mechanics, it's like dropping a beckoning worm into a pond full of hungry bass: every mind in the room will rise to the bait.

I'll give you an example of how this works. Could you put me in personal contact with someone who speaks and writes fluent Chinese and could translate into English? It doesn't have to be someone you know personally; it could be a friend of a friend, or a waiter in your favorite Chinese restaurant, or a professor at a university where a friend of yours teaches. But I want a name, an address, a phone number, and the name of the go-between, so that I can go in and say, "So and so sent me."

I'll bet that the farthest thing from your mind just now was the people in your personal universe who know Chinese. But if you give it a few minutes' thought, I'll bet you'll realize that you can solve my problem. If, on the other hand, I had said, "I'd like to have a pen pal in Peking; can you help me?" the chances are that—unless I was making a clear request for brainstorming—you would have shrugged your shoulders and felt helpless.

Before you can get what you need, you've got to take responsibility for *knowing what you need.* Being clear and specific about your needs is one of the most important ways of treating yourself like a winner. It's also the signal to everyone else that you're serious about your goal. So if what you need is Hard Times—and an ill-defined problem often conceals fear or pain—ask for Hard Times. If you need ideas, ask for brainstorming. And if you need a tractor or violin, *ask* for a tractor or violin. The chances are excellent that you'll get it.

The second rule for getting the most out of a barn-raising is: *always ask for the most specific information you can get*—names, addresses, phone numbers, book titles, etc. Remember that what you are aiming for is to get your flow chart down to *first steps*—things you can do today or tomorrow. If you want to make the move from executive secretary to executive, and Anne says, "Hey, I know somebody who *did* it," don't say, "Wow, great!" Get that woman's phone number and write it down. If you need a write-up in the local paper and Bill's best friend's wife works there as a copy editor, get her number so you can call and ask if she knows a reporter. If Joe knows three magazines you should run classified ads in for your book-find service, write down their names and ask Joe if he has copies you can borrow tonight.

Do you feel like saying, "Hey, wait a minute! Not so fast!"? Right.
That's because we're getting out of the nice, comfortable realm of
fantasy and into the frightening realm of real action. You're going to
follow up on the leads you get from barn-raising—tomorrow and the
next day and the next. That's what makes your goal really happen. It
can also make you very nervous. That's why the next section of this
book is all about how to set up a support system that will keep you going
when you feel like crawling into bed and pulling the covers over your
head. But one of the best things about throwing a barn-raising is that
you've already got some of the raw materials for your support system
right there with you in the room.

I've mentioned the importance of accountability—of having someone
else, like a teacher or a boss, who knows what you're planning to do
and cares whether you do it or not. Just knowing that someone else's
eyes have seen your plans helps to keep them from sliding back into the
never-never land of dreams. Once you've told your friends that you're
planning to write a novel or start a dairy farm, they'll be interested and
excited—and hopeful, because if you can do what you love, maybe they
can too. So they'll be rooting for you. And all of a sudden, if you don't
do it, you'll not only be letting yourself down—you've done that before
—but you'll be disappointing them, too.

Believe me, you will find this infinitely more effective than "self-
discipline." And it works right down to the step-by-step level. Because
if Anne should happen to call you next week and say, "Did you talk
to that lady executive I told you about? What did she say?" you're going
to feel pretty sheepish if you didn't call her. That may not be enough
to get you to pick up the phone when the midweek willies strike (more
first aid for them in the next section), but it helps. So whenever the
person you get a lead from is a friend, it's a good idea to work on the
"report back" principle. Say, "I'm going to call you next Sunday and
tell you what happened." That's a firm date. Write it down.

When your barn-raising group has given you all the suggestions
they can, it's the next person's turn to take the floor and tell what
s/he wants to do and what s/he needs. As you go around the room,
you'll be astonished at the variety of resources a small handful of
people can offer each other for achieving goals of all kinds. Here are
some of the kinds of things people I know have asked for—and gotten
—in barn-raisings.

INFORMATION

I'm a great believer in libraries—and in librarians, bless them. You can go to the library in any moderate-sized town, college, or university and find out almost anything you need to know, from the regulations of the American Kennel Club to the Gross National Product of Paraguay. You can also accomplish wonders by browsing through a bookstore, if yours allows browsing. But before you spend precious hours searching for the facts and addresses you need, try a shortcut. Ask your friends.

Stacy had a bottom drawer full of poems she had always secretly thought were pretty good. She got up her courage and showed some of them to her friends, and they urged her to make it her first target to get at least one poem into print. Stacy was a school nutritionist in a small midwestern city, not a literary person at all. She had no idea who would publish the work of an unknown poet. One of her friends had taken a course in women's writing at a nearby community college and was able to give Stacy the names of the best women's literary magazines. She promised to check copies out of the college library so that Stacy could see the kind of work they printed and get their addresses.

Carol, a cartoonist, had signed up with a top agent and gotten some encouraging responses from TV people, but she needed a special kind of assistant: a gifted cartoonist who would be willing to work with someone else's concepts. She had no idea how to find such a person, or why that person would want to work with her. She brought up the problem at her barn-raising. One friend knew a professional illustrator who had done animated commercials. She called the illustrator and got the names of two trade magazines that deal exclusively with cartoonists. Another remembered seeing a recent magazine article by a freelance cartoonist that mentioned trade associations, and offered to track the article down. By following up on this information, Carol was able to place classified ads that led to interviews with three eager potential apprentices.

All of us have more odd bits of information floating around in our heads than we know we've got. We're constantly reading and overhearing things—TV features about women stockbrokers, newsletters on volunteerism, reports on new solar collectors or supersonic cockroach zappers—and filing them away, forgetting we even have them until someone else's need suddenly yanks them into the limelight. We can be eyes and ears and memory banks for each other. It's a lot less lonely than the library stacks, and it works just as well, if not better.

THINGS AND STUFF

"Pathological individualism" is the single factor that has done the most to give money its awesome power over our lives. Why be "self-reliant" and pay the going market price for all kinds of things we can help each other get for less—or for free?

Starting with that classic cup of sugar, *borrowing* is the world's most time-honored and legitimate way of getting something for nothing. Friends will very often be willing to make you the short-term or long-term loan of something they're not using. I know a penniless playwright whose first off-Broadway hit got written on an old mechanical Royal portable that had been gathering dust in a friend's closet. And a Siamese cattery that survived its first lean year because its owners could borrow a car to make trips to a wholesale pet-food warehouse.

My writer friend Julia is the most successful "borrower" I know. People just seem to walk up and offer to lend her things, and not just things, but whole houses. She needed a work studio for $100 a month or less; the third person she asked offered her the free use of an enormous gothic apartment with a view of the Statue of Liberty where she now writes her articles for a total cost of $25 a month in subway fares. (She stumbled on an exceptional situation—an empty apartment that its country-dwelling owners only used on occasional weekends. But that's just the kind of wonderful surprise that barn-raising can turn up! It's a more common solution to "borrow" temporary living or working space from vacationers in exchange for routine house, plant, or pet care.) Julia has also spent months writing in her parents' beach cottage, borrowing a neighbor's bicycle for trips to the grocery store. Most borrowers are equally enthusiastic lenders, and in return for all this bounty Julia arranged for me to use the same little beach house for free at a time when I was in desperate need of a cheap and solitary vacation. It gave her almost as much pleasure as it gave me.

When Shakespeare's Polonius told his son, "Neither a borrower nor a lender be," he was telling him to miss out on one of the small joys of life. Of course, he was talking about money. And money can be tricky. We'll be talking about that a little later. But there is rarely any problem about borrowing tools, books, tape recorders, tennis rackets, musical instruments, or a string of pearls to look classy for an interview —provided that they are not in active use and that you use them with care and respect.

Second-hand: Anything you can't borrow, or would rather have for your own, you can usually buy second-hand from someone you know or someone they know: a truck, a flute, a desk, a film projector. Ellen, who wanted to start a horse ranch, brought up her need for second-hand riding tack at her barn-raising. Within a week she had offers of two used saddles and three bridles, in good condition, cheap. Second-hand shops naturally mark things up. So do people who put ads in papers or throw garage sales for strangers. Friends give each other rock-bottom prices. The mark-up is in the pleasure of knowing that your old couch, camera, or Chevy van is filling a need in your friend's life.

Homemade: Do you need display shelving or a hand-lettered sign for your store, a handsome business card, a special costume for your stand-up comic act? Don't go out and buy them before you've checked out the talents in your network. If you can make a personal contact who knows carpentry or graphics or sewing, you'll get exactly what you want for less—and you'll be giving someone else the chance to do what s/he loves.

I know a free-lance sales rep in textbooks, the creator of her own business, who got a unique and beautiful business card designed by the friend of a friend, a graphics designer. Kate didn't charge Helen anything for the design (she was employed full-time), but she enjoyed it so much that she produced a whole sheaf of stationery designs for another friend who was starting a film production company. Both delighted noncustomers passed along so many inquiries—"Hey, who did your letterhead?"—that Kate wound up quitting her job and starting a free-lance custom design business.

Freebies: If you know someone who works in an office, s/he can sometimes bring you small quantities of pens, pencils, stationery, envelopes, rubber bands, and paper clips for free. Many a poet has broken into print on the strength of photocopied duplicates made on some more gainfully employed friend's office lunch break. My friends who breed Siamese cats got introduced to a restaurant manager who was happy to give them all the chicken gizzards that would ordinarily have wound up in the garbage. Free samples, out-of-date but still perfectly good merchandise (like dated film or photographic paper), and usable scrap (like mill ends from a lumberyard or empty fruit and egg cartons, the primary school teacher's and shoestring interior decorator's dream) can be carted away by people who work in many businesses. Get in touch with them and they'll give it to you.

Discount and wholesale: Here is another privilege that employees in anything from retail stores to giant corporations can often share with their friends. The old joke, "I can get it for you wholesale," is no joke if it saves you hundreds of dollars. One woman who was starting a small dance company on a shoestring got a personal contact to the friendly young manager of a hosiery store. He provides all the company's leotards and tights at wholesale prices in exchange for credit on their recital programs. A man I know who works for a large electronics corporation used his employee's discount privilege to buy videotape equipment for a friend who wanted to produce a series of health-information programs for community cable TV.

Shopping skills: Find that special person who knows where all the bargains are in your town. There's at least one in every network. I know a woman who has made it her business to find every thrift shop in a three-state area. Rae is a book designer with terrific taste, and she can make herself look like she just walked out of Saks Fifth Avenue for about $7. (I'll bet she loved to play dress-up when she was a kid.) She'll not only let you make the rounds with her—she'll design you from head to foot, just for the fun of it, if you've got a public appearance or an interview coming up.

Which brings me to another valuable kind of help you can get from your friends . . .

SKILLS AND SERVICES, OR MIXING BUSINESS WITH PLEASURE

Lorna, a weaver, ran a barely-surviving craft shop called Fabric Arts, selling weaving, knitting, crocheting, and macrame supplies. To meet her goal of getting the business into the black, she needed her shop remodeled, and she needed expert marketing advice. By announcing her needs at a barn-raising, she found a young interior designer and a marketing consultant who were friends of friends. The interior designer was willing to accept payment in kind—in hand-woven fabrics. The marketing consultant didn't charge her for his advice. In a couple of hours over coffee, he gave her some fantastic ideas—and invited her out to the movies the next week.

John, a psychiatrist who lives and sees his patients on a sailboat (believe it or not), had a further dream: to make his living by turning people on to nature. He got a bunch of people together for brainstorming, and they came up with a brilliant idea: he should promote himself as an expert on "success stress" (which, as an ex-workaholic himself, he was) and take small groups of executives on fishing and camping weekends as a form of play therapy. But how to do that and earn enough money to keep three children in school—and maintain a sailboat? His friends put him in touch with a professional PR person who was immediately delighted with the idea. Because John came to her through mutual friends, she didn't have to spend a lot of time interviewing or investigating him; there was an immediate feeling of warmth and "let's get to work!" She proceeded to prepare a campaign of press releases, media appearances, and newspaper interviews that would make him known and attract a clientele.

Whoever said that mixing business with pleasure was a bad idea? Since so many of us spend one-third of our lives doing business, it might as well be as pleasant and as personal as possible—and save us money besides. So if your goal calls for the know-how of an electrician, typist, editor, literary agent, publicist, lawyer, accountant, or auto mechanic, check out your network before you open the Yellow Pages. Services delivered on a basis of friendship, even a couple of times removed, are generally higher quality, lower cost, and a lot more fun than exchanges based strictly on money. If a friend or a friend's friend types your manuscript . . . or frames your drawings . . . or keeps the books for your store . . . or takes the pictures for your portfolio, you'll have the assurance of personal care and the added satisfaction of contributing to his or her survival. If you're setting up in business yourself, your friends will be your first and best source of customers and clients. Exchanging professional services with people you know does more than anything else to recreate the community of mutual aid that is such a natural form of human relating. And it often cuts costs even further by developing into a spontaneous system of barter—swapping services and skills instead of paying for them. (More on that a little later, when I talk about how to keep a considerate balance between giving and getting help.)

By supplementing your own skills, the skills in your network can save you time and energy as well as money. They'll set you free to concentrate on what you do best, instead of having to struggle with all the little side tasks that clutter up every goal. For instance, there are published books—good ones—that tell you how to write an effective resumé or grant proposal. I've listed the best ones I know in the Resources appendix at the back of this book. But if you know someone who's a whiz at resumés, you can get one written up in a pleasant evening over coffee, instead of wrestling with it for a week by yourself! If your network can put you in touch with someone who's applied for grants and gotten them, you'll get personal advice and feedback you can't get from any book. If you're applying to school and you draw a blank on one of those awful essay questions—"In 1,000 words or less, what are your reasons for wishing to enter the medical profession?"—you can get a friend with the gift of blarney to write it for you! In short, *you don't have to do everything by yourself.* Save your energy for what you love—and delegate as much of the rest as you can. You deserve help—and you don't have to worry about "using people" as long as you observe the "Safeguards for Barn-Raising" on p. 165.

If there are skills your goal requires that you really want to learn for yourself, like bookkeeping for your small business or auto maintenance for your delivery van, ask your barn-raising group to get you an introduction to someone who can teach them to you. For instance, if your goal is to open a bookstore because you love books, but you have no idea how to *keep books,* tap your network for an experienced small business owner who's willing to show you how to take inventory and use a ledger. (Again, I've provided a list of good books on starting your own business in the Resources appendix. But the best book is no substitute for the personal advice of a seasoned veteran.) If you're interested in photography but have never touched anything more complicated than a Brownie, get a photographer to give you a short lesson on f-stops and light meters so you can go out and start taking pictures tomorrow. A miniapprenticeship is the quickest and most direct way to get your hands on any skill, and barn-raising is the ideal way to set one up. Most people are as glad to share the secrets of their trade with a personal acquaintance as they are reluctant to teach them to a stranger or a customer.

Another valuable resource we can offer each other is something called *a day in the field.* This is especially important if you have one or more tentative goals that you think you might love, but don't really know much about. Suppose you're attracted to the life and work of a newspaper reporter, but you suspect that you got your idea of what it's like from the movies. It sure looks gritty and glamorous and exciting when Bette Davis or Robert Redford does it, but what's the reality?

The way you find out is, you ask your network to find you someone who works at a newspaper. And then you arrange to spend a day or two or a week hanging out with that person—soaking up the atmosphere of the newsroom, going along on assignments, carrying notebooks or cameras, toting coffee and copy. You won't be in the way. Most people love to talk about their work and enjoy the novelty of having an audience. It makes them feel like *they're* Robert Redford or Bette Davis! And that goes for doctors, stockbrokers, teachers, and craftsmen. Like volunteering, a day in the field is a great way to find out whether a particular goal is for you—and if so, to make contacts that will help you get your start toward it.

MONEY

Jeannette's Appalachian photography trip is a good example of how the exchange of ideas, goods, and services through barn-raising can reduce the cost of any plan to the absolute minimum. When you've reached that rock-bottom amount you've still got to have, your network will help you get it.

Friends can help you dream up and carry out fund-raising schemes, like Jeannette's did. They can find you a contact who's had personal experience with Small Business Administration loans. I know a couple who are close friends with the vice-president of a bank, an unpretentious sweetheart of a man; they have helped friends of theirs get bank loans by acting as references and go-betweens. If you have a promising scheme and a steady income, a friend will sometimes be willing to co-sign a loan with you or put up collateral—or even lend you the money directly. A woman I know put up her savings passbook for a doctor friend who had helped her through a difficult hospital stay and was now starting his own practice. And a young sculptor and his wife were able to buy a brownstone in Manhattan by arranging to borrow money at interest from a friend. If you know someone who has a few thousand dollars lying idle, there can be a special mutual advantage in this arrangement: you pay your friend less interest than you'd pay a bank, but more than he or she gets from a savings account. (Important note: a loan to or from a friend is a business arrangement. It should always be undertaken on the basis of financial reliability, not emotional trust, and the terms should always be drawn up on paper. That's not crass or cynical. It's the way to protect both your money and your friendship.)

If you're looking for a business partner, investor, or "angel," your network of personal contacts can find you one. There are an amazing number of mildly-to-massively wealthy people in this world who are looking for something interesting to do with $3,000 or $25,000—as a tax deductible contribution, a hedge against inflation, or just a sporting gamble. Where are they? They're hiding—for very good reasons. But even they have friends and cousins and grandchildren. And the odds are that someone you know knows one of them. It may take four or five or six links in the chain, but you can find that little old lady who loves murder mysteries and will back your little bookstore if you'll put up her name on a brass plaque.

I know people who've done it. Like the chess master—brilliant but broke—who opened his own chess shop with two partners: a former pupil and a fourth-generation multimillionaire who'd been in several business ventures with the pupil. And the theatrical director who financed a Shakespeare festival with a $14,000 gift from the grandfather of an actress in her company. Before you can look for a backer, of course, you've got to demonstrate your seriousness by getting your plan precisely defined on paper—and that means *figures.* And projections. It's the projections—where you expect to be in six months, one year, two years—that really turn on a creative entrepreneur. If you don't know how to do them, your friends will help you.* They'll dig up someone who's run a boutique, or managed a restaurant, or packaged a movie, and who can sit down and give you a short course on capital

*See the Resources appendix for books that give you sample business plans.

outlay, overhead, percentage points, projections, and whatever you need for a financially sound proposal.

CONTACTS, CONNECTIONS, CLOUT: "JOE SENT ME"

It should be getting very clear by now that the most important resource people can offer each other is *other people*. And it's never more important than when your goal is to get in through the door of a closed professional world. Not all goals require clout. But if yours does, your network will help you get it.

I'm sure you've heard those conversations about how hard it is to get a good job in business—or to get into medical school, or get a movie part, or get published, or get reviewed—that end with an angry sigh: "It isn't how good you are. It's *who you know.*" Damn right it is! Some seeds have wings to travel on the wind; some have stickers for hitching a ride on animal fur or human clothing. The seeds of human genius happen to travel by a system of personal contacts. Why sit around bemoaning that fact when you can put it to work for you?

I'm not saying that how good you are isn't important. *It is.* It just isn't *enough.* Talent or merit alone will rarely get you past the smiling receptionist, the protective secretary, the wary agent, the routine hiring or admissions screening. A personal introduction to someone on the inside will. And that's not because magazine editors, movie producers, and personnel directors are "corrupt." It's because they're human. Like you, they tend to be a little suspicious of total strangers, but happy to meet anyone bearing the seal of approval of a respected colleague or a trusted friend. Personal introductions are the strength of the old-boy network. And by drawing on your own network, you should never have to walk into a job interview, publisher's office, or record company cold. At the very least, you'll go in with the name of a common acquaintance; at best, you can have an introductory phone call precede you.

Incidentally, this is one place where the generations can really be of help to each other. Your kid may be in school with the daughter of a film director; your friend's father may be a doctor who'd be willing to recommend you for medical school. You'll never know until you ask. And don't ever think this is "cheating." It's not a substitute for a strong sense of what you have to offer, or a willingness to be judged on your merits. It's simply the smart way to get your merits the recognition and opportunity they deserve.

If you're ambitious, there are two especially valuable kinds of inside contacts to ask for in any field. One is an equally ambitious young man or woman whose career needs complement your own. Ask your network to help you find and meet the brightest young agent or editor in town, on the lookout for new best-selling writers; a gifted young actress or director looking for scripts; a young record producer eager to turn an unknown talent into a smash hit; a young fashion designer looking for marketing help. And hitch your wagon to that rising star. When you're just starting out in your own career, this can be easier than getting the attention of someone already established, and the two of you together will have more than twice the chance of breaking into the big time.

Remember Andrea, the photographer who wanted to be famous for her portraits of celebrities? Since she was timid about marching straight up to big stars and major magazines, I suggested that she pick out a promising new rock star, follow his or her career, and offer her pictures to the editor of a young women's magazine that was just getting started. The singer would be grateful for the publicity, the magazine would be grateful for the scoop—and all three of them could get famous together.

The other kind of person you want to be put in touch with is the man or woman right at the top. If at all possible, get your novel manuscript to the editor-in-chief, your film script to the famous movie star, your marketing proposal to the vice-president in charge of sales. It may make you nervous (Chapters 9 and 10 will help you prepare), but it will save you time and uncertainty. Assistants and trainees may be friendly and sympathetic, but they hardly ever have the power to make decisions—especially positive ones.

This is where you will really need a personal introduction. People at the top, like people with money, are well protected against extra demands on their attention and time. They have to be. That's why letters of inquiry and phone calls to secretaries won't get you anywhere. But your network of friendships will.

Do you doubt that a modest gathering of friends in your livingroom could put you in touch with the likes of Robert Redford or an executive of IBM? Well, it can. It's already been mathematically proven that if you get any fifteen or twenty people together in a room and start asking them who they know, in five or six steps you can build a bridge of personal contacts to anyone—*anyone*—in the United States. Geography is no barrier. You can take a phone book from any town in the country—say, Bozeman, Montana—pick a name at random, and say, "All right, who knows somebody in Montana—or somebody who *knows* somebody in Montana?" And within five days you can have a message delivered personally to that sheep rancher or liquor-store owner in Bozeman. That's been done!*

I don't know if anyone has ever tried the same deliberate experiment across the tougher barriers of celebrity and power—getting together fifteen people in a room and asking for a personal contact with Marlon Brando or Jimmy Carter. But two friends of mine have done it in pursuit of their goals, and they're no more "well-connected" than most people. One, a man whose agent had failed to sell his exciting adventure novel to the movies, got copies of the book personally delivered into the hands of Telly Savalas and Robert DeNiro. The other, a woman journalist, arranged a rare telephone interview with the then ailing and reclusive Anaïs Nin through a network of trusted friends. If they could do it, so can you!

Given modern mobility and communications, every one of us has "connections." We just don't know they're there because they've never been plugged into the juice—the determination to reach a goal.

Let's just suppose I had written a screenplay, and I had a strong, irrational hunch that if Marlon Brando could see it, he'd do it. I wouldn't try to find out who Brando's agent was and mail it to him, because I'm no dummy. I know that that would be the surest way of getting my screenplay shipped back to me unopened and unread, with the unspoken message, "Who do you think *you* are—William Goldman?" What I'd do is, I'd take it to a barn-raising. And instead of asking my friends who they knew in Montana, I'd ask them who they knew in the movies. Once I'd gotten one or more contacts inside the movie biz, I'd say, "All right, now please find me someone who knows someone who knows someone . . . who's buddies with Marlon Brando." And just by following that chain of acquaintanceship, sooner or later I'd get my screenplay placed directly into Marlon Brando's hands. I wouldn't try to do it in five days, of course. I'd give myself, oh, maybe

*It's called the "small world experiment," and was done by psychologist Stanley Milgram.

six weeks, just in case Brando was on his island in the South Pacific.

I have a strong suspicion that there's no one in this world a chain of helping hands can't reach—however high, however far. If you still doubt that your own personal network will reach far enough fast enough, you can try expanding your barn-raising beyond the circle of your friends. But first, I want to deal with some of the problems you may anticipate arising when you start sharing resources with your friends.

SAFEGUARDS FOR BARN-RAISING

Most of the resources you can get from your friends in a barn-raising will make a minimal demand on their time and energy. But what if you're asking for a favor that will really cut into a friend's life space —like help writing a grant proposal or term paper, or painting a coffee-house, or getting a loan? Or what if *you're* blessed or cursed with skills many of your friends need, like editing or typing or carpentry or therapy? How do you keep from taking advantage—and being taken advantage of? Isn't there a danger that this barn-raising business could get out of hand and afflict our friendships with imposition, resentment, and guilt?

Getting and giving help is an art. It takes tact and sensitivity—and blunt honesty. Fortunately, there are two simple rules for restoring an optimum amount of community—enough to provide everyone with support and help without asking the impossible of anyone.

Rule 1: The Principle of Mutuality

"You scratch my back, I'll scratch yours" is the old, old secret of effective cooperation. And there's nothing crass or calculated about it. You don't help out a friend with the deliberate intention of putting him or her in your debt so you can demand something in return. You help because you care, and giving practical help is one of the most satisfying ways of saying so. But like all expressions of affection, this one has to be roughly equal and mutual, or a feeling of imbalance creeps into the relationship that makes both parties uncomfortable.

The economy of gratitude between friends is very deep and delicate and fascinating. When you help a friend, you establish a sort of fund of willingness to help you that you know you can count on if you need it. No one keeps books or writes up mental bills; each friend simply tries to keep the "account" more or less in balance. Most of us do this kind of balancing act instinctively. We know that simple favors are compensated by the pleasure of giving—and even so, we'll often take the giver out to dinner just to say thanks. But if we ask for a major investment of time or skill, we're aware that we're making a big draft on our "account," and we feel the need to make more substantial compensation. Here's where *barter* can really come to the rescue.

Informal barter is simply a matter of offering something you're able and willing to do in exchange for something you need. "If you'll help me with my resumé, I'll babysit for you when you have your interview." "If you'll build my bookshelves, I'll teach you to play the guitar." I know people who've traded professional typing for group therapy, scientific writing for free medical care, and clerical work for karate lessons. Most such "bargains" are spontaneous and approximate, made by feel rather than by a reckoning of hours spent or dollar value. After all, what someone else does for you gets its chief value from the fact that you can't or don't want to do it yourself, and that's a matter of quality, not quantity.

In case you're intrigued by barter as a cost-cutting strategy, I've listed some published accounts of both formal and informal swapping arrangements in the Resources appendix. But the principle of fair exchange isn't just a good way to save money. It's the best way of saving feelings—of getting help without guilt and giving it without resentment. In many close friendships, this kind of exchange takes place without a word being said. But if you're in any doubt, talk about it! Say, "I really appreciate your doing this for me, and I want to know what I can do for you in return." Your friend may not need to take advantage of your offer right now, but s/he will know s/he can, and that's what counts.

A word of warning, however. There are two kinds of people who seem to lack that instinctive sense of balance between giving and taking. I call them "mamas" and "babies." The terms have nothing to do with sex or age; there are male "mamas," and there are 55-year-old "babies." You will probably recognize someone you know in the portraits of them I'm about to draw. You may even recognize yourself.

Mamas are the compulsive fixers. They run through the streets hoisting people on their backs, and then they say, "See? Five hundred people on my back, and who ever carries me?" They are building up a case that they're all alone in the world with these tremendous burdens, but it never occurs to anyone to take care of them for the simple reason that *they never ask.* They don't know how. "Listen, I've got a problem, can you give me a hand?" is not a sentence that's ever in a mama's mouth. If you ask them, "Say, how's it going with such and so?" they get a stiff look on their faces and say, "Fine. Fine. I've got it all under control" —even if they're collapsing. And if you actually offer them help, they get terribly defensive, because what they hear is that you don't think they've been trying hard enough!

Mamas believe that they're supposed to do everything for themselves —after they finish doing everything for everybody else. If they can't accept help, by the same token they can't turn down a request for help. In fact, they will interpret a conversational complaint—like, "Gee, I'm having a rough time with my income-tax forms"—as the call of duty, and before you know it, they'll have taken over your life. That might be very convenient, if it didn't have a high price for mamas and their adopted charges alike.

Mamas need to help and help and help because they believe that's the only way to give and get love. (It's no accident that so many women are mamas—and that the majority of mamas are women.) But what happens is, first and worst, the mama's own dreams and talents get lost in the shuffle, because she or he is always giving them last place. And second of all, that kind of "love" really isn't very loving. Consciously or not, mamas regard their self-inflicted broods with resentment and sometimes contempt. That's not friendship. It is noticeably lacking in respect.

"Babies" are mamas' opposite number. They are the people who seem to lack all sense of moderation about asking for favors. The sentence that is always in a baby's mouth is, "I've got a problem. What are you going to do about it?" Babies have usually grown up as some-body's prize poodle. Lurking in the background is a parent who was going to prove what a good parent he or she was by taking such good care of that baby that it would never have to do a thing for itself. Babies believe that the way to love and get loved is to act cute and helpless. They know how to charm almost anyone into doing things for them that they would get much more satisfaction and self-respect from doing for themselves. Of course, it's the mamas who fall for it.

Mamas and babies are each other's natural prey. They're both con artists. They hustle each other. And they both miss out. Mamas are secret orphaned babies who can never relax and find out that life doesn't have to be so lonely and hard. Babies are private, angry adults who've been cheated out of feeling capable and needed. Neither mamas nor babies can marshal the resources to reach their goals, because mamas are always walking around on the cross, and sooner or later babies wind up wailing alone in the playpen.

You've got to be very careful of mamas and babies in barn-raising. If you run into one—or if you are one yourself—you've got to watch out that the mama doesn't take on everyone else's goals at his or her own expense, and that the baby doesn't turn the whole room into an army of private servants. There's a very useful little tool that serves both purposes.

If the magic word in brainstorming is "How?" the magic word in barn-raising is "No." Learning how to say it is the second safeguard for cooperation.

Rule 2: The Right to Say "No"

Every person in a barn-raising has the God-given right to say no both to offers of help that are unwanted or excessive, and to requests for help that he or she cannot reasonably fulfill.

Suppose, for instance, you're looking for a lawyer, and instead of just giving you a name and a phone number, your friend goes into a whole spiel about why her lawyer, Jane Jones, is the best, and it becomes more and more obvious that your friend is going to feel personally rejected if you detest Jane Jones on sight. You have the right to pick and choose what *you* want—not the obligation to make helpful people feel good. Real help is offered as neutrally as fruit on a tree, for you to take or leave as you wish. If you can use it, fine. If not, it doesn't mean you're rejecting the giver.

By the same token, if someone eagerly offers you a big chunk of help and refuses to accept any compensation at all, you're probably dealing with a mama, and if you accept the offer, you may pay in subtle ways. "No, I will *not* let you type my three-hundred-fifty page manuscript for free even if you've got nothing better to do" is one of the most important kinds of "No" you can say. You can insist on the principle of mutuality even—or especially—when the other person doesn't. It's better for you and better for the mama, who needs to learn to place a higher value on his or her own time and skills.

It's even more important, since so many of us have "mama" tendencies, to say no promptly, firmly, and without guilt when someone asks for a kind of help you don't want to give or don't have time for.

Sometimes, for instance, you will have to refuse professional services to friends, if giving them would jeopardize either your friendship or your profession. If you are in a position to make creative judgments—for instance, if you're the director of a local TV station, a talent agent, or a PR person—you've got to be very careful about acting as a resource for everyone you know. You must reserve the right to turn down material you can't work with, or even to refuse to consider something if you sense that more than an honest opinion is expected of you.

Similarly, if you have skills you'd rather not use—if, say, you can type really well, but you would rather die than type another word—don't ever feel obliged to volunteer them just because somebody needs them. You're not the only person on earth who can type, and you'll help just as much by recommending someone else who doesn't hate to type. Your friend will understand. After all, she doesn't want to type the damn thing either!

If a friend approaches you for a loan and you can't spare the money or can't be sure of getting it back, saying "No" is a kindness. In the long run it will only protect your friendship.

Finally, never, ever forget that *your time belongs to you and your goal first.* It's fun and exciting to be involved in other people's projects—but it must not be at the expense of your own. The time you can offer or trade to others should be spare time, after you've done your goal-work and anything else you need or want to do. True giving is from surplus, and the only way to keep your reservoirs full is to take good care of yourself.

The only people who will react to a "No" with real hurt and indignation are babies, and it should relieve your guilty conscience to know that a "No" is usually good for babies. It throws them back on their own resources—especially if you give them ideas and leads they can follow up themselves, instead of agreeing to do it all for them. Otherwise, an honest "No" between friends is an act of mutual respect, offered with regret and accepted with understanding, and often followed up by some joint brainstorming on alternatives.

On the other side of the ledger, you must respect your friends' right to say "No" to you—and don't let the possiblity make you afraid to ask. If it's so hard for you to ask that by the time you finally get up your nerve a "No" will kill you, you're doing something wrong—and you're putting an intolerable burden on the person you're asking. You should ask a *lot.* Just make your requests as *specific* and *direct* as possible, so your friends will know they have the option of saying "Yes" or "No" to the request, not to your whole existence. People love to be asked as long as they know they are free to say "Yes" or "No."

With these two safeguards in mind, you can now discover the magic of turning friendships into resources. It's like a connect-the-dots puzzle: the pattern of community is already there, but you don't see it until you draw in the lines of purpose. Most personal networks will reach as far as you need to fill in the gaps in your flow chart and get started toward your goal. But if you'd like to cast the net even wider on the first throw, you can invite your whole office, neighborhood, school, or town to a barn-raising in your conference room, church community hall, or school auditorium. Buy an ad in your neighborhood paper or on the local radio station announcing a resource-sharing gathering; put up invitations on every bulletin board you can find, and tell all your friends to bring *their* friends . . . the more people in a room the bigger the pool of possibilities, talents, and connections—and the higher the energy level. In Success Teams seminars, we start with a roomful of forty or fifty strangers and end up with a crackling resource network

When you've got a big group of people gathered together, you establish the rules:

1. Be as *specific* as you can about what you need.
2. *Do not* offer anything you are not truly willing and able to give.
3. If you can provide what someone else needs, or use what someone has to offer, raise your hand and give your name. Write down each other's names and get together after the formal part of the meeting is over.

Then each person gets up in front of the group, introduces him- or herself, and says, "I'm Ellen Johnson. I'm a Gestalt therapist trained at Esalen, and I'm starting my own workshops. I need clients and loft space. Does anyone have any ideas?" "I'm Joe Jones. I'm a sculptor, but I make my living by carpentry. I'll build anything out of wood for a reasonable price. I could use contacts to art galleries that might show my work. Does anyone have any ideas?" "I'm Mary Smith. I want to go to dental school, and I'd like to talk to a woman who's actually done it." "My name is Joy Greenberg. I've written a screenplay, and I'd like to get a production together and act in it myself! I need lots of advice, any contacts in the movie business, and maybe financial backing." And so on around the room.

When everyone has had a turn, the formal meeting breaks up and everyone goes looking for the people whose names they've written down. Ideas, leads, advice, and phone numbers are exchanged over refreshments. It happens to be a great way to meet people, as well as goals. Many of the participants will stay in touch and develop fruitful professional and/or personal relationships. If you ask everyone who comes to write his or her name on a master list by the door, you can call a "reunion" in three or six months to see what's actually happened as a result of one evening's barn-raising.

Once you've got a master list of interested people, it's a very short step to starting a *resource bank.* This is a bit of a project— one that could even become a fascinating goal in its own right for anyone interested in the interconnections that bring community alive. The simplest way to start a resource bank is to ask everyone on the list to fill out a large file card with: name and address; goals; specific needs; and resources to offer. This last category should include not only professional skills and services, but hobbies, interests, abilities, experience, anything the person knows and loves: fluency in Spanish, time spent living in Greece or Alaska, knowledge of cooking or ballet or backpacking. It should *not* include any skills he or she does not want to share. Whoever takes responsibility for the resource bank then has a brain-teaser of a job: devising a filing or cross-referencing system.

In Success Teams, we started out by giving each name on the master list a number. Then we could file the cards in numerical order and make a separate, alphabetical classification of skills and resources. After each resource we'd list the numbers of the cards on which that resource was offered—like this:

Animals: 5
Carpentry: 17, 29
Cars: 10, 27
Greece: 19
Public Relations: 15
Spanish: 10, 12, 23, 36
Typing: 8, 43, 61

That way, when a request came in by mail or phone ("I need to meet someone at the Ford Foundation," "I need to know people who raise Labrador retrievers"), we could just look up the appropriate numbered cards and give the caller names or phone numbers. Whenever someone new called in, we'd say, "Would you like to be part of our resource bank?" and, if the answer was yes, we'd fill out a card for that person.

We've got over 2,000 participants now, and we're working on computerizing the network. Our goal is to make it nationwide, with a geographical cross-referencing system, so that you can call a toll-free 800 number at any time of the day or night and get the name of someone in Chicago with a kennel full of Labradors; or a recording engineer in Seattle; or someone in Houston who has pink canaries and will ship you one by Christmas; or the only woman plumber in Sacramento; or someone who's taken that new career-counseling course and can tell you "It's great," or "Don't waste your money." We're going to have our own network all over the country.

I've put our address under Resources, in case you'd like to send in a card and plug into *our* network. I've also given the names of books that list some other experiments in community-wide and nationwide resource-sharing: education, information, and employment networks, barter organizations, apprenticeship clearinghouses, etc. You might want to investigate and see whether one of them meets your needs— or you could use any or all of them as models for setting up your own local resource-sharing system.

There are infinite variations on the theme, but the theme itself— lending each other helping hands—is an ancient good idea whose time has come again.

–8–
Working with Time

After a successful barn-raising, you should be able to finish your flow chart, with every major branch of action developed right down to first steps. You don't actually have to write all your first steps into the chart —you'll probably have too many to squeeze them all in. Just complete the basic structure of your chart.

Then make a separate list of your first steps, checking them off as you get them done and adding new ones.

Like Jeannette:

FIRST STEPS	GOAL
call mechanic	publisher accepts
call A	book
call friends	
look	
network	
get maps	

or Mary:

FIRST STEPS	GOAL
notes	enter medical
research corporations	school
call B	
study for exams	
call about review course	

The purpose of a flow chart isn't to map out every tiny detail of your plan. We're going to be using other tools for that, like a pocket calendar. The flow chart is to guide you so that you'll always know what *phase* of your plan you're in, and exactly what you have to get accomplished at that phase before you can move on to the next.

Flow charts are as individual as fingerprints: no two are alike. Try drawing your own on a sheet of blank paper. Once you've done that, you've turned your dream into a *structure*: a logical sequence of actions designed to lead you step by step to your goal. But that structure hasn't begun to exist in reality yet. A flow chart is like an architect's blueprint: it's a lot more specific than a mental image of your dream house, but it still isn't the house—it's only a guide for building a house. To turn it into a reality you can live in, you've got to start building. And the only way to build a dream is brick by brick, action by action, day by day, *in real time.* So our next task is *to map your flow chart onto time.*

That will mean, first of all, setting a target date: an actual day, like January 1, 1981, by which you'd like to have your goal and think you might be able to get it. Then you will mark a wall calendar with target dates for each major phase or step in your plan, corresponding to each circle on your flow chart, so you have a rough schedule to measure your progress against. And finally, you'll start assigning the small specific actions that really make it all happen to specific days in your pocket calendar, so that they actually get done, one by one.

Before you can start working with time, however, you've got to have the time to work with. If you think you don't, there is a very simple way to solve that problem. Just get into action. Start fitting little bits of your goal-work into your life however you can. And it's like being in love: the time will find itself.

Whenever people complain to me that they can't afford to do what they love full time, I tell them, "Start doing it in your spare time and watch what happens." Ellen, an elementary-school teacher on a small salary, dreamed—and despaired—of having her own horse ranch. I told her that as a first target she ought to have a horse to come home to evenings and weekends. She thought horses were terribly expensive because every birthday of her childhood she had asked her mother for one and her mother had said, "We can't afford it, dear." So I suggested she schedule some first steps of the "go-out-and-find-out" variety. To her astonishment, she found a wonderful, gentle 11-year-old bay gelding for all of $150! She stabled him in her tiny backyard and paid for his feed by giving riding lessons on weekends.

Having that horse changed Ellen's life and her whole personality. She was such a joyous teacher that word spread all around her New Jersey area, and the demand for riding lessons grew to the point where she needed—and could afford—a second horse. Next year she's going to be teaching riding full time.

The same thing happened to Diane, the city planner, who started her career by going to block-association meetings in the evenings after work. And the same thing will happen to you. If your goal is to make your living by doing what you love, start doing it just for love.

Whenever someone still protests that I don't understand, she or he really has no time, I say, "Try a Hard Times session." Because "I don't have time" can be an emotional problem. It means you're scared, and keeping very busy is your way of staying safe. You'll be learning techniques for defusing that kind of fear in the next two chapters. But in the meantime, you can go ahead and start freeing blocks of time for your goal-work. The way to do that is by analyzing the way you spend your time now—and then pinpointing those time-filling, time-killing activities where the fear and pain are hiding. I call them *avoidance patterns,* and it's from them that most of your new time will come.

PRESENT PATTERNS OF SPENDING TIME

Most of us have very little idea of how we actually spend our time —and it can be pretty hair-raising to find out. But if you think you have a time problem, I really recommend doing this next exercise if you can stand it, because *the way you spend your days is the way you spend your life.* It's right here, in the little details of your days, that you will have to make the changes if you want your life to change. And before you can change those details, you've got to take a good frank look at what they are.

Try to record, without flinching or falsifying, *what you actually do with your time* every day for a week. This is even harder than keeping track of every penny you spend to figure out where the money is going, but it can be done. Fill in this chart:

PRESENT PATTERN OF TIME SPENT			
	Morning	Afternoon	Evening
Sunday			
Monday			
Tuesday			
Wednesday			
Thursday			
Friday			
Saturday			

Most people have one of two reactions to what they find out: 1) "I had no idea I was wasting so much time!" Or, 2) "What's going to be on my gravestone is, "Good Person. S/he kept a lot of people clean, well-fed, and happy." We will call 1) The Procrastinator, and 2) The Good Woman/Good Provider.

The Procrastinator

If you have discovered that a lot of your time is going down the drain of avoidance patterns, don't be too hard on yourself for it. Above all, *don't make any drastic resolutions to reform.* You know perfectly well that "I'll never watch another late movie or read *Cosmopolitan* again!" leads straight to a guilty orgy of whatever it is you're not supposed to be doing. It's an invitation your inner brat cannot resist. The strictest Puritans are the worst and sneakiest time-wasters, because they demand so inhumanly much of themselves that their brats are in a constant state of rebellion.

The fact is, you cannot get rid of your avoidance patterns—and you shouldn't. You need them. You have to have some self-indulgent goodies—a few late-night movies, some time to read paperback bestsellers, drink beer, talk on the phone, or do nothing at all. The whole trick is to schedule them. That's right, absurd as it may sound, *schedule your avoidance patterns,* so that you can look forward to them, instead of allowing yourself to fall into them whenever the impulse strikes.

Unless you are a mother with two children under the age of 3—in which case you'd better find another mother to swap afternoons with —your "Present Patterns" has probably turned up at least an hour or two a day that you habitually fill by napping . . . or watching football games or soap operas . . . or rereading the morning papers . . . or cleaning a closet or desk you already cleaned last week. It's probably a time when you're alone, a lull between storms of activity and demand: lunch hour at work, afternoon before the kids come home, evening after they're in bed. That's the ideal kind of time for working on your goal —but you need the idleness and relaxation, too.

So here's what you do. First, pick one of those time periods and mark it off simply as *time that belongs to you.* (Note that you're not stealing time from anything or anybody else—not yet. Right now, all you're doing is making official and positive something that's already true in fact.) Try to define its borders—say, from 1:30 to 3:00 P.M. in the afternoon. If you use the kind of pocket calender that shows the hours of each day, draw a red line around those hours and label them, *"My time."*

You don't have to set a formal block of time aside every day, unless you want to. It can be once or twice or three times a week—but try to make it the same time every day or every week, like "One-thirty to three P.M., Tuesdays and Thursdays." That's because ritual is a terrific antidote for procrastination. Setting a definite and regular time for getting certain things done makes it much likelier that you will do them, as you well know if you pay your bills on the first of every month. I happen to think you owe yourself at least as much promptness and reliability as you owe the phone company. If you forget to pay them, they just shut your phone off. Forget yourself for long enough, and you'll shut your soul off. So you establish a regular time period that's just for you. I don't care how short it is at first.

Now, *divide that time period in half.* The first half is your time slot for doing whatever goal-work you'll schedule into each week: writing a paragraph, sketching the cat, running over to the library, making phone calls. The second half is strictly for goofing off. *Promise* yourself that when half your time is up, you'll drop whatever you are doing for your goal and start reading *True Romances* or watching "Columbo" with a vengeance. I promise you that you'll eventually break that promise, but never mind. It's there for as long as you need it.

That's how you start getting goal time out of "wasted" time, like gold out of dirt. And a start is all you need. Once you really get going on your goal, a lot of other things you thought you absolutely had to do are suddenly going to start taking second, third, and eighth place. Like housework, for instance.

The Good Woman/The Good Provider

I've got a couple of radical statements to make about housework and other role-related "shoulds." The first is: If you love keeping a house shining clean, cooking, and taking care of people (or mowing the lawn, washing the car, and weeding the garden), do it. Have a good time, and don't let anybody tell you that you should be doing something more Important and Creative. But if you find you're bored and overwhelmed by the *sameness* of it all, stop. I did. And I found out that a lot of things I thought were important—like a clean floor and a full refrigerator— weren't. My friend Joe made the same discovery—just in reverse. Joe had grown up with the male myth of the Good Provider. That meant that it was a real man's responsibility to get a secure high-paying job and work long hours, so he could supply his wife and children not only with food, shelter, and clothing, but with ten-speed bikes, Florida vacations, and Airstream trailers. A man who would really rather spend long evenings at home, make jewelry in his garage, and take the kids camping in a 6-year-old Volkswagen bus was considered shiftless, self-indulgent, and an evader of responsibilities. It cost Joe a bleeding ulcer to quit driving himself in an accountant's job he hated and start keeping books at home part-time while he worked on his cabinetmaking and woodcarving. He discovered to his surprise that his kids felt proud when they earned the money for something they wanted, and that his wife infinitely preferred the pleasure of having him at home to the convenience of having two cars.

So my second outrageous pronouncement about housework . . . or any other paying or nonpaying job—is:

If you don't love doing it, *stop.*

You're only going to live once. *You must have what you want.* So draw up a list of all the things you think you have to do. Then cross out everything you would cross out if you were going to die in six months! And then stop doing them. Your house may not run right. Your lifestyle may go through some interesting mutations. But no one is going to die, no one will get scurvy, no one's teeth will fall out—and no one is going to throw you out on the street for not being a Good Woman or a Good Provider.

Of course you need to take care of other people. It makes you feel connected, and it's rewarding to protect and nurture living things and watch them grow. But *you have no right to give away everything.* If you have two children and a husband or a wife, that's three people you need to love, but there's a very important fourth one—you. There shouldn't be *any* second-rate children in your house. If you treated yourself like a favorite child you would know how to help your husband learn to be nurturing and attached . . . your wife to be a person in her own right.

You would help your children see you as someone who loved life, loved them, and encouraged them to love themselves.

"Selfish" people love with all their hearts. They may not take care of their loved ones from the cradle to the grave, but they do something better: they give them the gift of self-respect and strength and freedom. Self-sacrificers create bonds of guilt. If your children look into your eyes and see delight, they've got a good world. If you're so tired and angry you can't enjoy them, what they're going to feel is, "I don't care about my Christmas present or my lunch. Why don't you ever smile?"

Just try this exercise and ask yourself how you felt about your own parents:

OBLIGATIONS

Did you ever feel guilty about either of your parents? How do you think you would have felt if your mother or father had done a little less for you and a lot more for her/himself?

Here's how some other people answered:

John, 32 years old: "If my mother, instead of making all the beds and making sure I had my lunch, had kept coming in to me—when my bed was unmade and nothing was picked up—and telling me how excited she was about some poem she was writing, I think I'd have had the best life in the world! I think that I'd have felt so enthusiastic about her, so free to go out and do what I wanted, so happy to have some real company instead of a devoted maid who made me feel sad and guilty, that I'd have adapted to the rest."

Harriet, 45 years old: "I can think of no greater single pain in my life than knowing that my mother, 'because of us,' was less than she could have become. And I can think of no greater gift she could have given us than to have been a full, complete, and happy person—because if she had, then I would have had a much easier time finding the full and happy person within myself."

Grace, 27 years old: "My father was the martyr in my family. There were four of us kids, and he worked for years at a routine job to keep us in braces and vacations. I didn't really know what he believed or felt, except that he thought it was good to be the way he was—self-denying for other people's sake. I could never enjoy the "selfishness" he made possible for me, because he made me so ashamed of it. There's a happy ending to this story, though. After we all got out of school my father went through an incredible transformation. He quit his job, pooled his savings with another man, and started a restaurant and jazz club! It's almost as if he was inspired by the changes in his kids' lives and values. I love him so much. I swear, I would have worked my way through college if he could only have been himself when I was growing up."

How would *you* like to have had no guilt about your mother or father?

How would you like your kids to have no guilt about you?

OK. Now let's get back to planning.

YOUR PLANNING WALL

We've talked about finding time for yourself. Now you're also going to need a space that's all your own: one wall of one room in your apartment, house, or garage, preferably with a desk or a table in front of it. If you've got a real space problem—you share a bedroom with your mate, and you've got a small living room and kitchen and that's it—buy a cheap folding screen with which you can temporarily block off one corner of either room. Use the screen, or a moveable bulletin board, for your wall space.

That's your *planning wall,* and on it you're going to put up a series of charts that will map your plan of action out *across time*—month by month, week by week, day by day—like a general mapping out both the broad strategies and the details of his campaign.

The reason for blazoning your plans across a whole wall, instead of hiding them away in a drawer or a notebook, is that you can glance up at any time and see exactly where you are in your flow chart, whether you're ahead of or behind the schedule you've set yourself, what you have to get done *this week,* what you have to do *tomorrow.* (And when you get to knock off work for a while.) When it's all right in front of your eyes, constantly updated, you won't ever get lost—and you won't be able to run away from it! This wall is going to be your conscience and your guide, your security blanket and your boss. And your planned vacation. You might as well have fun designing it.

You can cover your wall with corkboard, and put up your charts with bright-colored push pins. You can stick them on the wall with masking tape, and tear them down and tape up new ones every time your plans change. Or paper a whole wall with glossy shelf paper, and scribble all over it with water-color markers that can be wiped off. Or use the side of a metal filing cabinet—or your refrigerator!—and tack up your plans with magnets. No matter how you design your wall, though, put up a picture of your personal "saint"—the person you chose in Chapter 5 to inspire you and cheer you on. (You can put up pictures of your whole imaginary "family" of winners from Chapter 3, if you want a really substantial cheering section.) You can "report back" to that imaginary friend as a way of acknowledging your own progress whenever you don't have a real friend waiting in the wings to hear how things went.

The real meat of your planning wall begins with:

Your Flow Chart

This belongs right in the center, because it's the master plan that coordinates everything else. If you're one of those wonderful maniacs who plans to pursue more than one goal at a time, like running for City Council and learning to play the piano, you can put up two (or more!) flow charts in different colors.

On the left-hand side of your flow chart it should say "Tomorrow." Now you're going to pick a *target date* and write it under your goal, over on the far right. (You might also like to draw or cut out a picture that symbolizes your goal—a published book, a well-dressed executive at her desk, a house in the country, a horse in a field—and put it up at the end of your flow chart. Some people find that it helps them keep their goal in their mind's eye.) That date is the other end of your "bridge" of actions, and it is what makes it a solid bridge, of a measurable length, with a real destination, not a rainbow with its other end in the clouds.

Of course your target date can only be a rough estimate. After all, we're planning without facts. Once you get out there, a hundred things can roll in that there's no way of predicting—from an unforeseen problem that sets you back two months to a fabulous job offer that advances you six. Life is full of chutes and ladders. Even without major surprises, you'll almost certainly have to adjust your target date simply because you can't know in advance how long things are going to take. For instance, you may have thought you could write a book at the rate of ten pages a day, and then discover that you can only write ten pages a week—or vice versa. In other words, you can and probably will change this date—*but it is very important to set it anyway.* Here's why.

Anybody who's ever gotten married knows that setting the date is a declaration of serious intention—the promise that makes the goal real. Because a date is also a deadline, and you know from experience that that makes the difference between acting like you have all the time in the world and getting yourself in gear.

A 17-year-old boy was standing in line to apply for college. He turned around and discovered that standing right behind him in line was a white-haired old man.

The boy said, "Excuse me, are you . . . I mean, I don't mean to be rude, but what are you doing here?"

"Why, I'm applying for college," said the old man, smiling.

"Would you mind if I ask you how old you are?" said the boy.

"I'm seventy-four."

"But . . . don't you realize that you'll be seventy-eight by the time you graduate?"

"Son," said the old man, "I'll be seventy-eight anyway."

That's the whole point. You'll be 78 anyway. You can do a thousand fabulous things between now and then. If you get with it. And a deadline will make you do that.

If setting deadlines for yourself has never worked before, it's because you kept those dates in your head (or your pocket calendar, where you never look six months ahead). *In your head there is no time!* In your head it is always now. That's why you need a planning wall. On it, you're going to be able to see time blocked out ahead of you as clearly as a hopscotch game, with instructions for each square, each "now."

Only two words of caution about setting your target date. Don't set it so close that it's totally impossible. That's a dirty trick to play on yourself—it will only make you feel inadequate. You are not a machine. You've got to allow some time for Christmas and summer vacation, for laziness, love, and fun. But on the other hand, don't set the date so far away that it gives you lots of slack "just to be safe." You want some pressure and urgency. This piece of work isn't less important than a term paper for your professor or a report for your boss. It is more important, because it's for you. If, after your best efforts, your target date turns out to be "unrealistic," you'll change it with no sense of failure. But if you give yourself three years to write your book, you'll never know what you could have done in one.

Your Goal Calendar

A GOAL CALENDAR is a large sheet of paper divided into boxes, one box for each month between you and your target date.

It can be a six-month goal calendar:

	Jan.	Feb.	Mar.	Apr.	May	June
1980						

or a two-year calendar:

1980												
	Jan.	Feb.	Mar.	Apr.	May	June	July	Aug.	Sept.	Oct.	Nov.	Dec.
1981												

or whatever you need.

Now look at the major steps of your plan—the circles on your flow chart. Important: If your goal is something like writing a novel that doesn't have clearly defined steps—just demands a steady pace of work —invent some big steps: "Finish first draft," "Finish 100 pages," "5 chapters." You will need these landmarks, both to regulate the pace of your work so you don't hit a panic two weeks before target, and to reward you with a frequent, reachable sense of accomplishment. Assign each of these steps a target date of its own, and write *those* deadlines into your goal calendar.

Again, you're going to be doing some fairly wild guessing. It doesn't matter. You can change every one of these dates, if necessary, as you find out what the realities are, but they are guesses you must make in order to get yourself in motion.

Your goal calendar is really what maps your flow chart onto time, giving you a tentative schedule against which you can check your pace and progress.

Jeannette—the would-be traveling photographer—really had a first target: the day of departure for her trip to Appalachia, with a fully-equipped rolling photo lab, a list of places to stay for free, and enough money for traveling expenses. When she got back from her trip, she could draw a new flow chart for the process of putting together and selling her book. So she set a target date for her departure: June 15, 1979. She chose that target date not only to allow enough time to get everything together, but so that she would be driving through Appalachia in summer, when children were out of school.

To leave on June 15 there were three things Jeannette would have to have—goals she would have to meet: equipped truck, addresses, and money. Jeannette decided to allow a good four months before departure for fixing up the old van she planned to buy—two-and-a-half months for the mechanical repair work, and six weeks for converting it into a darkroom. So the van would have to go into repairs no later than February 1. While it was being repaired, she would have time to send out a call through her network of friends for second-hand cameras, as well as for places to stay along her route—which meant, of course, that she'd also need to get her route planned out in February. She then had January to take advertising pictures for the mechanic in trade for repairs. She decided to aim for a pre-Christmas flea market on November 25 to raise the money to buy the truck. She also realized that her best chance of getting a job in a photo store would be during the pre-Christmas rush—and that a lot of film and photographic paper would probably go out of date on January 1. Jeannette marked all of these deadlines on her calendar. She had now organized the tangle of tasks on her flow chart into neat blocks of time that didn't overlap too heavily in any one month, and her calendar for the nine months between her starting point and her target date now looked like this:

Oct.	Nov.	Dec.	Jan.	Feb.	Mar.	Apr.	May	June 15
call mechanic call re truck call friends start looking	organize flea mkt. by 25th	buy truck	advert. pix for mechanic try to get old. film, paper, etc. after 1st	start fixing truck by 1st	network call for cameras	outfit truck network call for cameras	outfit truck	Lab
	look for photo store job							
call re grants				grant applica-tions				$
			get maps	plan route	network call	network call		addr.

For Mary, whose goal was to get into medical school, drawing a goal calendar required meeting an outside-world timetable. So Mary had to do a little research. What was the deadline for medical school applications each year? When were applicants informed about their admission? When were the MedCATs given? When did review courses start?

Mary had begun working toward her goal in March, 1978. A few phone calls to nearby universities quickly informed her that this semester's review courses were already under way, that the MedCATS were given in June and December, and that the deadline for medical school applications was in September. Mary realized that she would have to take the review course starting in the coming fall, and that since she had to work and couldn't possibly study full time, she would probably have to take it over a time span of two semesters. She couldn't apply to medical schools until the fall of 1979, and that would make her target date for entering school the fall of 1980. Mary had a two-and-a-half-year goal calendar!

Now you can begin to see how different a flow chart is from a goal calendar—and how necessary both of them are. Your flow chart gives you the *logic* of your plan. Your goal calendar gives you the actual *timing*, accounting for reality factors like Christmas rush and summer vacation, test dates and application deadlines—and just how long things are likely to take. Your flow chart works each branch of action down to first steps, things you could do tomorrow. Your goal calendar lets you know which of those first steps you *should* start doing tomorrow.

When you've completed your calendar, you've got your plan planted firmly in real time. You've defined your *first steps*—clear-cut, short-term tasks with fairly pressing deadlines. Now you can focus in on those and forget about everything further down the line for the time being. You've entrusted it all to paper; it's there, it's real, it's not going to go away. You don't have to try to carry the whole structure around in your head. Any time you need to know if you're on schedule, you can look ahead at the next deadline on your calendar. And any time you need to be reminded why you're doing what you're doing, you can just glance up at your flow chart and see exactly where today's small action fits into the context of your plan.

Scheduling Your First Steps

Right now you've got your list of first steps to launch you on all the branches of your plan: places to go, people to see, numbers to call, information to look up. Your goal calendar makes it clear to you which of these first steps must take immediate priority and which can wait. What you're going to do now is tack up a list of those immediate-priority steps on your planning wall—and then start scheduling them, one by one, into the days of this week, next week, and the week after that.

We're going to schedule one week at a time. Some of the steps you take may turn out to be blind alleys, and you'll have to come up with new ones to replace them. (For instance, Jeannette might call and find out the man with the broken-down van has already sold it. Then she'd have to start looking for another one: asking her friends, checking classified ads in the paper, putting notices on bulletin boards, etc.) On the other hand, one step may hit the jackpot and catapult you into the next phase of your plan, making five other steps unnecessary. (Jeannette might walk into a photo store and strike up a conversation with a store manager who couldn't give her a job, but liked her plan and was willing to donate old film and paper.) Once you get into action, each week is really going to be a whole new ball game.

Weekly Calendar

You're going to put up a fresh weekly calendar each week, at your own personal Sunday night planning meeting (see p. 239). Use a week-at-a-glance calendar, or hang a whole pad of paper on your planning wall and just tear off each week as it's finished.

How many of the steps on your master list you can schedule into any week depends, of course, on how much time you've been able to set aside for goal work. Jeannette had a full-time job, but she'd cleared most lunch hours, one hour two evenings a week, and Sunday afternoons. Her list of first steps read:

1. Call Ned in Susan's office about van
2. Call Abby's brother about van repairs
3. Call friends to arrange flea-market planning meeting
4. Call Tony A. for advice on grants
5. Check Yellow Pages for photo stores near my office
6. Start looking for photo-store job
7. Call Abby: report back

Obviously, after talking to Tony about grants, checking out the Yellow Pages, and having her flea-market meeting, she'll have a number of *follow-up* steps to add to her master list on Sunday night and to start scheduling on her next week's calendar.

Mary, by contrast, had an even fuller schedule of responsibilities—and only one immediate first step to schedule over the next four months: reviewing her old college science notes. Your weekly calendars may look like Mary's if your job is to make slow, steady progress toward a subgoal like researching a particular business or topic—or a goal like writing a book. (If your life is as crowded as Mary's, you may also want to schedule your relaxation time to remind yourself that you need and deserve it.)

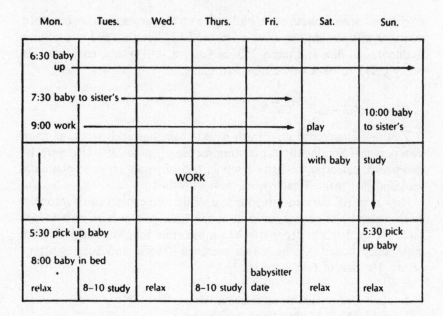

Mon.	Tues.	Wed.	Thurs.	Fri.	Sat.	Sun.
6:30 baby up →→						
7:30 baby to sister's →→→→→→→→→→→→→→→→→→→→→→→					10:00 baby to sister's	
9:00 work →→→→→→→→→→→→→→→→→→→→→→→→→→→→→→→→				play		
↓			WORK		with baby	study
					↓	↓
5:30 pick up baby						5:30 pick up baby
8:00 baby in bed						
relax	8–10 study	relax	8–10 study	babysitter date	relax	relax

The next step is very easy—and very important. You transfer the information from the weekly calendar on your planning wall into your purse or pocket calendar. *This is the step that really gets things done.*

Purse or Pocket Appointments Book

This little calendar is the piece of your planning machinery that travels around with you and reminds you what you're supposed to do at lunchtime today and at 3:00 P.M. tomorrow. Most of us already use pocket calendars to remind us of business lunches, dentist appointments, birthdays, and social engagements. If you don't, I recommend starting now—you'll discover that a pocket calendar is at least as indispensable as a wristwatch. If you do use one, you know that writing something in that calendar virtually assures that you will do it. And that's because you've got an *appointment.* Not an option; not something you may or may not do depending on whether you remember, whether you feel like it, and the weather; but something you've contracted to do at a particular time. In this case, the contract is with yourself—the most important person in your life, and the one person to whom you may never have accorded the simple respect you give your doctor or your date. But once you write a goal step in your pocket calendar, it becomes as real as a doctor's appointment. And like a doctor's appointment, unless there's a blizzard, it doesn't make much difference how you feel—when the time comes you'll do it.

This is that wonderful thing called *structure*. It has a momentum of its own, and it will keep you rolling along with it through all your ups and downs. You don't have to be solemn and military about these plans. They are an aid to help you get what you want—and they will. Even if you sometimes skip a scheduled step, you'll get many, many more of them done than if they weren't assigned to specific days in your calendar. (When you have no structure, you can just bury the whole idea the first time you get discouraged or scared.) And as you do those steps, you'll be making real progress toward your goal.

Each phone call you make, each article you read, every office or museum you visit, forges another link in the chain. Many of these steps are so small that you don't need "self-confidence" or "self-esteem" to do them. And yet they're going to give you the self-esteem of cumulative accomplishment—the only kind there really is. At the end of each day, you can note down what you did in the Actions & Feelings Journal you started keeping in Chapter 5. At the end of each week, you can look back at your weekly calendar and see how many things you've actually done. (Whether they've all worked out or not, they will have given you what you need most: the experience of goal-directed action.) And then you can check your progress against your goal calendar and see how far you've already come. If you're making more rapid progress than you anticipated, shift your deadlines forward. If you're slipping behind schedule, step up your pace—scheduling two steps a day instead of one or using Saturday afternoons as well as Sundays—or decide that your deadlines are unrealistic, and push them back.

You'll make many other changes in your planning wall. You may get a totally unexpected job offer; you may fall in love and go off on a two-month cruise to the Bahamas; you may decide to change your goal. So you'll pull down all your charts and start over. You may want to draw a new flow chart halfway through your plan, when the details of the later stages are much clearer. What I'm giving you here isn't an absolute, it's a flexible set of skills for building large plans out of small, steady actions *without losing sight of either the detail or the whole.* Gloria, 36, who had conceived a complex and ambitious plan to found a textile-design and learning center, had this to say about it:

"My plan seems big and I'm nervous about it, but I know there's one thing that's going to make me feel secure, and that's my planning wall. Even if there are unknowns ahead that frighten me, I'll feel fine now that I understand how to work with these different kinds of charts. I'm a visual person in my work, and it really helps me to be able to see it all in black and white."

Speaking of the detail and the whole, there are two more items that are very handy to have on your planning wall. They frame the whole vista of time, from your very next step to the far horizon, and remind you that to make the best of your one stay on Earth, you've got to think both large and small.

The Next Five Years

At the end of your Goalsearch, when we did "Five Lives," I encouraged you to think about a larger life plan that includes all your dreams and goals. Here's where you put that life plan into a real time frame. Of course, you have no way of knowing what you'll really be doing—or wanting—in five years. But of all the forces that will be operating on your life over those years—chance and love and loss and luck, health and economics and history—your wish and will, your own unfolding, should be one of the strongest. And it can be. That's what this book is all about.

Here, for instance, is what my writer friend Julia put down:

1980	1981	1982	1983	1984
write	write	live in Mexico learn Spanish	house in country have baby	study violin

Having this sketch of the next five years on your planning wall serves two purposes. It gives you an extra nudge to meet your deadlines, because it reminds you of all the adventures that are still waiting for you. And as you log in solid progress toward your current goal, those future dreams are also going to start looking much more real and possible. Your reach will grow with your grasp as you realize from experience that you really can shape your destiny with your own hands.

The Next Step

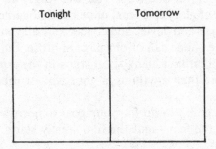

Tonight | Tomorrow

Like your weekly calendar, this is most conveniently drawn on a pad of paper you hang on your planning wall. You can tear the top sheet off every day and fill out a new one, entering the information from your weekly calendar.

It may seem redundant to write down again what you're going to do tonight or tomorrow when you've already got your actions laid out day by day on your wall and in your pocket calendar. But it can be tremendously helpful, and I'll tell you why. First of all, it lets you clear your mind of everything but what you have to do the next day. You can focus on that one action and make sure you're prepared for it. If you have a phone call to make at lunch hour from the office, you'll want to make sure you've got the number written in your pocket calendar. You may want to run through what you're going to say, or even make cue notes for yourself. If you have an interview coming up, it might be a good idea to rehearse it, and to pick out what you're going to wear so you won't be frantic in the morning. I'll have a lot more to say about preparation in the next chapter. It's one of the world's greatest antidotes for the shakes.

Second, a tonight/tomorrow sheet is a forceful reminder that action is always *now*. The present is where it's got to be happening, or it isn't going to happen at all. The most important action in your whole plan isn't that big meeting next week, or even your goal—it's what you're going to do *tomorrow*. Your goal is only as real as that step! Handle it as best you can, and your goal will take care of itself. Don't handle it—and the biggest talent or the best imagination in the world won't budge you one inch off dead center.

That's reassuring, in one way. You can forget all about the exaggerated fantasies of glory and fears of defeat that gather around a large ambition like angels and devils, and concentrate all your creative energy on the text of one phone call or one page of prose. But in another way, that first call, or that first blank sheet stuck in the typewriter, is going to scare you more than anything in your wildest dreams.

Because it's real.

What are you going to do for your goal tomorrow?

This is where the fear—and the fun—really starts.

Four

Crafting II:
Moving and Shaking

—9—
Winning Through Timidation, or First Aid for Fear

Up to this point, everything you've done—with the possible exception of throwing a barn-raising party—has been on paper. If you haven't been too nervous, it's because you haven't had to do anything dangerous yet.

The structure you've built on your planning wall has led you right up to the threshold of action, and it has taken away a lot of your old excuses for not acting—like not knowing where to start, or despairing of ever getting there (your flow chart shows you exactly how you are going to get there), or thinking you'll get around to it someday. So having a structure makes it a lot likelier that you will act. But it can't *make* you act at the moment when you encounter what Carlos Castaneda's Don Juan called "the first enemy"—*fear.*

Fear strikes when you feel as if you'd been so busy building and climbing a ladder that you forgot there was a thirty-foot diving board at the top. All of a sudden you're teetering out at the end of that board, with your toes curling over the edge, and the loudspeaker is booming, "Hello! Are you ready?" And as the spotlight hits you and the drums begin to roll, you feel like yelling, "Wait a minute! I thought we were just having fun! I didn't know I was actually going to have to *jump!*"

That may not happen to you the first day you start work on your goal, because many first steps are as small and simple as just walking down the steps into the shallow end of the pool. There's nothing particularly intimidating about a trip to the library or the newsstand. But you keep taking those little steps, and one day very soon you're going to find yourself out on the end of your first thirty-foot board. It may be a job interview, or a dramatic audition, or the first day of a class, or the day you finish your nice safe research and have to start writing. But whatever it is, it will have an element of *the unknown* (you've never done this before); a strong *investment* (both your dreams and your self-image are at stake); and a corresponding *risk* (you may get hurt, mess up, make a fool of yourself, find out you're not good enough).

The funny thing is, you may or may not know it when you encounter the first enemy. The physical symptoms of fear are unmistakable: icy hands, wobbly knees, blushing, stammering, a runaway heart, and a seasick stomach. The body has a candor that's refreshing, if sometimes embarrassing. But the mind is much sneakier. It thinks fear is beneath its dignity, so it will try to save face by persuading you that you're not scared at all—you just suddenly remembered you had pressing business elsewhere. Since it's important to know when you are dealing with fear, I'm going to show you some of its most common disguises, so that you'll be able to unmask it in a flash.

KNOW YOUR ENEMY

If you've ever had any of the following thoughts, feelings, or experiences in the course of trying to do or get what you want, you have met fear. Put a check mark beside the ones that are familiar to you, because you're going to be meeting them again very soon.

☐   An overwhelming desire to sleep: you're suddenly so tired
☐   An overwhelming desire to eat: you're suddenly famished
☐   An overwhelming attraction to the paperback rack: you must read *Love's Tender Fury* or the latest Travis McGee mystery *now*
☐   The soothing thought, "I've got plenty of time. It can wait till tomorrow."
☐   A suddenly blank mind: you were fermenting with plans and ideas, now you're the Village Idiot

☐   A sudden ferment of plans and ideas about eighteen other dreams you'd rather have first, before this one ("Gee, I've never been to Europe . . . I can always start my business when I get back.")

☐   A sudden loss of interest in your goal: it fascinated you in theory, but in reality it's boring, not for you at all (NOTE: Hidden fear will try to trick you into changing your goal whenever it starts getting challenging. That's why so many of us have picked up and dropped so many activities—not because we're "dilettantes" who can't make up our minds.)

☐   A sudden conviction that you don't have what it takes for this goal ("Whatever made me think I was aggressive enough for a job in sales? I'm really a very shy, retiring person.")

When fear strikes—whether it's bare-faced or in one of these disguises—what's to stop you from saying, "I've changed my mind. I'm not ready yet"? What's to stop you from tearing up all your charts, stuffing them in the wastebasket, kicking this book into a corner, and deciding that goals are just a bad ego trip and you'd rather join a Zen monastery or get pregnant instead?

I'll tell you what's to stop you from letting fear stop you. *Everything in this section.* Because I happen to believe that missing out on your dreams and never finding out what you're capable of is a hell of a high price to pay for peace. You have the right to get what you want and become all you can be—and sometimes that means you have a right to *act* even when every nerve in your body is screaming "Stop!!" The secret is to turn the "first enemy" into a stimulating companion, advisor, and friend.

Fear is the natural companion of creative action. There is only one way to live free of fear—and that is to live without hope, change, or growth. Do you want to know what "self-confidence" really is? Just think about how you feel when you're doing something you've done so may times you could do it in your sleep—like tying your shoes. That is self-confidence, and that's all it is: know-how verging on boredom. Do you remember the first time you tied your own shoes? You weren't self-confident then. You were nervous, excited, and unsure. But you mastered shoe-tying, and you soon moved on to bigger things in which, once again, you had no self-confidence—like arithmetic . . . and jitterbugging . . . and driving a car. That's the game we're playing. That's the law of human growth. Would you like to do nothing but tie your shoes again for the rest of your life so you'd never have to feel nervous again?

There's no way around it. When you start moving, you start shaking. Every time you try anything new, anything that really summons and stretches your capacities—in short, anything worth doing—you're going to feel uncertainty and self-doubt as well as challenge and exhilaration. That is the healthy fear called *stage fright,* and I'm going to let you in on what all accomplished people know: how to live with it and love it. It's a good friend that lets you know you're on the right track, that what you're doing is big enough for you. There are easy ways to make yourself move right through it, and as soon as you do, it turns into pure excitement.

For many of us, however, stage fright is complicated by another kind of fear, much deeper and more disabling. I call it *survival fear.*

Survival fear is most common in "first-generation winners"—people whose families didn't know how to prepare them for action. The people it doesn't afflict are the rare ones who've had lots of loving support and who've been shown *how* to do things, so they could start getting experience early. To those lucky people, the unknown is just . . . the unknown. There could be a lady or a tiger behind that door, but they're prepared for either one. They've handled both before. They know they can call on reinforcements in an emergency. They aren't going to open that door without nervous palpitations, but you can bet they're going to open it. They have had the security human beings need for risk and adventure.

For those of us who haven't had emotional and practical backing, however, the unknown is the part of the map with the dragons in it. When we don't know what's coming, we expect the worst. If you feel a mistake or a failure would be so devastating that you don't even dare try, that's survival fear. So is the paralysis that strikes when you demand a performance of yourself that's far beyond your skill and experience—like trying to write the Great American Novel the first time you sit down to write. If you think someone you love will be hurt or hate you or divorce you if you start getting what you want, that's survival fear, too.

All survival fear is exaggerated. It gets its intensity from a child's-eye view of the world that many of us were never helped to outgrow. Of course one mistake isn't going to be the end of you. Every great novelist, salesman, doctor, or anything else began as an inexperienced beginner.

And it's an extremely rare husband who's really going to divorce his wife for painting instead of ironing his shirts. Your *mind* knows that. Your *feelings* don't. The best antidote for those feelings is the adult experience of going ahead and doing the thing and finding out that nothing so terrible happens after all—*but it's precisely that experience that the fear prevents us from getting.* So we're caught in a vicious cycle, a lot like the old circular saw about a job: "Can't get self-confidence without experience; can't get experience without self-confidence."

How can you tell stage fright from survival fear? With just a little encouragement and Hard Times, you can push right through stage fright. Survival fear is too strong. You can't bluff and brave your way through it—and for a very good reason. As exaggerated as it is, that fear has a real message for you. It's trying to tell you that there's something you need and have got to get before you can afford to take risks and have adventures. It may be practical preparation or emotional support; it may be permission to lower perfectionist standards or to make mistakes. The message will be different for different people. But whatever it is you need, if you don't get it and you try to go ahead without it, you really will get hurt. And your body knows it.

So the only way to break the vicious cycle of survival fear is to *respect the fear and pay attention to it.* If you decode the *survival message* and take care of your need, all that's going to be left of your fear is stage fright—and that's the easy part.

SURVIVAL MESSAGE NO. 1: PREPARE

Suppose you have something to do that you've never done before —say something that involves presenting or selling yourself, like going for a job interview, asking for a raise, or taking samples of your handmade greeting cards around to gift shops. You're scared. Being scared just makes you feel more inadequate, more sure that you're going to lose the power of speech and trip over your own feet. So what you usually do is try to fight the fear, either steeling yourself with will power or relaxing yourself by deep breathing. That doesn't work very well, and the reason it doesn't is because it misses the most important point: you have never done this thing before, and *you don't know how.*

In this situation, self-doubt is not a weakness—it's a valuable warning signal. It's telling you you're about to go off the thirty-foot board without ever having had a diving lesson in your life, and that's dumb! The worst thing about Positive Thinking is that it tries to override this natural signal and push you into the arena full of blind, unfounded confidence. That can get you so badly hurt that you'll never try again. *A positive attitude is a rotten substitute for knowing what you're doing.* If I told you, "You're wonderful, you can do it!" and sent you into the ring against Muhammad Ali, I'd be guilty of murder. The least I could do for your self-doubt in that case would be boxing lessons.

The survival message here is an urgent request for *preparation: information, instruction,* and *rehearsal.* You aren't supposed to be born knowing everything—although some men and most women think they are. If you don't know something, say, "I'd better find out." Don't say, "There's something wrong with me, and if I ask, everybody will know."

Information and Instruction

This is where you can really *use your network.* If you have a difficult phone call, interview, or sales pitch coming up, find someone who's done that kind of thing and ask: "What should I say? How do I act? What should I wear?" Get a close approximation of the actual words you're going to say. *Write them down.* If you like, you can use them as a little script for rehearsal, or as cue cards for a phone call.

Another thing you need to know is the questions that are likely to be asked of you, so you can be ready with the answers. If the owner of a gift shop likes your greeting cards and then asks you, "Advance or consignment? And what's the retail discount?" you don't want to stand there opening and closing your mouth; it doesn't look professional, and it feels awful. Again, someone who's had experience is the source to go to. If you're scheduled for a job interview in a particular company, it will help you to know as much as you can about that company in advance: what its priorities and objectives are, what kind of ability and personality they're looking for, even what kinds of questions they ask in their job interviews! Read about the company. Talk with somebody who works there. You'll get a better sense of what you have to offer in the context of that company, and you'll impress the interviewer with your initiative and interest.

Rehearsal

It may seem silly to you to actually practice a phone call or interview, but it's one of the most reassuring things you can do if you're nervous. Knowledge hastily filed in your head is more likely to desert you under the pressure of stage fright than knowledge you've programmed into your behavior so it's at least semiautomatic. Actors know that. They don't just memorize their lines and then walk on stage opening night. They rehearse.

It helps a lot to have someone to rehearse to, who plays the other part, throws you your cues, and helps you shape up your performance. It's good practice to stand up in front of someone and talk, whether it's your mate, your child, or a friend. (The next chapter will tell you how to enlist that kind of help.) But there are also two very useful kinds of rehearsing you can do by yourself, in fantasy.

SuperMe/SuperFool

Know how you sometimes lie awake in the safety of your bed imagining the perfect conversation or argument, in which you are devastatingly witty, utterly poised, and say all the right things? And how, on the other hand, when you're in the throes of stage fright, you imagine utter catastrophe? Both kinds of fantasy have a purpose. They are instinctive efforts to *prepare*. Here's how you can help them help you.

Whatever it is you've got coming up, sit back in a comfortable chair, close your eyes, relax, and imagine how you'd do it if you were perfect. A flawless performance by the person you wish you were, the person you've only seen in movies and daydreams . . . who doesn't exist.

Now change the scene. Shut your eyes, tense up, and imagine the worst disaster that could possibly befall you. You walk into the office smiling with your hand stuck out, trip over the rug, and fall on your face. You stutter. The magazine editor, leafing through your short story about the death of your dog, starts to laugh. You forget your own name. Whatever. Just make it a real pratfall—the worst.

Now open your eyes.

This exercise will bring you the great relief of realizing that *you're not either one.* SuperMe doesn't exist, it's true—but SuperFool doesn't either. Since you can't possibly be perfect (and no one else is either), why torture yourself trying to be, or punish yourself for failing to be? On the other hand, no matter how badly you mess up, you'll never live down to your SuperFool fantasies. So you can stop worrying on that score. You've now explored the most extreme possibilities, and you can be sure that the reality is going to fall somewhere in between. But you can get a few helpful hints from your SuperMe fantasy. That paragon may have come up with some genuinely elegant ideas, gestures, or lines. It was your imagination that scripted them—it won't be plagiarism if you use them!

Role-Play the Opposition

It will help you to be prepared for an interview or encounter if you sit in a chair and imagine that you are the person you're going to meet, watching *you* come into the room. You've had practice at this way back in Chapter 3—"Seeing Yourself as Others See You." That time, you wrote down everything nice that the person you were role-playing could see in you. This time, however, you are role-playing a prospective employer, backer, retailer, or customer—someone who has wants, needs, and expectations you will have to meet if the encounter is to be a success. Useful questions to ask yourself are: "What is this person looking for in the way of an employee/investment opportunity/retail item? Would s/he be more impressed by a conservative, casual, or strikingly original appearance? What kinds of questions is s/he likely to ask? How do I look to this person? Is there a mismatch between his or her expectations and the way I present myself? If so, what is it and how can I fix it?"

I disagree with people who think it's possible to be "overprepared." I really don't think there is such a thing. Just as long as you don't forget that the real situation will be different from your practice sessions, that it remains fundamentally unpredictable, preparation can do you nothing but good. There are going to be enough unknowns in the actual encounter without adding unnecessary ones! Preparation doesn't cure stage fright, but it does make you feel a lot more secure than if you were walking into a strange situation cold. And once you've had some experience, you won't need as much preparation, because your experience will be your preparation.

SURVIVAL MESSAGE NO. 2: LOWER YOUR STANDARDS— AT FIRST

This is the merciful message fear is trying to get across to you whenever you freeze with your paintbrush in midair . . . or your fingers an inch above the typewriter keys . . . or your mouth open to make your first insurance sales pitch. No matter how prepared you are for your first day on a new job, or the first real page of a novel you've been making notes on for months, this is different. This is *real*. You've never done it before, and if you expect yourself to do it the first time with the finesse of someone doing it for the thousandth time, you'll be in trouble. You won't be able to do it at all.

There are many reasons for becoming this kind of premature perfectionist. You may have had overly high standards imposed on you as a kid. Or, like me, you may have been told that you were a wonderful genius who could do anything in the world, but never told *how*. Or maybe you grew up in what I call an "audience family": people who regard great achievements as the effortless products of a superior species, and can't see the long, slow, human process of development that leads up to them. Any of these early experiences can create a humiliating gap between your fantasy of what you *could* do and the reality of what you *can* do.

Your vision of what you could do isn't necessarily wrong. The problem is that your vision and ambition have outgrown your experience and skill. To give them a chance to catch up, you have to allow yourself to do what you never got a chance to do as a child: *start at the beginning*. I know it feels funny to be an adult beginner in our precocious society, but there are wonderful rewards. The world is kind to beginners the way it's kind to preschool children. They get lots of help and praise, and they're allowed to play.

Professional First Steps: 'Fess Up, Don't Mess Up

Bernadette, 46, had passed her real-estate certification course with flying colors, but it was her first day as an agent and she was facing her first customer. The man had asked a routine question about mortgage rates, and Bernadette knew she was supposed to have the answer at her fingertips. But her mind had gone blank. The seconds ticked past as she waited for the man to realize that she wasn't a competent professional at all, just an impostor pretending to be one. Then she'd lose the sale. But finally she had to say something, so she admitted, "This is my first day on the job. I'm sorry, I'll have to look that up."

The customer said, "Oh, are you just starting out in this business? Great! I'll have to bring my wife over to meet you. Now that our kids are growing up, she's wondering whether it's too late to get some kind of professional training."

You know from your own experience that if a tour guide, taxi driver, or librarian fumbles around, takes too long, and makes mistakes, you get annoyed—unless he or she tells you, "It's my first day. I'm new at this." Then you immediately become sympathetic and curious! If it's the other way around and you're the one in the hot seat, the worst thing you can do is try to act experienced and suave. The strain of keeping up the act will make you twice as clumsy and prone to mistakes. Admitting you're a beginner, on the other hand, instantly creates a warm, relaxed, low-risk atmosphere in which—paradoxically—your performance improves. Even medical students new on the wards, who are terrified of hurting someone with a misplaced needle, are often soothed and reassured by the patients themselves! You won't be a beginner for long. More will be expected of you even a week or a month from now. But by that time you'll be ready for it.

Creative First Steps: Start Badly

When you're starting a first creative project or beginning the study of an art or craft, what I want you to do is lower your standards until they disappear. That's right. You're not supposed to be any good at the beginning. So you might as well give yourself the liberating gift of joyously expecting yourself to be *bad*.

Forty-three-year-old Matthew wanted to take up drawing and painting again after a twenty-year lapse, but he found all kinds of excuses not to start. The biggest thing stopping his hand was the fear that he wouldn't be any good. So I told him that his first step was to go home and do a bad drawing of the cat, the coffeepot—anything, just as long as it was *bad*. He had to do at least one terrible drawing every night for a week. The point was simply to get his hand moving—by getting rid of the paralyzing expectation that he demonstrate a skill he couldn't possibly have. And it worked. He looked through his first sheaf of "bad" drawings with surprised pleasure. Of course they weren't that bad at all.

Elaine, a 30-year-old English teacher, did not want to be an English teacher all her life. She had a secret fantasy of becoming a best-selling mystery writer, which she was embarrassed to confess because she had never been able to get past page 1 of a thriller. The solution for Elaine was to set herself the unthreatening task of writing just ten *bad* pages a week, working early in the mornings before school. She is now 150 pages into her first book, and she's having so much fun working out the intricacies of the plot that she's forgotten to worry about whether it's good or not. When it's finished, maybe she'll revise it and get it published to hosannas and dollars, or maybe she'll decide to put it away in a drawer and write another one, using everything she's learned from the first. But she's a working writer now, instead of a wishful thinker, and her talent is getting the exercise it needs to grow.

First steps are supposed to be small and manageable, remember? That's what makes it possible to do them. And "Become a good painter" or "Write a best-seller" is not a small, manageable step. It's a major goal. If you ever want to get there, take my advice and make your first steps something like, "one *bad* page a day" or "one roll of *bad* photographs a week." You will tighten up your standards later—when you have the experience to match them. In the meantime, remember the lesson of SuperFool: the worst you produce can't possibly be as bad as the worst you can imagine. And you might also like to remember this cheerful piece of advice from Robert Townsend: "Anything worth doing is worth doing badly."

The Graduated-Risk Principle

Raising a talent or ability is like raising a child. When you start out, you need to be allowed to make any kind of mess you want. No one should criticize you—least of all yourself. As your competence grows, it can be given simple tasks to master, then gradually harder ones; it can be introduced little by little to wider and more discriminating audiences. You've got to pace new challenges and demands so that your skill gets stretched a little more each time, but never snapped or hopelessly outdistanced. A good basic principle is: "Your reach should always be one step ahead of your grasp." You can build this kind of graduated risk right into your planning.

The safest arena is solitude. You don't want to get stuck there, but it's the place to start if other people's eyes make you feel judged and self-conscious. Robert, a New Journalist, developed his own distinctive style by keeping journals that no one ever saw. Matthew didn't have to show his first "bad" drawings to anyone. When no one is watching, you can play freely, and that freedom of movement is crucial for discovering and developing the natural direction of your talent. Training and discipline can come later.

Unless your creative goal is just for your own private pleasure, the next step should be to set a *target date* for venturing out and showing your work to someone else. Make it your family or a close friend—someone who is not an expert in your chosen field. At this stage of the game you don't want professional critical judgment, you want loving appreciation. You need to experience the world as a welcoming place. Your family and friends will think you're fabulous, and their praises and suggestions will help you discover that it's safe to be your growing self in front of others' eyes. Only then can you move into a more impersonal and demanding arena.

After Matthew had been showing his drawings to his friends for a few weeks, he wanted to start getting some training, but he still got the shakes at the thought of being up against other students in the competitive atmosphere of a classroom. He realized that he knew a woman painter who taught in her home, so he arranged to take private lessons for a while. After just a month he had gotten enough guidance and encouragement from that teacher to sign up for drawing classes at a small art school. From there he "graduated" a few months later to painting classes at a major art school.

Matthew had to cope with the fear of not being good enough, and he was only studying painting for his own pleasure! That's how tyrannical our inner critics are. But what if your goal requires that you meet a combination of inner and outer standards—like Andrea, who wanted to become a famous photographer? Her first goal was "To publish one or more photographs of celebrities in a quality national magazine." And one of her problems was, "I'm afraid I'm not good enough." Since creative "self-confidence" breaks down to nothing more mysterious than practice and graduated outward confirmation, you can brainstorm it just like any other strategic problem. That's what Andrea did.

"Problem: I can't because I don't have X—X, in this case, being 'Knowing I'm good enough.' Then Question No. 1, 'How can I get it without X?' becomes, 'How can I get my goal without knowing I'm good enough?' I can't. If I don't have at least some confidence in my ability, I know I'll never even approach a magazine editor. I don't want to make a total fool of myself. So I'd better try Question No. 2: 'All right—how can I get X? How will I know when I'm good enough to show my work to magazine editors?' "

Notice that that's a question like "How will I know when I'm a movie star?" It cries out for a *target*—a clearly-defined action or event. If Andrea waited till she felt good enough, she'd never march up to an editor's door, because that kind of subjective self-confidence vanishes like a mirage in the throes of stage fright. So what Andrea did was to set up an *external confirmation* of her ability that she'd have to accept even if she was terrified: "I'll know I'm good enough when a professional photographer whose work I respect tells me so."

Now Andrea could ask herself, "How will I know when I'm good enough to show my work to a professional photographer?" She set an adequate but firm limit to the amount of "safe" practice she allowed herself: her answer was, "After three months of taking pictures and showing them to my friends." At that point, she could ask her network of friends to give her a personal introduction to a photographer, which would put the "test" in an informal context and make it less intimidating.

The fact is, however, that no matter how prepared you are, *each time you move to a higher level of performance or a more exacting audience, you're going to get scared all over again*—like a diver who's gotten very comfortable on the three-foot board, but feels sick the first time he has to go off the ten-footer. If it's true that you cannot be overprepared, it's equally true that you will never be ready. That's why you had to set definite dates for each step in your plan. The moment comes when you've got to act, ready or not.

I sometimes think the biggest single difference between men and women is that if a boy is scared of something, he has to do it anyway or face ridicule, while a girl is allowed to chicken out without too much disgrace—and sometimes even with approval. Timidity is supposed to be "feminine." Of course, that ethic is changing now. But it's one of the reasons why so many of us grown women missed out on the experience that would have freed us from the witch's tower of inaction, fantasy, and fear.

I want you to have the experience of moving right through fear. Because there's only one way to get really burned—and that's to stop because you're scared. *That's what* real *failure is.* Look back over your life, and I think you'll find that your cop-outs have cost you much more than your worst mistakes. When you fell on your behind, at least you learned that the ground is hard and you're not made of glass. But when you quit, you didn't learn anything.

Let's suppose that you've taken care of Survival Message No. 1 or No. 2. (There's a third powerful survival fear—the fear of being alone —that we're going to deal with separately, because you can't deal with it by yourself.) All that's left now is the last barrier: stage fright. You bust through that once, and you're home free. The next four steps are to help you do it.

HARD TIMES REPRISE: BE SCARED

If you feel scared before you make a difficult move, don't fight it. Let yourself be scared. It's your body's natural response to novelty and uncertainty, and it's designed to tune you up to peak readiness—not to paralyze you. It's only the fear of fear that can do that, not fear itself.

The hard time is the day or the hour *before* you go into action. This is when all the frank physical symptoms of fear show up. You may feel like you're going to have a heart attack, or not make it to the bathroom. But all that's really happening is that you're anticipating, the energy of readiness is revving up, and it doesn't have an outlet yet. So give it an outlet. Move. Pace the floor, punch the wall, shred paper, shiver, dance. Make noise. Moan, complain, growl, swear, scream, and cry. I will never understand why we were taught that we had to behave like Mature Adults under these circumstances. Let's dispense with maturity. If you're doing difficult, scary, grown-up things that are right for you, that's enough. You shouldn't have to act like a grown-up too. You have the right to act like an absolute infant—right up to the moment when you walk through that door or the voice on the other end of the phone says "Hello?"

Obviously you can't allow yourself to fall apart in an "onstage" situation. A bad mood under fire is the luxury of losers. So just do your falling apart beforehand—and afterwards! Throw a tantrum in the wings before you make your entrance—it will get the energy flowing. Then, when the heat is on, be a pro. When you come "offstage" and it's all over, you can go to pieces—you have that relief to look forward to. Minimize the heroics. It will help you concentrate them where they really count—in the action itself.

TASK THERAPY

When the moment comes, and your hand is on the doorknob or your toes are wiggling out over thirty feet of space, follow one simple rule:

DO IT RIGHT, DO IT WRONG, BUT DO IT.

Squeeze your eyes shut and jump. Because a wonderful thing happens then. Your focus shifts from yourself, your nervousness, and your imagined inadequacies to the task at hand.

The trouble with the debate about "self-doubt" versus "self-confidence" is that it has you thinking about yourself at all. You may have noticed that at the times when you're feeling best, you do very little thinking about yourself. You are a background of awareness, not an object in the foreground. You only focus attention on yourself when you feel bad. And then, of course, you can't see anything else. It's hard to tear your eyes away from the worry: "What's *wrong* with me? Why am I depressed/scared?"

Insight therapy takes those questions seriously and seeks the causes in your past. It's fascinating and helps you feel better, but it doesn't necessarily lead to action. "Task therapy" says, "All that's wrong with you is that you're human. You're full of mixed feelings and unresolved conflicts. So what? You've got a job to do. Do it." The funny thing is that the minute you switch your attention from the unsolvable problem inside you to the solvable problem in front of you, you feel a surge of energy and relief. And afterwards, looking at what you accomplished in one hour will do more to heal your self-doubt than ten hours of self-analysis.

DON'T BE AFRAID OF MISTAKES

"Yes, but what if I make a terrible mistake? What if I fail?"

Well, what if you do? What's so terrible about that?

Many grown-up people feel that one failure, setback, or mistake will be a sign of ultimate defeat and worthlessness. But look at any child learning to walk! That child will have to fall down at least a hundred times before it masters the art, and instinctively it knows it. Watch what any 1-year-old does when she falls down. She has a fit—not so much in pain as in impatience and fury. Then she crawls over to the nearest chair leg, pulls herself up, and tries again. If that child fell down once and gave up, she would never learn to walk. And that's a beautiful model for every kind of learning.

You will never learn or accomplish or create anything of value if you cannot let yourself make mistakes. All successful people know this. You tell a top achiever in any field, "I failed. I feel like giving up," and she or he will say, "You're crazy." Herman Melville, of *Moby Dick,* went so far as to say, "He who has never failed somewhere . . . cannot be great. Failure is the true test of greatness." And this is from a *Quest* magazine profile of rock climber Royal Robbins:

It's disturbing, perhaps, to think of Robbins, one of the greatest climbers alive, as losing his hold and falling—after all, if *he* falls, what about us? —but the reason has nothing to do with lack of ability. Robbins falls

when he attempts something that is at the very limit of his powers, and
it is his nature always to extend these limits. He expects a fall and is
prepared for it.*

There is a strange and comforting relationship between failure and
preparation. It's a common assumption that if you really try your
hardest to get something and don't get it, you'll be shattered—so it's
safer not to risk going all out. That is totally false. The exact opposite
is true. If you've prepared for every contingency you can imagine, and
then it doesn't work out, you won't feel so bad. You'll just say, "Damn!
Well, three cheers for me, I really tried," and go on to the next thing.
You never feel really bad when you've given something your best shot.
You may be disappointed, but you don't blame yourself. But if you
haven't given it your best shot, you feel terrible. Because you never
really know whether you could have done better . . . but you do know
you could have done more. Win or lose, all-out efforts leave you feeling
clean and good about yourself.

REWARD YOURSELF

I do not happen to be a believer in the cliché that "Virtue is its own
reward." As far as I'm concerned, the reward for virtue should be at
least a chocolate sundae, and preferably a cruise to the Bahamas. Virtue
is damned hard work and frequently uncomfortable. Yes, the results are
satisfying in themselves—immensely so. But the satisfaction of accomplishment is much too complex, adult, and uncertain a reward to promise the frightened child in you. S/he needed something simple, sure, and
sweet to look forward to, like a lollipop after getting a shot. And I bet
you never said "No, thanks," to the lollipop afterwards because your
relief and pride were enough! You took all the goodies you could get.
And you still should. The more you give yourself, the less vitamin
deficiencies you'll have.

There are not one but two kinds of rewards you should plan to make
a regular feature of your success program.

The first is the kind of reward you earn. You get to look forward to
it before you do a hard thing, and then to savor it afterwards. It could

*James Salter, "Man Is His Own Star: Royal Robbins and the Art of Pure Ascent," *Quest,* vol.
II, no.2, March–April 1978, p. 28.

be a big helping of your favorite food—or your favorite avoidance pattern: an old John Wayne movie, a fat paperback family saga, a long-distance phone call. It could be a daydream of lying on the beach on the most beautiful island in the Caribbean, or of the life you'll lead when you've reached your goal. It could be a day in the country, a hot oil massage, a new pair of earrings, or that fishing rod or Picasso poster you've been wanting for so long. Give yourself little extravagances for little steps, big ones for big steps, and a real whopper when you reach your goal: a whole new wardrobe or a set of matched golf clubs or a fabulous vacation. This kind of reward keeps things sweet instead of Spartan and prevents you from developing a permanently stiff jaw on your way to success.

The second kind of reward is the kind you should give yourself often just because you're you, and worth it—whether it's cooking a gourmet meal for yourself, taking a long, hot bath, or buying yourself a new sport jacket, a jazz record, or a theater ticket. This kind of reward is as important for the health of your self-image as physical exercise is for the health of your body. You must treat yourself like a first-class person, no matter what you've done or not done.

Don't ever punish yourself for skipping a step—or ten steps—in your plan by cutting out these little ways of being good to yourself. You need them more than ever when you're feeling down. They remind you that you have every right to be on earth and enjoy it just because you're alive. You need and deserve some pleasure at all times. When you've accomplished something, you get an extra helping on top of that for having been willing to undergo the discomfort of risk and change.

So, to sum up my six-point program for coping with the shakes:

1. *Survival Message No. 1:* PREPARE. Get information, advice, instruction, and practice.
2. *Survival Message No. 2:* LOWER YOUR STANDARDS—AT FIRST. Begin in a risk-free arena and gradually work your way up.
3. BE SCARED. Use Hard Times to release fear and tension before and after a difficult step.
4. TASK THERAPY: Focus your attention on the task, away from yourself.
5. DON'T BE AFRAID OF MISTAKES. They hurt you much less than stopping for fear of them.

6. GIVE YOURSELF REWARDS. Be nice to yourself at all times and extra nice to yourself when you've done something hard.

SURVIVAL MESSAGE NO. 3

Now, however, we have to talk about the third survival fear and its message. I'm talking about the fear that success will be cold and lonely —that gut feeling that you'll leave your friends and loved ones behind, or that they'll be mad at you for being "selfish" enough to put your dreams and plans first. "It's lonely at the top" is a common cliché, one powerful enough to scare many women and men away from the highest peaks of achievement. But it's even truer to say that it feels like it's going to be lonely *outside*—outside the comfortable, if constricting, nest of other people's expectations. When you start moving, changing the status quo, you shake up everyone around you, too. And yet, that is the moment when you need their support the most.

You need much more emotional security for risk-taking than you do if you stay within the safe, predictable bounds of habit. Going for your goals involves not only uncertainty, change, and the unknown, but a new and scary feeling of being visible. You are no longer hidden behind a low profile that attracts little attention, expectation, or envy. You're laying your real self on the line, making promises you'll be expected to keep, and making waves people are bound to notice. And that feels dangerous. But if you have even one positive partner around saying, "Your idea is wonderful. You're wonderful. Stick with it. I'm with you," you've got the warm weight of another body right beside you on that line.

I don't know if anyone's ever done a statistical survey, but I have the impression that the overwhelming majority of successful men get this kind of support from their wives (with booster doses from their secretaries and sometimes their mistresses). I can't remember reading a book by a man the acknowledgments of which didn't end something like, "And last, but not least, my wife, without whose unfailing support and help . . ." A well-turned-out woman smiles beside every senator, and it's a truism in the business world that an unmarried young executive is handicapped for the climb. There is also the fact that the majority of widowers remarry within a year or two of their loss. They can't make it alone and they've got sense enough not to try. Less well known is the fact that successful women have had exactly the same kind of support in their lives, sometimes from a woman friend, but very often from a man. Look at Virginia Woolf and George Eliot. Look at Bella Abzug and Jacqueline Susann!

Where does that leave those of us who aren't getting that kind of support? In trouble. In double trouble, because at the moment when we need *more* love and encouragement—when we start moving out for our goals—we're likely to get *less*. If you're a woman, your husband, lover, and/or kids may react angrily to the rerouting of so much of your attention away from them. After all, they've been used to getting the whole pie! That not only leaves you all alone out there, it puts you under fire at a time when you're shaky enough already. It can make you feel like giving up your goals or your family, neither of which is a very happy solution. There are men who have this problem too—men whose wives are willing to support some kinds of success but not others, the secure or managerial but not the creative or domestic, the executive but not the carpenter or restaurateur.

If you are one of those women—or men—your survival fear is real. The fear of being alone becomes a self-fulfilling prophecy if you think you have to walk out or sue for divorce in order to be free to pursue your goals! That fear isn't a weakness, to be overcome by toughening up and caring less. It's a survival message: "You can't go for your goals without emotional support. So *get* it." That's going to take some strategy. The next chapter tells you how.

–10–
Don't-Do-It-Yourself

A lot of women these days are talking about getting all the support for their professional goals from other women. I think that's fine, up to a point. There's no question in my mind that women can and should be a primary source of support for each other, especially when they're just beginning to exchange old roles for new goals. Later on in this chapter, I'm going to give you a format for sharing goal-support with a friend—a format men can use equally well to make going for their goals less of a solitary struggle.

FAMILIES: TURNING RESISTANCE INTO SUPPORT

For women who live with men and/or kids, however, those people are very important and dear. No matter how much new emotional nourishment we're getting from women, we still need our families or lovers, too. It's sad to leave them, and it's sad to live with them in a state of armed truce, defensive about our goals and resentful of their demands. We really want them on our side. What we don't realize is that they want to be on our side, too, if we would only give them the chance. But we're so guilty and frightened about *putting ourselves first* that we've got our dukes up from the word go, expecting nothing but trouble. And people who expect trouble usually get it.

And what about the men who love and puzzle over women who are trying to change their lives? And the men (*and* women) who would like to liberate their talents and loves, but feel responsible for economic dependents? What about the male poet and teacher in the middle of a divorce who told me, "I felt as if I had to do all the living, as well as all the earning, for two"? We know now that the rigid breadwinner/ nurturer split along sex lines has been as oppressive for many men as it has for women. But it's difficult to change any behavior that since childhood has spelled "love," whether it's clean socks or a regular paycheck. Here are some of the strategies—developed by my usual scientific technique, trial and error—for making it through the rough transition in roles with your sanity and your relationships intact.

Let Them Be Mad

When I decided to start Women's Success Teams, I told my husband about it, with some trepidation. He scowled and said, "I don't like that. I don't like women working with women. It worries me."

I panicked.

"What do you mean, you don't like it? How can I go ahead if you don't like it? What am I supposed to do now?"

He looked at me like I was slightly bananas and said, "Whatever you want!"

I said, "What do you mean, do whatever I want? You'll be angry!"

He said, "So what? You get mad at me frequently, and I do what *I* want! Where did I get all this power to stop you from doing things? So I'll be mad! The fact is, women working together make me nervous. I'll get over it. Why do I have to love it right away?"

And I thought, Well. He's right. How did I get to be such a sissy?

Just about every grown-up person still has a scared little kid hiding inside. That's why we so often react to our mates as if they were our fathers or mothers. We give them much more power over us than any adult really has over any other adult. We don't go home and say, "Hi, I've decided I'm going to be a veterinarian." We're afraid they'll be mad at us. So instead, we say, "Can I be a veterinarian? Please? Is that OK with you? Will you still love me?" And then when we don't get total, instant, 100 percent approval, we feel like we've been stopped. We say, "He won't let me do what I want," or "They're forcing me to choose."

I call that the "S/he won't let me" syndrome.

If you think someone won't let you do what you want, take another look at yourself. Because *he or she can't stop you.* You are not 4 years old, and that person is not your parent. S/he's just a person and s/he's scared. The people who love you are bound to be at best ambivalent about the changes you're making in their lives. They liked having everything nice and safe the way it was, and change makes them nervous!

Of course, what's really killing you isn't so much that you have to start doing things for you. It's that you're going to have to *stop* doing certain things for them. In the time-planning chapter, we've already dealt a blow to the guilt many women feel when they stop taking total care of everybody from the cradle to the grave—and some men feel when they stop being the Iron-jawed Provider. But of course there's survival fear there too, very deep. We're afraid that if we stop delivering the way we've always delivered, they'll never love us again. That's why, if they get mad or grouchy, we overreact—with terror or rage.

What they really deserve is compassion. These are people you love, don't forget it, and they're in trouble. All of a sudden, this man and these kids have got to become aware of a few facts of life which, thanks to you, they never had to think about before—like, when you wear something or eat off it, it gets dirty, and then what? To make matters worse, they have been trained to associate *care* with *love*—at the price of feeling eternally guilty toward their mothers. And you've fallen right into the trap. You've been giving them lots of attention and service. Now all of a sudden a lot of your energy is going someplace else. That feels to them like you're going away. And when they express their apprehension in the form of resentment, all of a sudden you feel oppressed!

Or: all of a sudden this woman and/or these children have got to become aware of a few facts of life which, thanks to you, they never had to think about before—like, when you want something it costs money, and money takes work. And work is sometimes scary, hard, or dull, and then what? To make matters worse, they may have grown up associating *financial support* with *love*—at the price of feeling eternally guilty toward their fathers (and sometimes their mothers too). And you've fallen right into the trap, carrying the whole household on your shoulders. Unfortunately, most men endure this trap in silence till they crack, and then they run off with another woman who represents the free and romantic side of them.

Do you see what a crazy thing we're doing to people we love? We're adding insult to injury out of our own insecurity and guilt. We've got a new love in our lives, which is a threat to them for starters; we've stopped taking the old compulsive kind of care of them; we've thrown their lifestyle into total disorder—and on top of it, we're ready to kill them or leave them! Of course they're going to blame and resent our new goals, because it looks to them like that's where all the trouble started.

Don't give up your goals. Go ahead and make the changes. Come home and announce that you're going to be writing a novel or running for City Council, not making beds or folding the laundry any more; or that there will have to be some changes around here because Dad wants to get out of the wholesale sporting-goods business and become a college philosophy teacher. *And give them the right not to like it.* Let them be scared and mad. Let them sulk and throw tantrums. Instead of getting all up in arms, say "I know, it's rough." Give them some time to get used to it. And one day somebody's going to look at you sheepishly and say, "You know, this is kind of fun. I like it a lot better than I thought I would."

We all need to learn a new language for love—a language that speaks not in socks, pancakes, and paychecks, but in shared fascination with physics or poetry, delight in each other's uniqueness, and *mutual* practical and emotional support. If you think your family loves you for the role you play, there's only one way to find out. Throw the role to the winds and go right through the fear of losing love. You aren't going to lose it. All you're going to lose is some peace. And only sissies think they're the same thing.

Working It Out

I've been talking about the *emotional* turbulence of changing roles, and how you can anticipate and weather it. But what about the *practical* rearrangements? In any shared household, certain things have to get done. The bills have to be paid, food, clothing, and other necessities have to be shopped for, and somebody has to bring in enough money to pay for them. And while people can survive on a bare minimum of cooking, housecleaning, and laundering, life is a lot more pleasant if those things get done at least some of the time. If you can't afford a maid, who's going to do them?

There's been a lot of talk about drawing up marriage or living-together contracts in which each person's responsibilities are spelled out very explicitly. You can do that if you want, but in my experience, imposing rules doesn't work as well as *defining common dreams, needs, and priorities*—in other words, finding a shared touchstone.

Economics: The Family Goal Conference

What if you are the primary breadwinner in your family—man or woman, partner or single parent—and your goal involves a temporary or permanent drop in either the amount or the regularity of your income? Carl, a married cartoonist, wanted to give up his newspaper job and try to make it as a free-lancer. Laura, a divorced teacher with two grammar-school children, wanted to make a living by marketing her own coloring books. Herm, the father of six, wanted to leave the real-estate firm where he was a vice president and take a lower-paying job with a nonprofit housing organization that got its funding renewed from year to year.

If that's you, the people you live with are simply going to have to make some changes. Either they will have to make their own economic contributions to the household, if they're old enough—like the teenager who takes a paper route to pay for her bicycle, or babysits to supplement his allowance—or they'll have to decide on what aspects of their lifestyle they are willing to economize. That sounds harsh. In practice, it's fun. If you sit down with your partner and/or kids and give them a full voice in the decision making, they're not going to feel deprived, threatened, or abandoned. They're going to feel like partners in an adventure.

Carl and his wife Sherry sat down and agreed that they would both actually enjoy the challenge of living more simply and self-sufficiently. They planned a move from their big-city apartment to a small lakeside town where rents were low and they would be able to catch fish and grow a vegetable garden. Sherry decided to contribute a little extra income by finding an outlet for her knitting and crocheting.

That's a fairly extreme example of two people who were willing to make a major overhaul of their lifestyle. What if you're not? Laura stayed where she was, in a Minneapolis apartment; she and her daughter and son decided to bake bread and cook "from scratch" and exchange homemade Christmas presents—things Laura would have more time for when she worked at home. Herm's wife got her first paying job —something she had been wanting to do for a long time—and his three youngest kids, who were in college and high school, gladly agreed to work summers for money instead of just for fun, so that their father could do what *he* loved.

The questions to ask when you sit down for a couple or family goal conference are very much like the questions you asked to arrive at your pared-down ideal day:

1. Which elements of our current lifestyle do we *need?* (Living space, health insurance, and—in some cities—private school might be examples.)
2. Which elements do we *want?* (An annual trip to the ocean, pets, a color TV? These items may be adjustable, or ingenious substitutions can be found by brainstorming.)
3. Which elements could we do without or economize on? (Our own washing machine, lots of eating out, second car, summer camp, private health-club membership instead of YMCA?)

Like your adjusted ideal day, this strategy isn't meant to be a permanent compromise, or to prune life down to the bare essentials. It's meant to get your priorities straight—in this case, your *shared* priorities. If you love each other, one of the things that's important to you is to have each other be happy. So each of you should define those areas where you're willing to compromise and the ones where you can't and won't. ("I don't mind eating out less, but I *refuse* to give up going to the movies." "Mama, I'd rather babysit every weekend than stop my ballet lessons.") Now ask yourselves two more questions:

—What long-term goals do we have in common? (Each other's happiness, more money, a house in the country, a trip to Europe, etc.)

—What is each of us willing to do *now* to help reach those goals? (A small sacrifice, a part-time job, help with the housework, etc.)

Housework: How Not to Nag

Note that I said, "Help with the housework." One of the things men and kids are going to have to pitch in and do if they want a happy lady and/or a second income is a share of the shopping, mopping, dishwashing, and bed- and dinner-making. And I promise you that they're going to make all sorts of noble resolutions at your family goal conference, none of which are going to get kept. What do you do then?

I think it's safe to say that the great majority of working women have tried to keep the peace by continuing to take the lioness's share of responsibility for the household. We usually justify this by saying, "If I don't do it nobody will," or "It takes more energy to keep nagging and reminding them than to do it myself." But often what we're really doing is striking a bargain: "If you let me have my job (school, boutique, literary magazine, painting class), I promise I'll still be just as good a wife/mother as I was before." In other words, we're keeping one foot in the old role just to be safe.

I think that's a mistake, because anyone who earns love doesn't believe in it when she gets it anyway. You've got to find out that you are loved just for being you. (Then you can cook an occasional meal or wash the dishes because it's fun and relaxing for a change, or because it's your turn.) I personally believe in making the change abrupt. If that makes you feel guilty and scared, *be* guilty and scared—you have the right to feel what you feel. But don't give in. Brave it out.

Your family wants a clean house? There are four strategies for dealing with that one.

Democratic Chaos: If you're cheerful and willful and can play blind like me, and step over debris, you can simply say, "You're absolutely right. Everybody should have a personal maid, including me. However, since none of us has got one, I guess we're just going to have to do the best we can."

Just think of yourself as one in a household of roommates who are muddling through. No one person is the foreman. When you wake up one morning and say, "Oh, my God, nobody's got any clothes," the laundry has to be done, and somebody has to do it. You can fight over who's going to do it. Nothing makes a kid feel better than being able to say, "Hey ma, it's your turn to do the dishes, and you better do them!" It really brings it home to them that you're not that slave they used to feel so guilty about. Nobody's the "mother" in my house any more. We were just three kids in a mess until I got married again; now we're four kids in a mess. We hassle over whose turn it is to walk the dog. It's a warm, noisy household.

The Compassionate Autocrat: What if you have a lower clutter tolerance than I do, and you need cleanliness and order around you to hear yourself think? Don't fall into the trap of doing all the housework yourself because it's easier and takes less time than getting them to do it. There is a way of getting them to do it that takes no time at all. Like this:

The dishes need washing. Instead of saying, "You never help me!" or "You must help. That's the rule. This is discipline," walk up to the man or child who is reading or watching TV and say, "Please do the dishes. *Now.*"

He or she will stand up with a loud sigh, slam the book shut, kick the television, throw you an evil glance, and start moving toward the kitchen with about as much enthusiasm as if it were the guillotine.

At this point we usually say, "Oh, forget it!"

We have so much trouble asking for help that when we finally do ask, we're hurt if we don't get enthusiasm! Well, you don't need enthusiasm. You just need the dishes washed. So use the key sentence from Hard Times. Say, "I don't blame you. I don't like to wash the dishes either. *You don't have to like it, you just have to do it.*" And if they grumble and swear all the way through the dishes, when they finally slam the towel down on the counter, you say just two words:

"Thank you."

I Need You to Take Care of Me: Here's what my days were like when I first got to New York: I got up at 7:00, made breakfast, made my kids' lunch, took them to separate schools, went to work, came home, shopped, made supper, and screamed at them all evening because I was so exhausted. That obviously wasn't working very well, but it went on for a few years, both because my kids were still quite small and because I needed to be this frontier mother to hold myself together.

Then one evening I looked at my 8-year-old and 5-year-old, who were watching TV, and I thought, Hey! I'm working two full-time jobs, staying up half the night, and here are these two strong healthy kids who aren't doing anything. I opened my mouth to lecture them, like I usually did, but then I shut it again. I thought, You know . . . I'm complaining, but it really gives me a wonderful feeling to make their lunches because I know it makes them feel loved and not lonely. But what makes *them* feel that good? My God. They're being cheated. *They need to make my supper!*

So I ventured, "I'm so tired when I come home from work at night. It would really make me feel good if you made my supper."

And they lit up! They went to the supermarket the next day and shopped, did all the cooking, set the table, and when I got home from work and they saw my face, they felt like a million dollars.

During the years we were alone together, those kids were what kept me going, and they know it. They cooked my dinner, they made my lunch, they even occasionally cleaned house. And they felt valuable and loved—and proud and protective, because I was just one little lady, and I needed them to look out for me. They say, "You'd never have made it without us."

I am convinced that that's one of the major reasons why those kids grew up OK: somebody needed them. We don't give that to our children. We give them everything else, and then we wonder why they're not satisfied. I think it's because they need to feel needed. They need to know that they are truly important to someone they love—helpful, capable, and necessary.

Love Your Life: The most important strategy isn't a strategy at all. *Be really happy at what you're doing.* That's when you're irresistible to your family, because you're off their backs, and you're cheerful, enthusiastic, and loving. That's when they start willingly cleaning the kitchen, doing the laundry, cooking dinner. They don't cook, clean, and wash *first* and then say, "OK, now you go to school and work, and we'll take care of everything." It's the other way around!

All they really want is your loving attention—in any form. They want to feel needed, involved, and included. Therefore, the best and simplest way to have both love and success is to let your people help you with your goal. Let them pitch in with practical help and emotional support. Instead of a rival that divides you, make your goal a shared project that brings you closer together.

Sharing Ownership of Your Plans

Sharing your goal may require a little bit of psychological judo, especially at first. It took me a while to figure this out. I used to walk into the house with my jaw stiff and my boxing gloves on, and announce, "I've got a fabulous idea. I'm going to start a worm farm and make lots of money!" Then if anyone just said, "But do you really think that will work?" I'd burst into tears and say, "See? See? I never get any support," and stomp out and give the idea up. That was very unfair of me. I was shutting them out completely, and then expecting them to smile and applaud like a paid packed house.

When you walk in with a flawless plan, *everybody feels left out.* I know I do. When somebody says, "I have the most fabulous idea," no matter how helpful I'd like to be, I start thinking, "What has that got to do with me?" But if somebody says, "I have this idea, but I don't know if it's going to work—so-and-so hated it," I roll up my sleeves and say, "OK, what is it?" Then I've got a place.

That's very important to do with your family—and your friends and co-workers, too. *Share your hopes, fears, and failures, not just your triumphs.* Triumphs always shut people out, no matter how much they'd like to join. So don't try to sell them the positive aspects of your idea. Say, "I have an idea, but it's only half-baked. I think anybody can shoot it down, and I don't know what to do about it." And let them talk you into it!

This is where you can really put negativity to work for you. It isn't a trick, because those doubts are there. Don't try to hide them, use them! It works like a charm. Judy, 29, told me, "This had never dawned on me before; I always thought I had to present a confident front. Instead, this time I went home and told my husband I'd been thinking about starting my own craft gallery, but I was afraid I wouldn't be able to pull it off. I expected him to criticize me. And what do you know, just like I'd pushed a button he said, 'You can do it. Here's an idea. Why don't you try . . .'"

As you saw in Chapter 7, other people have so much to offer once you invite them to get involved. Men—husbands, lovers, colleagues—love giving suggestions and help. They often have skills, experience, and connections women don't, and being asked to share those things with us makes them feel big and kind and wise, like older brothers. They'll write your resumé for you, photocopy it in the office, teach you corporate strategy, get their friends to write you references on impressive stationery. Kids are especially fabulous at ideas and legwork. Their heads and feet are quick. They'll come up with brilliant solutions to problems that had you stumped, and they'll run around on their bikes sticking notices up on bulletin boards. Trust them to help you with actual procedures, and to figure out their own ways of doing the jobs you assign them. This is very important. The more problems you give people to solve on their own—unsupervised—the more commitment and enthusiasm you get.

It doesn't have to be done the hard way. People will give you all the help and support you need if you just give them a place in your garden.

As far as I'm concerned, the goal of goals is a system in which you and the people you love act as each other's mutual support team. There are only two problems with it. One is that it takes time—and turmoil—to get there, and in the meantime you need something to keep you moving toward your goal. The other problem is that it doesn't work for people who live alone. If your family or partner is still in the throes of adjustment to the new order, or if you happen to be single, what do you do?

You call your friendships to the rescue.

In particular, you find someone who's in more or less the same bind as you (and believe me, we're all in some version of the same bind), and you make a compact to help each other out—a conspiracy to succeed together. I call it the Buddy System.

THE BUDDY SYSTEM: TEAMING UP FOR SUCCESS

The Buddy System is a way of creating your "ideal family" in miniature. It's the most compact and efficient way I know to give yourself the kind of support system I've been describing throughout this book. Its principle is simple: you and a friend make it your shared goal to meet both your individual goals. It works because it's about a thousand times easier to have faith, courage, and good ideas for someone else than it is for yourself—and easier for someone else to have them for you. So you team up and trade those positive resources: your buddy provides them for you and you provide them for her or him.

How do you pick a buddy? She or he can be a close friend or roommate, but doesn't have to be. A new acquaintance or a neighbor can be just as good. This is an action-oriented arrangement first and foremost, and an intimate friendship only if you want it to be. Your buddy will be giving you emotional and moral support, yes, but for a purpose: to keep you in motion. In fact, if you are close friends, you're going to have to keep the long, rambling, heart-to-heart talks out of the business part of your relationship and save them for after hours.

Almost the only requirement for a buddy is that she or he be someone whose mind and values you respect and whose ideas and goals intrigue you. His or her goals don't have to be in the same field as yours, or even in a field you know anything about. I know a concert pianist and a department-store buyer who helped each other reach their goals! On the other hand, I also know a husband and wife, both book editors, who are each other's informal "buddies." (You can make a family member your buddy; I'm just putting the system in terms of friendships because they are often a firmer and steadier source of support, outside the emotional fireworks of intimate love.) So there are no rules. Just beware of picking someone who intimidates you, who is considerably more advanced in his or her career than you are, or who never admits to being doubtful or down. The buddy system, unlike the mentor system, is a relationship of equals.

You and your buddy will be able to give each other three overlapping kinds of help:

1. First and most important is *expectation*—the knowledge that someone is waiting to hear whether you did what you said you'd do and how it went. A buddy fills the need for that vital someone outside you who steadfastly believes in the importance of your goal and expects you to stick with it, as if you were doing it for him or her and not just for yourself. It's like my Ideal Environment fantasy of a boss who would make me do what I really want to do even when I don't feel like doing it!

Each week, you will tell your buddy exactly what steps you've scheduled for the following week, day by day. And s/he will tell you what's on his or her schedule. (See *Weekly Business Meeting,* below.) The next week, you'll report in and tell each other what you did or didn't do. It's as simple as that—and it makes all the difference in the world.

Elaine, the English teacher who wanted to be a mystery novelist, decided to start writing her first book at the rate of ten pages a week. She knew she was going to be meeting with her buddy every Thursday night, and she couldn't walk in there empty-handed. So as often as not, those ten pages got written on Thursday morning. But they got written. And at the end of eight months, this woman who had dreamed of writing for years but never done it had produced a 350-page manuscript.

The buddy system *works,* where attempts at "self-discipline" usually end in self-loathing. Alone, you can always find good excuses for falling off your schedule, but the minute you've got somebody else to answer to, it becomes a lot harder to fool yourself. Your buddy isn't your externalized "conscience" so much as the appointed representative of your best self. Once you've empowered her or him to keep you on the track, you don't have to try to sustain constant enthusiasm. You are free to be human—sometimes lazy, sometimes ornery, sometimes depressed—and still get things done.

2. You and your buddy will give each other the emotional support so necessary for staying with any plan: a sympathetic audience for HARD TIMES when you're down, someone to hold your icy hand when you're in the throes of stage fright, and above all, companionship in the enterprise of goal pursuit. Help over the rough spots is a necessity, but sharing the positive excitement of goals is a delight, as women and noncutthroat men are just beginning to discover. You can't always get that from your mate or kids, at least not at first when they may still perceive your new goal as a rival. With a buddy, you can share not only the weight of your problems, but the crackle of ideas, the camaraderie of work, and the festivity of success.

3. Finally, you and your buddy can provide each other with lots of *practical help.* You'll be each other's core brainstorming and barnraising team. When either of you has a tough strategic problem to solve, you can put your two very different heads together and they'll be twice as good as one. Your buddy will lend you the unused paints and brushes in her closet, or her fur coat when you need to look rich. You can

role-play her for her upcoming interview—and even make phone calls and pretend you're her if she hates the telephone more than anything on earth. He'll get his sister the journalist to write an article about your dance studio; you'll get your lawyer uncle to give him a reference for law school. You can share whatever ideas, contacts, materials, and skills will help you both meet your goal of mutual success.

The best format for all this give-and-take is a regular one: the *weekly business meeting*—supplemented whenever necessary by the *three-minute booster phone call.* First, though, you'll need to have an initial get-together to share your plans and set a joint target date.

Bring your flow chart, goal calendar, and the coming week's calendar to this first meeting—unless you prefer to do some of the detailed planning in this book together with your buddy. In either case, get a broad overview of each other's plans and a sense of the major time blocks for each of you. The later of your two target dates will become your *joint target date*—the day when both of you will have achieved your goals. Make a verbal contract to stay together until that date. Like all target dates, it is tentative and can be readjusted any time the circumstances warrant, but you've still got to set it. When that day arrives you can have a party—and then renegotiate whether you want to stop or to stay together because you've got six new goals to work on!

Now pick an afternoon or evening when you'll both be able to meet at the same time every week. It's important to be in frequent, regular touch—a contact you can count on and look forward to. And it is very important to make these business meetings an open, official, high-priority part of your life—not something you just sneak in when you have time. *The commitment to your buddy is a commitment to yourself and your goals.* It doesn't have to take up more than an hour a week, but family demands and social activities should be planned around it, not vice versa. If you're out of town or you have a sick child or some other good reason why you can't make it, you will report in to your buddy by phone at the regular time.

Before you end your setting-up meeting, go over your next week's calendars with each other. You write down what your buddy is planning to do each day. She writes down what you are planning to do each day. If either of you thinks you could use a "booster" phone call on a particular day, write that into your schedules too: "You call me Wednesday evening to find out whether I called the director of the museum. I'm going to call you Friday noon to see if you wrote your poem." (Note: don't always wait for your buddy to ask for a "booster" call. You ask him when he thinks he might need one. A little loving push every now and then is very much a part of the buddy system. So is the snarled reply, "For Chrissake get off my back!" Because you'll be urging each other to do things that are uncomfortable, an occasional flare-up of resentment is inevitable. It's just Hard Times. Handle it with awareness and humor.)

Now for your weekly procedure.

Weekly Business Meeting

I call this a business meeting because it is exactly that. It is not a kaffee klatsch; it is not a beer-and-football party; it is not a conscious-ness-raising group. It is a goal-oriented strategy session, and the minute it turns into anything else, it's not going to work.

The problem is, you're friends. You like each other. And it's very hard for people who like each other to get down to business, because they have such a good time together. On top of that, you may not be used to practical talk about goals, achievements, plans and problems, all of it taking place "between friends." Sometimes we have a lot of trouble taking ourselves and each other seriously in that dimension. Women especially tend to slide over into the realm of feelings, personalities, and relationships, where we feel at home and can go on for hours. To prevent this from happening, you've got to make your business meetings stick to a couple of rules.

1. Be on time. This sounds like a small thing, but it's the essence of self-respect. You try not to be late for an appointment with your doctor or your boss, because you respect them and you want the feeling to be mutual. Well, your weekly business meeting is an appointment with your future—with the person you can become. So no matter how you feel on the meeting day, try hard to be on time. And expect the same from your buddy.

2. Use a clock or a kitchen timer. This will structure the meeting and help you keep to the point. Each of you gets a maximum of half an hour, divided up roughly as follows:

5 minutes: Report in. Tell what you did—or didn't do—in the past week, and if you did it, what were the results. Your buddy will have it all written down from the previous week and will expect a report on each item. If you haven't done any of the things you said you were going to do, that isn't the worst thing in the world. You just come in and say, "I didn't do anything." But usually you did do something, and you just don't realize it. You start out, "I didn't do anything. Oh, well, I did call so-and-so, but he wasn't in." And so you get the confirmation you can't always give yourself that you've really done a great deal. (Here your buddy is fulfilling the same report-in and feedback function that an Actions & Feelings Journal fulfills when you're working alone.)

20 minutes: Problems and solutions. Now tell about any problems you ran into, and invite your buddy's suggestions. But watch out: if the problems you bring up have an *emotional ingredient*, air it out in a Hard Times session first, or your attempts at problem-solving will be a spectacular failure. Here's where you'll have to be alert and attentive to each other. You can't always pick up on the need to complain in yourself, but there's no mistaking the "yes-but" game or that heavy, dragging tone in someone else's voice. Try to have fun with Hard Times. Complain until you feel lightened and ready go on, but *set yourself a limit of 10 minutes.* Even bitching and moaning can be done efficiently in the service of your goal! Then get down to brainstorming and barn-raising.

Five minutes: Scheduling. Update your master list of unscheduled actions, adding any suggestions from your buddy that you want to act on, and then lay out your next week's plan of action: what you're going to do on what day. Be sure to write in any booster calls you're expecting from your buddy, because knowing those calls are coming in will keep you on the ball. Your buddy should write down a copy of your schedule, including the times s/he's promised to call you. And then it's his or her turn.

After this basic one-hour business meeting is over, you can do things like rehearse an interview or draft a resumé (you'll be very up for it); you can sit around and fantasize about how great it'll be when you both have your goals; you can open a bottle of wine and gossip all night; or you can go home. I really want you to experience what it's like to walk out and say, "I'll see you next week and tell you what happened—and I'll talk to you Wednesday on the phone."

The Three-Minute Booster Phone Call

A phone call from your buddy in the middle of the week can give you a shot of courage and motivation when you need it most: just before you've got to do something difficult, or just after you've done something difficult, or both ("Are you ready to leave for your interview? OK, I'll expect you to call me the minute you get out of there and tell me how it went"). I don't mean only those calls you've promised to make at your weekly business meeting, but also an occasional impulsive holler for help, advice, congratulations, or just to touch base. If you and your buddy make it part of your verbal contract to be available to each other over the telephone, it will help both of you not to feel alone. But like any other mutual-aid arrangement, it can get out of hand. If the person you team up with has any "baby" tendencies at all (see Chapter 7), after a while you're going to cringe every time the phone rings. Again, the best preventive is a rule.

No call should be more than three minutes. Besides being cheaper, this three-minute limit will remind you to value both your own time and your buddy's. Now that you have a goal, you are living in a *time frame*, and for women and other former nonwinners that's a whole new ball game, one that's going to take some practice. People who don't live in a time frame have nothing to do but pour out their concern for each other and take care of each other for years, but people in a goal-directed work situation have to distinguish between linear time, which is for getting things done, and free or "global" time, which is wide open for play and feeling. Linear time has to be used efficiently; global time can be squandered, like "mad money." You can call up your buddy, say "This is the business call I said I'd make," talk for three minutes, and then call back and talk all night if you like. Just so you get it into your head that business is business.

One more suggestion. If your buddy ever calls up and starts going on and on in a negative way, remember, whatever you do, *don't try to fix the problem,* or you'll never get off the phone. If s/he says, "My husband/wife doesn't love me, I'm too fat, " don't offer help. Saying,

"Oh, no, you're not too fat, maybe you can get another wife/husband" will only trigger the "Yes-but" game. Just listen a little more and then say, "What can I do to help? You tell me." That little sentence is magic. If more people knew about it, Ma Bell might go broke.

Intensive Care

I don't know where you first heard the term "the buddy system." I picked it up in grade-school swimming class, where you had to keep an eye on another girl and she had to keep an eye on you to make sure neither of you drowned. There are times when your success buddy can be a bona fide lifesaver, too.

I mean those bad moments when there's something you've got to do and you know you can't do it. The very prospect of calling a Montessori school and asking if they need a teacher's aide gives you appendicitis. Or you've got a thesis deadline coming up and you've got that sinking sensation that you're not going to make it; your mind goes blank when you so much as look at the blank sheet of paper in the typewriter. Or you're supposed to go in for an interview and you have a strong feeling that when you reach the door you're going to turn around and go home and eat a whole bag of Fritos. What you have to do is just too hard, or you're mysteriously and horribly blocked.

This is known as a *crisis*. Sooner or later it happens to everyone, and there are three danger points in the pursuit of your goal when it's particularly likely to happen:

Crisis Point 1: At the beginning, when the field you're venturing out in—or maybe directed action itself—is new to you, and you have no solid experience of success to counteract your fantasies of disaster.

Crisis Point 2: Whenever you have to do something you don't want to do in order to get to something you do. No matter how ingeniously you've done your brainstorming, almost any goal you head for is going to require a few steps you don't much care for. Like practicing scales when you want to play jazz improvisations. Like taking a calculus course when you want to be a marine biologist. Like finishing your thesis. (Nobody wants to finish a thesis.) These can cause major crises of inaction, because in the short run it feels nicer to sit behind the roadblock and daydream about your goal than to grapple with the roadblock so you can go get your goal. A roadblock is also handy to hide behind if the idea of actually getting your goal is still a little scary. I'd wager that most chronically unfinished theses owe their long lives to a combination of these factors.

Crisis Point 3: *When you face the jump to a new level of risk or visibility.* I know a burgeoning writer who had a field day with her first steps, but froze up on the day she reread what she'd written and realized that not only was she serious about her work, she was actually good. And Andrea felt very comfortable with her camera after three months of taking pictures on her own, but the day she made an appointment to show her prints to a professional photographer, she freaked out. That's only natural.

I've told you the story of Matthew, the man who hadn't painted for twenty years and whose goal was to get back into it for his own pleasure. He progressed without a hitch from making sketches on his own to taking private drawing lessons in his home, and finally to life-drawing classes at a small art school. Heartened by that triumph over timidity, he enrolled in a painting class at a prestigious art school —and he crashed. He walked in and walked out again and said, "I can't do it. Everyone in there can paint but me."

The first thing I said to him was, "You can't stop now. When you're through being scared, that's different. Right now you get to panic, you get to feel lousy, you get to hate yourself, but you don't get to stop painting!" And that's the first rule for you, too, any time you hit a crisis. Never, *never give up or change your goal when you're feeling scared, discouraged, or depressed.* Once you get past the rough spot and you're feeling good again, you are free to change your goal if it really isn't doing much for you. But *not while you're down!* When you're down what you need more than anything else is to keep going, but it's awfully hard to do that alone. You'll make it if you have someone to hold your hand every step of the way. That's *Intensive Care.*

What Matthew did was to get a buddy to go with him to that painting class every night for a week. To be more precise, his friend Sharon dragged him to class and to make sure he went in the door. Sharon would be waiting for him two hours later when the class was over, and they'd go out and have a stiff drink together. The second week Matthew went to class on his own—a little unsteadily, but he went. He met Sharon after class a couple of times, but mostly he just checked in with her on the phone right before class to say, "Here goes." At the end of those two weeks Matthew called Sharon up and said, "Thank you for making me do it. You couldn't drag me away from that class now."

You don't have to be working in the buddy system to set up Intensive Care for yourself, though it helps. But in a pinch you can ask a good friend or family member to see you through a crisis. It's important for them—and you—to realize that this isn't a full-fledged nervous break-down. It's just a temporary case of stage fright, and you need somebody to shove you lovingly out under the lights. With that understanding, if you're facing a difficult interview or performance, you can have someone come with you right to the door and be waiting to give you a big hug and a hot bowl of soup when you come out. You can also ask for *crisis calls.*

Crisis calls are indicated when you can just feel that you've got a bad week coming up. You might say to your buddy (or appropriate substitute), "Help. I've got a thirty-page proposal to write this week and I can't." Or your buddy might spot the signs of an impending crisis. So she or he says, "All right, I want you to call me at nine every morning before you sit down at the typewriter. I need to hear from you at eleven with at least one paragraph written. And then I want to hear from you at four." In a crisis, your buddy gets to give you orders just like a schoolteacher. (Remember s/he is "the appointed representative of your best self.") That way, when you're blocked, you're not alone with it. You have someone to get you started in the morning and someone to report to at the end of the work day. Frequent crisis calls also help to break up an imposing task into manageable units: one paragraph, one page, one phone call at a time.

You won't need Intensive Care very often. In fact, once may be enough. Once you've had the experience of keeping going through a crisis, the world will be a different place for you. You'll have a solid, tangible achievement to be proud of, and you'll be less afraid of your fears—if they couldn't stop you this time, why should they ever stop you again? But to crash through that barrier the first time, you need help. Matthew needed it. I needed it. And I still want a loyal team on my side whenever I've got something grueling or scary to do—or something wonderful to celebrate.

Let the lone cowboy walk off into the sunset. He's a movie myth and the director is yelling, "Cut!!" Real cowboys rode the range in twos and threes, so they'd have somebody to help them out when a cow got stuck in the mud . . . and someone to drink coffee and play guitar with at night. Sharing goals works. It's based on the way we are.

I ran into Matthew about a year after he successfully weathered his crisis, and I asked him, "How's your painting going?"

He said, "You know, thanks to Sharon, I really did what I wanted to do. I carried a sketch pad around with me all the time, and I filled our apartment with canvases. I've got to put some of them in storage now to make room for the piano. That's right, I'm buying a piano! I've found someone to give me lessons. Of course, I'm scared to death.

"But I know now that I can do anything."

–11–
Proceeding

You've got all your planning machinery in working order, and you've got a set of helpful hints for starting up again any time you're stalled. Only one thing remains, and that is to show you how to turn the key and get it all rolling. What I'm going to give you now is the *weekly and daily procedure* that really puts your plans into action.

Here's what you have to work with:

ON YOUR PLANNING WALL:
1. your personal "saint"
2. Flow Chart
3. Goal Calendar
4. First Steps
5. Weekly Calendar
6. the next five years
7. the next step: tonight/tomorrow

PORTABLE:
1. Purse or Pocket Calendar
2. Actions & Feelings Journal
3. Hard Times Notebook

Here's what you do every week:

SUNDAY NIGHT PLANNING MEETING

This is the night on which you meet with yourself and prepare for the entire week ahead. It may take as much as an hour, or even more, but it's vitally important. No sensible business would proceed without planning meetings, and you've got to learn to treat getting what you want as top priority business.

I've picked Sunday night because it fits in with most people's work week, but if your schedule is different, it could be Monday night or Thursday night just as well. If you are working in the buddy system, your weekly business meeting with your buddy will take care of some of the steps below. I've indicated which those are, so that you'll know which ones you will still have to come home and do for yourself to keep your plans up to date.

Step One: Looking Back. Review what you got done the past week, referring to your Weekly Calendar and Actions & Feelings Journal to refresh your memory. (This step is taken care of by the report-in to your buddy if you've got one.) Now tear off the past week's page to reveal a clean new one.

Step Two: Flow Chart and Goal Calendar Update. Check to see where you are now on your flow chart and goal calendar. If you're using colored push pins, move them ahead to your present position. Pay special attention to the *closest approaching target date* on your goal calendar. Does it look like you're going to make it? Many unforeseen problems and/or opportunities may have come up in the past week. If you're falling behind schedule, what can you do about it? Can you step up the pace of your actions, or will you have to push back your target date? Or can you actually move it forward? This is the time to make any changes in your flow chart and goal calendar—either of target dates or of actual plans—based on what's happened out there in the world.

Step Three: List of First Steps. Look at your list. You will have updated it in your *Daily Procedure* (see below) as new ideas and leads came in, but now make any further additions you can think of and cross out any steps that have become unnecessary.

Step Four: Problems. Did you run into any snags last week? Are there any upcoming steps on your list that you feel puzzled or pessimistic about? This is the time for the Problems List, and as always, dealing with it is a two-stage process. (Both stages will be taken care of by your meeting with your buddy if you've got one.)

a. Hard Times. If you're feeling discouraged, tired, or anxious, open your Hard Times Notebook—your private, negative, ornery, un-American "I Hate Success" book—and start writing down all the reasons why it can't be done. Look at the picture of your personal "saint" and say, "I hate you. Go jump in the lake with your bloody encouragement." Say, "I'm a woman and I shouldn't have to do anything," or "Nobody else ever works this hard to get rich. Tomorrow I'm going to sell out to the highest bidder." Sooner or later, if you keep it bright and are very bad, you'll start to laugh. At that point, say, "Oh, what the hell," and turn your attention to the strategic problems.

b. Brainstorming—and Barn-Raising. Now, turn your ingenuity loose and play around with possible solutions to the problems. If you need input—fresh ideas, practical help—reach for the telephone and call someone in your resource network. Enter the results on your list of First Steps.

Step Five: Next Week's Plan. Two parts here, too (you'll do them with your buddy if you have one):

a. Weekly Calendar. Assign the actions you've decided you can get done this coming week to *specific days and times* on your fresh new Weekly Calendar page. Don't forget also to schedule any crisis, booster, or report-back calls to your buddy or to a friend who's given you a lead.

b. Purse or Pocket Calendar. Transfer the coming week's "appointments" into your portable calendar.

Steps Six, Seven, Eight and Nine will be the same as Steps 1, 3, 4, 5 in the *Evening Procedure* below *(Journal, The Next Step, Rewards, Dreaming).*

DAILY PROCEDURE

Evening:

1. Journal. Enter in your Actions & Feelings Journal what you got done today and how you felt.

2. List of First Steps. Add any new steps you've come up with as a result of today's actions to your List of First Steps.

3. The Next Step. Tear off yesterday's tonight/tomorrow sheet and fill out a new one. What do you have scheduled for *tomorrow?* What do you have to do *tonight* to prepare for it—lay out your clothes, lay out your paintbrushes and paints, make sure a phone number is in your pocket calendar, rehearse an interview in your mind? *Now do it.*

4. Rewards. Give yourself something nice: a hot bath, an hour of reading, a late movie, a glass of brandy, your favorite record, your favorite fantasy.

5. Dreaming. The last thing before you go to sleep, lie awake in the dark and imagine yourself in your Ideal Environment—the one from Chapter 3 in which you would be your best self. Go to sleep enjoying that thought.

Morning:

1. Set your alarm for ten minutes early, so you don't have to leap out of bed in a panic.

2. After breakfast, go to your planning wall and look at the next step. That's all you have to do today, and you are prepared for it. Remember that it may turn up nothing, or it may turn up a hundred new possibilities. There's no way of knowing until you do it.

3. Look at your flow chart and see where this one small step fits into the whole plan that's leading you to your goal.

4. If your goal or job takes you out into the world, pack up your pocket calendar and Hard Times Notebook, take a look at your kindly personal "saint," and you're on your way. If you're doing your goal work at home, sit down, take a deep breath . . . and begin.

— EPILOGUE —

Learning to Live with Success

Congratulations. You're there.

Where? Maybe this is the day when you've actually reached your first target. Maybe you've arrived at the first major milestone on your way to it—you've written a whole chapter, gotten through a job interview and felt good about it, lost ten pounds, drawn up a business plan, or learned to use a camera. Or maybe you're just at the end of your first week—or day—of directed action. *Each small step you accomplish is going to feel like success*—not just the big ones.

Winning is a process, not a product. And as soon as you get out on your path, you're doing it. Now you've got to learn to live with it. That isn't quite as breezy as it sounds. You may not be used to being out there making things happen, and it can sometimes give you a headache. But it's worth it. It feels so much better than the depression and boredom you suffered just sitting around. And there's an art to making it easier for yourself.

1. Hurray for Me! Don't ever let anyone tell you that there's anything wrong with self-congratulation. When you've done something hard, you deserve cheers, from yourself and everyone around you. When you've done something hard and it's worked, you deserve a banquet! You may remember that when you were setting your target and your target date, I told you that you would need to be able to know beyond a doubt when you had arrived—at your goal and at each big step on the way. I can tell you now that part of the reason was so you would know when to celebrate!

Pausing to savor your own accomplishments and feel proud of yourself isn't "conceited" or "self-indulgent," the way our Puritan culture taught us it was. It's food for your unfolding self. And you don't need to worry about "resting on your laurels." You've got to rest on them a little bit, if only to catch your breath! Then you'll want to move on. So enjoy this moment of triumph, in private and with the people you love. Give yourself one of those big rewards we talked about in Chapter 9. Take a vacation. Throw a party.

2. Fake It . . . The party's over. It's the morning after. You got the job of your dreams—and now you have to walk in there at 9:00 A.M. and *do* it, and not just tomorrow, but every day after that! You got the contract; now you have to write the book. You came through the audition with flying colors, and they gave you the part; now you're going to have to get up in front of a real live audience and act.

Each new level of success (and this is true of even the smallest steps) brings new tasks, new challenges, new stresses, as well as new opportunities. The operative word is *new.* You're navigating in unknown waters now. But don't think that means all your old, familiar fears and uncertainties are going to vanish as if by magic. No way! You bring them right along with you, and they will be doing plenty of kicking and screaming long after the rest of the world considers you a dazzling, invulnerable success. If your history is anything like mine, for a long, long time you're not going to believe you can do something even when you've just done it and the evidence is right in front of your eyes.

So I would like to share with you my simple, one-sentence formula for how to live with success:

FAKE IT TILL YOU GET USED TO IT

The first time I was invited to be on national television, I said, "Yes!" —not because I was ready, but because it was too good a chance to pass up. (Success, no matter how long you've waited for it, always comes before you're ready for it.) Then I freaked out. "I can't do it. I'll open my mouth and nothing will come out. I'm too fat." And so on. But by this time I knew a thing or two. So I made a resolution—the very rare kind that really *is* written in blood: "I will not, repeat, will not sabotage myself, no matter how much I may want to."

I got everything ready—the clothes I would wear, my plans for what I was going to say. Then I was hysterical for two days before the show. On the big day, I pulled myself together, walked in, carried it off almost as smoothly as an old pro, thanked everyone (they were very impressed), went home and got hysterical again. Nobody who watched the show ever knew that they had been watching a total fake. Only my family, who had to live with me backstage, knew that there were *two* Barbara Shers.

There are two tricks to faking it. One is the Hard Times before-and-after technique you learned in Chapter 9. You need to express your hysteria without ruining your performance. So just do it in the wings! Be your nervous self until they call your name, and then go out there and be a pro.

The second trick is *costumes.* Every actor and actress knows that getting into costume is a tremendous aid to getting into a role, and that there's a huge difference between the last rehearsal in jeans and leotards and the first one in full dress. You can do the same thing. If you are now, by definition, a doctor, lawyer, wilderness guide, salesman, businesswoman, executive, or college teacher—that is, if you're doing the thing—*dress the part even if you don't feel like it.*

I know two former college roommates, now both successful—one a lawyer, the other an executive—who made the mistake of waiting until they felt self-confident in their professional roles to start dressing for them. They may actually have slowed down their careers, because dressing like a college kid or a stay-at-home mother creates a vicious cycle: it provokes the people you work with to treat you as someone not quite grown up or serious, and you'll respond in kind. On the other hand, something magical happens when you look in the mirror and see someone you don't recognize as ordinary you. (By the way, there's an "ordinary me" hiding behind the confident face of every celebrity, bar none.) Even if you still feel ordinary inside, believe me, the ham in you will rise to the occasion.

Note: The days when you least feel like dressing for the part are the days when you absolutely must do it. For two reasons. One: When you're feeling great, you can look rotten and nobody will notice because you'll be so radiant. When you're feeling down, you need outside help. Two: If you drag yourself groaning to the mirror and get your makeup on or your tie straight, you'll start feeling better.

Sooner or later, the day will come for you that came for me: I'd bought a dress to fool everybody . . . and I put it on . . . and suddenly I realized that the only person I'd been fooling was myself. *I belonged in that dress.*

3. Until You Get Used to It. The scenario of my first TV appearance repeated itself, with decreasing intensity, for about a year. It got a little easier each time. And now? Now I'm absolutely greedy about it! I love to show off and can't wait for my next chance. I speak in front of large groups, go on TV and radio, and have a wonderful time. My stage fright has diminished to a pleasant champagne-like tingle. Nobody knows I've changed but my very patient family, who no longer have to put me together like Humpty Dumpty beforehand and pick up the pieces afterwards.

When you reach this point, you've really arrived. You'll wake up one day and realize that you are living a version of the Ideal Day you dreamed about all those months or years ago, when you first started moving. It may or may not be just the way you imagined it, but in one crucial respect it's different—and better: this is real. There's something else that's better about it, too. You're not alone, the way you once feared you would be. On the contrary, you have to take the phone off the hook every once in a while to get some peace. Success is sexy. It puts roses in your cheeks, a swing in your stride, and a warmth and enthusiasm in your presence that people can't resist. If you ever notice that someone you care about is feeling left behind, don't feel guilty. Grab that person, say, "Stop crying in your beer, get up out of that chair and come with me! I want your company. If I did it, believe me, you can. I'll help."

At this point, it is also in the nature of the human animal to say, "What next?" Remember, I told you that when you had attained self-confidence in one thing, you would start looking around for something new to do in which you would have *no* self-confidence. But you've got something much more important than self-confidence now. You've got experience and skills. When my friend Matthew said, "I know now that I can do anything," that wasn't a delusion of grandeur. It was a statement of fact. He could go on from painting to playing the piano because he had acquired a *metaskill:* he had learned how to learn, he had gained mastery of the process by which things get done. When you reach your first goal, you've done this too. Now you've really got the luxury of choice.

Look at the next five years on your planning wall. Are you ready for the next goal? Do you still want to run a printing press, or would you rather study the Spanish Civil War? Do you want to go on running a business or would you like to be a beachcomber for a while? The shape of things has changed. Your efforts have changed it. So what about the shape of things to come? What would you like to do now?

What I always do is imagine a new Ideal Day, in detail and in full color. It is always completely different from the last one, and often quite the opposite of the life I'm living. That helps me set my course for the *next* two years.

You've discovered the ultimate secret all winners know: that "the journey, not the arrival, matters." Being on your path is what it's all about. Each destination you reach only opens out into wider horizons, new and undiscovered countries for you to explore.

PHOTO: © MINDY STRICKE

BARBARA SHER is a bestselling author of seven books, each of which provides a down-to-earth, nuts-and-bolts method for uncovering natural talent, pinpointing goals, and turning dreams into reality. She has often been named the "godmother of life coaching" by the media and her many fans.

Sher has presented seminars and workshops throughout the world to universities, professional organizations, Fortune 100 corporations, and federal and state government agencies. She has been called "a stand-up comic with a message" and "the best speaker we have ever seen" in evaluations. Joining forces with public television, she has also created five hour-long special programs that continue to air in cities around the United States.

She has appeared regularly in the national media, including on *The Oprah Winfrey Show, The Today Show, 60 Minutes, Good Morning America,* and CNN. She was a life coach columnist for *Real Simple* magazine in 2003. Sher periodically teaches seminars at the Smithsonian Institute, Harvard University, and New York University. She has a new Internet radio show at BlogTalkRadio.com. Visit her website at www.barbarasher.com.